Peter Berresford Ellis, historian and novelist, was born in 1943 in Coventry. A former journalist, he was deputy editor of the *Irish Post* and subsequently editor of *Newsagent and Bookshop*. He has written a score of books, many dealing with aspects of Irish history and culture. His classic *A History of the Irish Working Class* (Gollancz, 1972) was the first major study of Irish history from a socialist viewpoint since 1910. He has also written several pamphlets on Celtic history and culture, and he has contributed to a wide variety of journals in several countries on socialism, history and linguistics.

His most recent works include the successful novel *The Rising of the Moon* (Methuen, 1987) and *Dictionary of Irish Mythology* (Constable, 1987).

PETER BERRESFORD ELLIS

HELL OR CONNAUGHT!

THE CROMWELLIAN COLONISATION
OF IRELAND 1652-1660

THE
BLACKSTAFF
PRESS

BELFAST

First published in 1975 by
Hamish Hamilton Limited
This Blackstaff Press edition is a photolithographic facsimile
of the first edition printed by William Clowes & Sons Limited

This edition published in 1988 by
The Blackstaff Press
3 Galway Park, Dundonald, Belfast BT16 0AN, Northern Ireland

Printed by The Guernsey Press Limited

British Library Cataloguing in Publication Data
Ellis, Peter Berresford, 1943–
Hell or Connaught!: the Cromwellian
colonisation of Ireland, 1652–1660.
1. Ireland. Colonisation by England,
1652–1660
I. Title
941.506
ISBN 0-85640-404-7

Now for our Irish wars:
We must supplant those rough rug-headed kerns,
Which live like venom where no venom else
But only they have privilege to live.

Richard II Act II, Scene I
William Shakespeare.

CONTENTS

ILLUSTRATIONS

Ireland 1650

ATLANTIC
OCEAN

Mull of
Kintyre

Doagh
L. Swilly
Foyle
Coleraine
Scarriffhollis
DERRY
Bann
Island
Magee
Carrickfergus
Belfast L.
Donegal
L. Neagh
Lisburn
BELFAST
ULSTER
Benburb
Charlemont
Armagh
Enniskillen
Monaghan
Newry
Moy
Belturbet
Cullaville
Carlingford L.
Cloughoughter
Cavan
Dundalk
Carlingford
CONNAUGHT
Shannon
Boyne
Drogheda
Inishbofin I.
Ballintubber
Trim
Tuam
Athlone
Tyrellspass
Maynooth
Lucan
DUBLIN
GALWAY
Liffey
Leixlip
Bray
Loughrea
LEINSTER
Kildare
Naas
Kilrush
Portumna
Maryborough
Roscrea
Athy
Wicklow
Aran Is.
Carlow
Wicklow
Mts
Ennis
Leighlinbridge
Arklow
Kilkenny
Suir
Nore
Barrow
Slaney
LIMERICK
Cashel
Mouth of
R. Shannon
Tipperary
Old Ross
Clonmel
New Ross
Wexford
Harbour
MUNSTER
Waterford
Wexford
Rosslare
Ballyferriter
Blackwater
Fermoy
Waterford
Harbour
Carnsore
Point
Dingle
Bay
Killarney
Knockanoss
Youghal
Kenmare
CORK
Kinsale
Cork
Harbour
Bantry Bay

0   10   50
                         miles

— — — — — Provincial boundaries

CHAPTER 1

THE SETTLEMENT

'A fateful wound hath made of me a hulk of sadness'

Early on the morning of September 11, 1652, three English frigates, *Revenge*, *Providence* and *Expedition*, rounded Raven Point and sailed into Loch Garman, at the south-east tip of Ireland. Boatswains' pipes squealed urgently as barefoot sailors sped aloft to haul in the billowing canvas sails. The three ships, black and white against the grey-green waters of the loch, were a picturesque sight as they rode slowly across the choppy waters to drop their anchors in front of the small port of Wexford, standing at the south of the River Slaney.

The quayside of the harbour, where the acting governor of the town, Colonel Thomas Sadler, with 'divers officers and gentlemen of the garrison of Ireland', stood waiting to greet the arrivals from the ships, was a blaze of colour. Along the grey stone quay of the old port, which the Viking settlers had called Waesfjord—the harbour of the mud flats—and which had been, until recently, the main harbour of the Irish insurgents' navy, detachments of soldiers stood at attention. Lines of infantry were drawn up in red coats, the different colours of the facings denoting their regiments. Yellow knee-length stockings and stout leather shoes added to the brightness of their uniforms. Each man shouldered a pike or musket. Behind them, on sturdy horses, sat troops of cavalry with buff coats of thick leather, shining back- and breast-armour and iron head-pieces which gave them a curiously menacing appearance. Every infantryman stood stiffly at attention under the anxious gaze of their officers, for the three ships now in the loch contained no ordinary arrivals to Ireland. On board *Revenge* was the new Commander-in-Chief of the Army of the Commonwealth of England in Ireland, head of both military and civil government in the country.

Revenge, commanded by Captain Clarke, who had won

fame earlier in the year with his blockade of the Irish garrison of Galway, began to edge in closer to the quayside. From the quarter-deck of the frigate, thirty-four-year-old Lieutenant-General of Horse, Charles Fleetwood, surveyed the lines of soldiers with a critical, professional eye. His appointment to command in Ireland had pleased him greatly. Nearly six years previously his regiment had been ordered for service in Ireland but, to his chagrin, they had mutinied and refused to serve there. Now his appointment helped to console the bitterness, and loss of face, he had felt then. The officers and soldiers of the army in Ireland had also been pleased at the appointment, for Fleetwood had a fair reputation as a soldier and had risen quickly from the ranks during the English Civil War from an ordinary trooper in the Earl of Essex's Life Guard to command of a cavalry regiment in the New Model Army at the second battle of Naseby. He was well favoured by the Puritans, especially by the Anabaptist faction who called themselves Christian Brethren. They repudiated baptism in infancy as a blasphemous formality and considered their entry into the covenant of a good conscience with God sealed by adult baptism. They maintained that Christ had wiped out the consequences of Adam's fall for all mankind, therefore infants were not punishable for sin until an awareness of good and evil emerged within them. By the exercise of their own free will through repentance and baptism could the people thus be saved. The sect had been founded in January, 1525, in Zurich, Switzerland, by Conrad Gretel, and many had, in strict obedience with the teachings of Christ, been opposed to the use of the sword. Many others, nevertheless, during the course of the English Civil War, had entered the army, and some had won high rank in it. They were a constant challenge to the leaders of classical English Protestantism and also to the civil administration for they argued politically that the government should be in the hands of 'the godly' and that there was no need of a written civil constitution because the Bible was enough by which to rule the Commonwealth. Fleetwood had drifted into their camp, causing one Presbyterian Member of Parliament to comment: 'Look at Colonel Fleetwood's regiment, what a cluster of preaching officers and troopers there is!' On that account his appointment in Ireland had been joyously greeted, for the majority of the senior officers there were Anabaptists.

With the new Commander-in-Chief on the *Revenge* were his children, eight-year-old Smith Fleetwood and his little sister Elizabeth, watched over attentively by their nurse. They were the children of Fleetwood's first wife, Frances, whom he had buried scarcely a year before at St. Anne's, Blackfriars, London. Now by his side stood his second wife, 'a comely Puritan lady', Bridget, eldest daughter of the Lord General of the Army, Oliver Cromwell. They had been married nearly three months before and for Bridget, now in her twenty-eighth year, it had been her second marriage also. Two days after Fleetwood had buried his wife, Bridget's husband Henry Ireton, Commander-in-Chief in Ireland, had died of the plague in Limerick. So, for the second time, Bridget found herself returning to Ireland as the wife of its military ruler. Naturally, the marriage of the pair, a mere six months after the deaths of their respective spouses, was the subject of much malicious gossip. Lucy Hutchinson, the vivacious wife of Colonel John Hutchinson, maintained that Oliver Cromwell had married off his daughter in order that she should 'be restored to the honour she had fallen from'. But Bridget was far too pious for a marriage of convenience. In fact, her piousness and serious approach to life was a cause of great concern to her father. At one point he felt compelled to write to her telling her to avoid being 'a bondage spirit' and rely on love rather than fear.

Apart from several Puritan divines and some prominent merchants, there were few civilian inhabitants of Wexford waiting on the quayside to greet their new ruler. Indeed, Fleetwood could not have wondered at the reason for the lack of enthusiasm of the citizens of Wexford as he surveyed the ruined, powder-blackened walls of the old town; the breaches where Oliver Cromwell's artillery had pounded its ancient fortifications, allowing his infantry to pour in. The Parliamentary soldiers had surged through the narrow streets pushing the people towards the market place, Market Cross, in the north of the town. There the soldiers had slaughtered nearly 1,500 of the inhabitants, including 250 women, as many children, five Franciscan priests and two Franciscan friars. The charred ruins of the Franciscan Friary in John Street bore mute witness to the massacre. The memory was too sharp for the survivors of Wexford to make a pretence of welcoming Cromwell's son-in-law.

Fleetwood and his party began to disembark. As well as his personal staff he was accompanied by several young men who had come to take up office in Ireland. There was the new Physician-General to the Army, twenty-nine-year-old William Petty, who had been enticed to Ireland for the annual salary of £365 plus £35 out of 'the States Apotheca and without being debarred from private practice'. Petty, who came from Rumsey, Hampshire, was something of a flamboyant character. He had studied at Caen University before entering the navy. But his nautical career had not lasted long and on the outbreak of the civil war in England he had remained in Europe, studying at Utrecht, Leyden, Amsterdam and Paris, returning finally to Oxford where he took a doctorate degree in physic and went on to become a Fellow of Brasenose College and deputy professor of anatomy. Later, as professor of anatomy, Petty had won a certain notoriety as the man who had brought a hanged woman back to life. The unfortunate woman had been sentenced to death for killing her illegitimate child but the executioner had fumbled the operation. Some of her relatives, in order to quicken suffocation and end her agony, had clung desperately to her legs. But she was still breathing when she was cut down. The executioner jumped on her chest a few times in a brutally clumsy effort to finish off the job but still the woman was found to be alive when she was taken to the mortuary. Petty had nursed her until she recovered and she had gone off to lead what normal life she could after such a gruesome experience.

Another medical man was among the arrivals, Dr. Benjamin Worsley, soon to be appointed Surveyor-General, with whom Petty was to maintain a contemptuous dislike and intense rivalry, though strangely enough not in medical fields, throughout the next ten years. According to Petty, Worsley, 'having been frustrated as to his many several great designs in England, hoped to improve and repair himself upon a less

knowing and more credulous people'. There were also Fleetwood's two chaplains, Edward Wale and Samuel Ladyman,
the latter not being in the best of humours, his entire library
having been swept overboard and lost during the voyage from
Bristol. Fleetwood eventually paid Ladyman £30 to refill his
bookshelves.

Once ashore, with the greetings over, there were messages
and despatches to be seen to. None of the four Commissioners
of the Parliament of the Commonwealth of England for
Ordering and Settling the Affairs of Ireland had been able
to meet Fleetwood in Wexford, there being still much to do
in the country. Remnants of the Irish army in Ulster had not
surrendered and there were several isolated garrisons holding
out. Also, a few weeks before Fleetwood's arrival, the Commissioners had been sent copies of an Act of Parliament laying down legislation for the confiscation of the property of
Irishmen who, for the past eleven years, had been in arms
against England. The legislation provided for the redistribution of the confiscated property to those who had financed the
English army in Ireland and to the soldiers of the army who
were to receive grants of land in lieu of their pay arrears. The
Commissioners had not yet published the Act as they were
concerned with planning how the 'forces may be best ordered
for the prevention of disturbances in the country upon the
publishing of the Act, which may probably be endeavoured
. . .'

Fleetwood's first priority was the despatches from the Acting Commander-in-Chief of the Army, thirty-five-year-old
Lieutenant-General of Horse Edmund Ludlow, who had
served in that capacity since the death of Ireton. He was a
West Country Englishman with, according to one contemporary, 'a gruff, positive humour, resolutely bent upon whatever his own will suggested'. In some ways he had followed a
similar career to Fleetwood's. Having matriculated from
Trinity College, Oxford, he had gone to study law at the
Inner Temple. Like Fleetwood, who was at Gray's Inn, and
so many young law students, he had opted for Parliament in
the civil war and joined the Earl of Essex's Life Guard. In
May, 1646, he became active in politics, representing his
native Wiltshire, as a member of a popular republican party

led by Henry Marten called the Commonwealth Men. In Parliament Ludlow had been a poor speaker and took little part in debates. He had been appointed to the commission to try Charles I and had appended his signature to the death warrant. When Oliver Cromwell returned from Ireland in 1650 Ludlow was offered the post as deputy to Henry Ireton and since the latter's death in November, 1651, the military successes against the Irish had been of his designing. Ireton had been a poor soldier but a brilliant administrator; Ludlow tended to an opposite position.

The month before Fleetwood's arrival, Ludlow had concluded a military campaign against the Irish clans of O'Byrnes, O'Tooles and Kavanaghs in the Wicklow mountains and had effectively crushed their resistance. He had then gone north to supervise military operations against the Irish General O'Farrell and Philip Mac Hugh O'Reilly's Ulster force, which was the only remaining group of Irish soldiers with any semblance of a field army. There were also isolated garrisons like Aran, Inishbofin and Ballyleague, to be reduced. These considerations, plus the added headache of preparing a strategy for the publication of the Act of Settlement, had prevented Ludlow from travelling to Wexford to greet his new commanding officer. But 'the news of his arrival was very welcome to me having found my care and fatigue recompensed only with envy and hatred...' There was, however, no love lost between Fleetwood and himself, for Ludlow, a staunch republican with no strong religious belief, was in opposition to Fleetwood's Anabaptism and anti-democratic tendencies. There was another reason, apart from Ludlow's 'fatigues', why he was glad to receive the news that Fleetwood had arrived. It also meant that the frigates *Revenge, Providence* and *Expedition*, which he had despatched to Bristol on August 12 to pick up Fleetwood, were once again available for service in Irish waters. For the past six weeks two Irish ships, *Patrick* and *Frances*, had been raiding Commonwealth coastal installations and the only vessels available to counter their attacks had been *Tenth Whelp*, which was laid up in the Kenmare River, in Co. Kerry, and *Hector*, which had only just been released from the arduous duty of transporting gunpowder from Limerick to Waterford.

Ludlow therefore sent greetings to Fleetwood and said he would meet him towards the end of the month in the town of Kilkenny, where ten years previously the Irish insurgents had convened their own parliament and given formal existence to a new state, the Irish Catholic Confederacy, with Kilkenny as its administrative centre. Letters from the other three Commissioners agreed to the meeting in Kilkenny. There was the Norfolk barrister, Miles Corbet, another of Charles I's judges who had signed the King's death warrant, along with a second Commissioner, Colonel John Jones. Jones had been a Commissioner since July, 1650. He was a bombastic Welsh-man from Maes y Garnedd, Merioneth, who had served in the Parliamentary forces with some distinction. He was a staunch republican and, as such, won praise from Ludlow but, according to the Lord General's youngest son, Henry Cromwell, was 'cunning and close'. The third member of the Commission was John Weaver, a Lincolnshire lawyer and former Judge-Advocate of the Earl of Manchester's army. A vociferous independent Member of Parliament for Stamford, he had been summoned to sit as a judge at the trial of Charles I but had never attended any of the sittings. He had come to Ireland in September, 1650, and during 1652 had been closely involved with the framing of the legislation for the confiscation of Irish lands.

Fleetwood and his entourage spent three days in Wexford dealing with the various despatches, messages of welcome and petitions before they set out for Kilkenny.

In East Cork, a twenty-seven-year-old poet called Dáibhí Ó Bruadair of Cnoc Rátha heard the news of the coming of the new English Commander-in-Chief and was filled with foreboding at what might be in store for his country. He articulated his anguish at the defeat of the Irish army in the words

Créacht do dháil me im árthach galair

A fateful wound hath made of me a hulk of sadness,
Stretched in fitful weakness, robbed of active vigour,
Since the martial genius of those sturdy soldiers
to earth is stricken and their valour's record silenced.

Now the conquerors were pouring into the country and the Irish soldiers were being sent into exile, or worse.

To take their place there will come the fat rumped jeerers,
after crushing them, their culture, and their cities,
laden all with packs of plates and brass and pewter,
with shaven jaws and English and braggart accent.

Every dowdy then will wear a cape of beaver
and don a gown of silk from poll of head to ankle.
All our castles will be held by clownish upstarts
crowded full with veterans of cheese and pottage.

What mental agony would Dáibhí have felt if he had known then that within a year the 'fat rumped jeerers' would take over, not only the castles, but the entire land of Ireland with the exception of the province of Connaught and Co. Clare, into whose confines they would order the Irish to move on pain of death, giving them the choice between 'Hell or Connaught!'. In 1649 Oliver Cromwell had told the Irish: 'We are come to ask an account of the innocent blood that hath been shed, and to endeavour to bring to an account all who by appearing in arms shall justify the same.' The account was about to be settled with a terrible vengeance.

'*There is no laughter at children's doings*'

The country which Charles Fleetwood had come to govern had been devastated by eleven years of vicious and bloody warfare. It was a country which had lost over a third of its population by war, pestilence and famine. Colonel Richard Lawrence, the governor of Waterford, recalled in 1655:

About the year 1652 and 1653 the plague and famine had so swept away whole counties that a man might travel twenty or thirty miles and not see a living creature, either man, beast or bird, they being either all dead or had quit those desolate places; or soldiers would tell stories of the place where they saw a smoke; it was so rare to see either smoke by day or fire or candle by night. And when we did meet with two or three poor cabins, none but very aged men and women and children, and those, like the prophet, might have complained: We are become as a bottle in the smoke; our skin is black like an oven, because of the terrible famine. I have seen those miserable creatures plucking stinking, rotten carrion out of a ditch, black and rotten, and been credibly informed that they dug corpses out of the grave to eat.

The new Physician-General of the Army, Dr. William Petty, wrote that the inhabitants of Thomond, Upper Ormond, and several other parts of the country 'were necessitated by hunger to eat their garrans [small horses] and plough horses and to buy and steal from one another the worst kind of horse to eat'. On May 12, 1653, the Commissioners reported on 'the great multitude of poor swarming in all parts of the nation ... frequently some are found feeding on carrion and weeds and some starved in the highways, and many times poor children who have lost their parents, or who have been deserted by them, are found exposed to, and some of them fed upon, by ravening wolves and other beasts and birds of prey'.

According to Petty '... about 504,000 of the Irish perished and were wasted by the sword, plague, famine, hardships and banishment between the 23rd October, 1641, and the same day in 1652'.

October 23, 1641, had been the day on which the Irish had risen in arms against the English administration. Their aim was simple: to drive out the English and Scottish colonists, regain the land that had been confiscated from them and establish the independence of their country. From 1172 until the reign of the Tudors, the conquerors and colonists that England had sent into Ireland had been gradually assimilated into the Irish nation. Despite attempts to impose the English language, customs and laws, the Irish showed a remarkable resilience and capacity for survival and were able to induce the settlers to adopt their language, customs and laws in spite of the severe punishments threatened from England. The Master of the Court of Wards, Sir William Parsons, had declared: 'We must change their course of government, apparel, manner of holding land, language and habit of life. It will be otherwise impossible to set up in them obedience to the laws and to the English empire.' The first serious attempt to do so was made by Mary Tudor in the province of Leinster. English colonists formed settlements, driving out the native Irish from their lands. They agreed to become colonists on condition they 'should use for the most the English tongue, habit and government' and make no appeal to the native Irish Brehon Laws. This colonisation was then extended to Munster and threatened in Connaught. But within a few years the Lord Chancellor, Sir Robert Gerard, writing in 1578, reported that 'all the English, and the most part with delight, even in Dublin, speak Irish'. In 1600 Fynes Moryson, an official arriving from England, complained that even the 'English-Irish', as he termed the colonists, would not speak English with him in Dublin.

Clearly the Tudor attempt at colonisation had failed. But a change began with the accession of James I, which coincided with the defeat of Hugh O'Neill, Earl of Tyrone, and his Irish armies which had fought for eight years against the armies of Elizabeth I. Following this defeat, English common law began to be enforced throughout the country, displacing the old Brehon system, and a sterner policy of colonisation was followed in which English and Scots took over confiscated lands, particularly in Ulster. Aindrias Mac Marcais summed up the despair of the people when he wrote

Gan gaire fa ghniomhradh leinbh

There is no laughter at children's doings,
Music is prohibited, the Irish language is in chains.

In spite of the conquest and colonisation the Irish were far from subdued. The clans remained loyal to their chieftains and the scattered nomadic septs lived in the shelter of the hills, bogs and vast forests, raiding the colonists' settlements with the approval of the entire native population. The colonists, however, were pushing the Irish further and further into the bogs while they took over the rich, low-lying, springy meadowland and introducing to it breeds of cattle from England, while the herds of lean, shaggy Irish cattle began to decrease for want of suitable pasture.

The clan system was gradually being eroded. Absolute private ownership in land had been alien to the Irish communal way of life. Land had been the common property of all the clan, and each clansman was allotted land for his personal use but he could not dispose of it without the consent of his clan, even the disposal of cattle or other goods needed such approval. All chieftains were elected by the clánsmen on two basic qualifications: one, they had to be capable of carrying out the job involved, and, secondly, were therefore usually elected from one particular family acquainted with the problems a chief would encounter. The feudal principle of primogeniture was unknown in Irish law. The Brehon system put the basis of power in the decisions of the people made at the clan assemblies. The philosophy was expressed in the old saying '*Is treise tuath no tighearna*'—a people is stronger than a lord. The law provided for election to every office with the addition that the most worthy be elected. It was therefore difficult for a chief to usurp his power for he was so limited and hemmed in by his office and so dependent on his clan that it was easier for him to promote the clan welfare and conform to the intention of the law than to become either negligent or despotic. The chief was president of the clan assembly, commander of its forces in war and a judge of its courts. But gradually through the years, as the influence of the colonists was felt, many clans became feudalised. In 1585 the Connaught chiefs, frightened by the colonisation policy, decided to swear allegiance to Elizabeth I as a feudal monarch, introducing rents and claiming full ownership of their clan lands in total contradiction to the Irish social system. Other chiefs held out. Morrogh O'Flaherty, who died in 1593, made a will recommending his successor as chief and dividing the clan lands between his sons as he feared, rightly, that the Irish law would be superseded by that of the English law of primogeniture. Nevertheless, Dubhaltach Mac Firbisigh of Lecan, writing in 1650, when compiling a dictionary of Brehon Laws, claimed that he still knew many chieftains at that time who ruled their clans according to the Brehon system.

The English and Scottish colonisation in the early seventeenth century had witnessed the proscription of the ancient bardic schools, the universities, and the academies of Irish literary and poetical activity. But this suppression had released hidden springs of new poetical expression in Irish. Poets still used old metres but new concepts and loosened measures began to take shape. These were known as *amhrán* (song) based on musical stress and did not depend on the strict counting of syllables, nor were the new poets shackled by an elaborate system of vowel and consonant correspondences as were the bardic metres. A new and vigorous folk poetry was gradually to grow from the ruins of the old bardic poetry as part of the European movement in which governments had seized on the potentialities of printing to channel the publication of works in vernaculars, creating national literatures. In Ireland, printing arrived relatively late. In Louvain, however, Irish Franciscan friars established a printing press using an authentic Irish typeface and began to print numerous books in Irish. These were smuggled into the country keeping alive literary activity in the language. Among them were masterpieces which were to become classics, such as the *Annals of the Four Masters* and Séathrún Céitinn's famous history of Ireland *Foras Feasa ar Eirinn*. These works preserved the national consciousness of the Irish, together with their desire to be rid of the English overlords. The insurrection of 1641 was consequently inevitable.

In October, 1641, Ulster chiefs, led by Sir Phelim O'Neill, seized the opportunity offered by the growing split between the English Parliament and Charles I, to unleash the might of the northern clans against the colonists. Within a few days—following a well-coordinated plan—the clans in all parts of the country had turned on the colonists. The King, busy intriguing to overthrow Parliament, could only spare 2,000 soldiers under Robert Monro to protect the colonists in Ulster. Irishmen who had been exiled after previous insurrections were soon flocking back to Ireland to take up arms. In August, 1642, Eoin Ruadh O'Neill, who would have been a possible nominee for the O'Neill chieftaincy under the Brehon system, landed on the shores of Lough Swilly. He had served as an officer in the Spanish army and now he used his military talent to turn the northern clans into a formidable army.

In order to raise money to suppress the insurrection London merchants were asked to loan the government sums of money in return for debentures. Those who had 'adventured' money would be rewarded with estates confiscated from the Irish at the end of the war. Naturally enough, an essential clause of the 'Adventurers' Act' of 1642 forbade any clemency to the Irish otherwise the investors would have no guarantees. The war became a gigantic capitalist speculation with Ireland as the prize. The scheme made the Irish insurgents re-

double their efforts and its threat drove new recruits to their
banners.

In the autumn of 1642 the insurgents convened their own
parliament at Kilkenny and gave formal existence to a new
state, the Irish Catholic Confederacy. A constitution was
drawn up by a lawyer named Patrick D'Arcy. The Confederate Parliament was divided into two bodies, a Supreme
Council of twenty-four members elected by a General
Assembly, and a second body comprised of lords, clergy and
commons sitting in one chamber, on the lines of the Scottish
Parliament. The commons were elected from 162 boroughs
and two members from each of the 32 counties. The Confederacy still recognised the English King as head of state and
adopted the motto *Hibernii unamines pro Deo, Rege et
Patria*—Irishmen united for God, King and Country. Their
aim was the restitution of confiscated lands, liberty of conscience and equality of status for Catholics, and above all the
repeal of Poynings Law (1494–5) which made any Irish parliament subservient to England. Ireland would become an equal
kingdom with England under the Crown. Ambassadors were
appointed to Paris, Madrid and the Vatican and many able
and competent Irishmen returned home to offer their services
to the new state.

King Charles now felt a desperate need to make a truce
with the Irish Confederates, having raised his standard at
Nottingham on August 22, 1642, and plunged England into
civil war. He badly wanted the troops which were tied up in
Ireland under James Butler, the 12th Earl of Ormonde. It
was not until September 15, 1645, that a truce was agreed
upon and five regiments of Ormonde's army were able to
reinforce the King's army in England. The Irish leaders were
invited to a conference at Oxford. They demanded a free
Irish Parliament, suspension of Poynings Law, repeal of all
Irish Acts and Ordinances since August, 1641, the freedom
of religious worship, and repeal of the penal laws against
Catholics, plus a general amnesty to all insurgents and an Act
of Limitation for Security of Estates, offices being granted to
Catholics as well as Protestants, and lastly an Act passed
establishing the independence of the Irish state and parliament. Charles I refused to accept these terms but the Irish

Confederacy, aware of his desperate need to make peace, believed they had only to hold out a little longer for him to agree.

In the summer of 1645 Pope Innocent X, who had succeeded Urban VIII the previous year, decided to send a Papal Nuncio to the Confederate government. He appointed Giovanni Battista Rinuccini, Archbishop of Fermo, an elderly and distinguished Florentine. Rinuccini's instructions from the Pope were to sabotage any settlement between the King and the Irish that did not restore the Catholic Church in Ireland and allow for a Catholic Lord Lieutenant. He was also to reorganise the Church. Priests had acquired 'dangerous' habits of independence as, with monks and nuns, they had been forced to live dispersed secretly in private houses and were no longer obedient to conventual discipline. People, used to hearing mass in secret, even found it troublesome to attend churches. Rinuccini arrived in Ireland in early October, 1645. He was immediately approached by the Earl of Glamorgan, sent by Charles I to conclude a secret treaty with the Irish above Ormonde's head. But another treaty was signed with Ormonde by which the Irish were to provide the King with 10,000 troops in return for the repeal of the penal laws against Catholics, and a suspension of all further colonisation. The treaty was too late. Chester, the last fortress of the King had fallen, and the King had surrendered himself to the Scots. Parliament was triumphant. The Irish Confederacy, however, was still in a strong position. On June 5, 1646, Eoin Ruadh O'Neill had met Monro's army, now fighting under the Parliamentary banner, at Benburb on the River Blackwater, and had almost annihilated it, Monro losing 4,000 men and O'Neill some 300.

Internal disputes were now splitting the Supreme Council of the Confederate government. Lord Mountgarret, President of the Council, was determined to conclude a peace with Ormonde as the King's representative so that both forces could unite against the English Parliamentary forces. A treaty to this effect was signed at the end of July against the wishes and advice of Rinuccini and the Irish Hierarchy. Eoin Ruadh O'Neill, considering the Irish cause betrayed by the Anglo-Irish lords, decided to overthrow the Confederate government and marched on Kilkenny, which he entered on September 18, 1646. Mountgarret fled, so did Lord Muskerry, who had supported him, and Richard Bellings, secretary to the Supreme Council, was imprisoned. The Ormonde treaty was repudiated by the new Confederate government.

In 1647 Michael Jones had become the Parliamentary commander in Ireland. The Scots had handed King Charles over to the English Parliament in return for payment for their troops during the Civil War, while in Ireland the Royalists were guaranteed their lives and property whether they left the country or stayed. Ormonde went to England, where he saw the King, before going on to France. In Ulster Monro had recovered from his defeat and had reorganised his army. In Munster Lord Inchiquin and his Parliamentary troops had captured Cashel, killing all inside, desecrating local shrines and gorging themselves on plunder. Lord Taafe, a local Confederate commander, tried to attack Inchiquin and was beaten off. Another Confederate general, Thomas Preston, lost two-thirds of his army in an attack against Michael Jones' forces. The only Confederate army of any size was Eoin Ruadh's army based in Roscommon. Michael Jones was trying to join Inchiquin and destroy Kilkenny, the centre of the Confederacy. Eoin Ruadh marched his men across Ireland to stand between Jones and the Confederate capital. There were more internal disputes among the Irish, and the Confederate government decided to negotiate a truce with Inchiquin in April, 1648, and declare O'Neill a rebel, in order that they could enter into negotiation with the Parliamentary forces.

In England Charles and his Parliament were spoiling for another civil war, which started with a series of uprisings in Wales, Kent and Essex during the spring and summer of 1648. But a battle at Preston, in which a Scottish Royalist army was defeated, led to the rapid collapse of all Royalist resistance. Ormonde had returned to Ireland to raise the standard once more for the King. Working on the dissension within the Confederate Government, he dissolved the Irish Parliament on the promise of religious freedom and of government of their own country if they came out for Charles I against the English Parliament. He declared Rinuccini a

rebel to silence the Nuncio's opposition and the Italian pre-
late fled to Galway. In spite of Eoin Ruadh's pleadings
Rinuccini left Ireland in January, 1649. With a major opponent out of the way Ormonde used his influence with such
Confederates as Lord Dillon, Lord Muskerry and Thomas
Preston, and they nominated twelve of their number to assist
him in government. The Scots in Ulster, since the ejection of
Presbyterians from Parliament for their refusal to take part
in the proceedings against Charles I, had joined with the
Irish against Parliament. Munro had taken his Scottish army
from Ulster to take part in the debacle at Preston. The
mauled remnants of that army had returned to Ulster and
found themselves in alliance with their former enemies.
Inchiquin, who had already changed sides once in the war
from Royalist to Parliamentarian, now changed back to
Royalist. Only O'Neill stood uncommitted, trying to remain
constant to the idea of an independent Ireland. In opposition
to the Royalist-Confederate alliance stood Michael Jones'
Parliamentary army in Dublin, Charles Coote's army in Galway and General George Monk's army in Ulster.

On January 30, 1649, Charles I was executed at Whitehall.
In February the English Parliament abolished the office of
king as 'unnecessary, burdensome and dangerous to the
liberty, safety and public interests of the people of this
nation'. By May, 1649, England was established as a Republic
which was to 'be governed as a Commonwealth, or a Free
State, by the supreme authority of this nation, the representatives of the people in Parliament, and by such as they
shall appoint and constitute under them for the good of the
people'. The major problem facing the English Republic
was the suppression of the Royalist-Confederate alliance in
Ireland. On February 13, 1649, a Council of State heard 'all
good ways and means for the reducing of Ireland ... and ...
the securing, advancement and encouragement of the trade
of England and Ireland'. On Tuesday, March 13, Oliver
Cromwell was appointed Commander-in-Chief and Lord
Lieutenant in Ireland.

He immediately immersed himself in reports of the situation. Michael Jones' main army consisted of 7,820 infantry
and 2,168 cavalry. Cromwell decided to reinforce this with

an army of 8,000 infantry, 3,000 light cavalry and 1,200 dragoons plus eight field guns. The forces were to consist of six regiments of foot commanded by Lieutenant-General Henry Ireton, Cromwell's son-in-law and Colonels Venables, Tolhill, Huncks, Stubber and Phayre, four regiments of horse under Colonels Hewson, Ewer, Deane and Cooke and five troops of Okey's dragoon regiment commanded by Colonel Daniel Abbott. By spring the forces of the English Commonwealth were ready to undertake the conquest of Ireland.

'these barbarous wretches'

It was in the Commonwealth army in Ireland that the most radical of the Parliamentary factions were to be found. Whether by accident or design they were sent to Ireland, where the task of conquest and land settlement removed them from English affairs and from participation in the political development of the Commonwealth. They were independent in religion, with the Anabaptists forming a hard core. Many were republicans, like Edmund Ludlow, some being even more extreme and involved in the Leveller movement. All shared an extreme dislike of Catholicism and regarded the extirpation of the Catholic Church as not only necessary but even meritorious.

The Leveller element in the army was quite strong in 1649. The Levellers were a republican and democratic party which had been originated in 1645 by John Lilleburn. Called Levellers because they wished to 'level men's estates', they claimed that the real sovereignty of England should lie in a Parliament elected by manhood suffrage, with redistribution of seats to make for fair representation in annual or biennial parliaments. The government should be decentralised to local committees. The Levellers put forward a programme of economic reform, complete equality before the law, abolition of trading monopolies, security of tenure for all, no conscription to the army, the laying open of enclosures, the abolition of tithes, complete freedom of religious worship and drastic law reforms. Oliver Cromwell told the Council of States: '...you have no other way to deal with these men but to break them in pieces ... if you do not break them, they will break you.'

While the Commonwealth was preparing the army for the reconquest of Ireland, the Levellers demanded to know why English soldiers should conquer another nation at the behest of men who had enslaved England to a government by will and not law. The Leveller journal, *Moderate Intelligencer*, of May 2–10, 1649, justified the 1641 insurrection as the attempt of a conquered people to throw off their conquerors. A pamphlet entitled *The English Souldiers Standard to Repaire To*, on April 25, 1649, echoed the argument. The Leveller leaders, Lilleburn, William Walwyn, Thomas Prince and Richard Overton, had been arrested on March 28. But on May 1 the Levellers published *An Agreement of the Free People of England* reiterating that England had no right to be in Ireland. Whalley's regiment mutinied in London but it was quickly suppressed and on April 27 a soldier named Robert Lockyer was executed in St. Paul's Churchyard, giving the Levellers a martyr for their cause. On April 14 William Walwyn smuggled another tract out of jail declaring the Leveller opposition to the conquest of Ireland. This pamphlet was attacked in a further one which commented that the Leveller leaders were 'arguing the cause of the Irish Natives in seeking their just freedoms, immunities and liberties, was the very same with our cause here, in endeavouring our own rescue and freedom from the power of oppressors ...'

On May 2 all but two troops of Scopes' and Ireton's regiments, stationed at Banbury en route for Ireland, mutinied. An officer, William Thompson, took over leadership. General Oliver Cromwell and Lord Fairfax immediately took the field against the Leveller troops and defeated them at Burford on May 15. Thompson was shot dead after a dogged resistance.

Although suppressed, the disgruntled Levellers, with other republican groupings, embarked for Ireland. Although the majority of officers and troops were Anabaptists, another large radical minority were the Fifth Monarchy men—a group of extreme Puritans who believed that the 'Fifth Monarchy' was at hand, a monarchy which would succeed Assyria, Persia, Greece and Rome and during which Christ would reign on earth for a thousand years. These radicals were the new colonists while the conservative section of the Commonwealth Army consisted of old Protestant colonists represented by such men as Lord Broghill, Sir Charles Coote and Major General Sir Hardress Waller.

Roger, Lord Broghill, was the youngest son of Richard Boyle, 'The Great Earl of Cork', who had arrived in Ireland in 1588 and carved an enormous fortune for himself. Broghill, who had fought against the Irish insurgents with his brothers, had turned twenty-eight years of age in the spring of 1649. His father, the first Earl of Cork, had died six years previously, two years after Broghill had married Lady Margaret Howard, the second daughter of the Earl of Suffolk. Broghill was a staunch Royalist and he had been in London in 1649 merely in transit to France to join Charles Stuart whom he recognised as Charles II. Oliver Cromwell was aware of the worth of Broghill in an undertaking such as the conquest of Ireland and went to visit him in his lodgings. Bluntly the new Lord Lieutenant of Ireland told him that the government knew of his plans and were about to commit him to the Tower of London. They would reconsider this if Broghill joined Cromwell in Ireland. In October, 1649, Broghill landed at Wexford as a colonel of a regiment consisting of twelve troops of horse.

Sir Charles Coote's father, also named Sir Charles, had likewise arrived in Ireland during Elizabeth's reign as a soldier of fortune, to become Provost-Marshal and Vice-President of the Province of Connaught. On the outbreak of the Irish insurrection he was very active against the Irish but was killed on May 7, 1642, 'whether by the enemy or by one of his own troopers was variously reported'. His son immediately took over his father's command and was soon made President of Connaught, committing himself strongly to the Parliamentary cause. Fifteen years after the Restoration, in 1675, an anonymous poet wrote in *The Moderate Cavalier or the Soldiers' Description of Ireland,* a tribute to Sir Charles:

> Brave Sir Charles Coote
> I honour; who in his father's steps so trod

> As to the rebels was the scourge or rod
> Of the Almighty. He by good advice
> Did kill the Nitts, that they might not grow lice.

Sir Hardress Waller, who had been born in Kent, settled in Ireland in 1630, marrying the daughter of Sir John Dowdall of Kilkenny. He acquired an estate at Castletown, Co. Limerick. During the years of the Confederacy he had fought under Inchiquin when Inchiquin favoured the Parliamentarian side. In December, 1648, Waller had acted as Colonel Pride's assistant in the seizure and expulsion of the Presbyterian members of Parliament. He was one of Charles I's judges and had signed the King's death warrant. Henry Cromwell wrote to his father:

> I have observed him to bear your Highness' pleasure so evenly, that I am more moved with that his quiet and decent carriage that I could by any clamour or importunity to give him recommendation.

On August 15, 1649, Oliver Cromwell, Lord Lieutenant and commander of the Army of the English Commonwealth in Ireland, stepped ashore from the frigate *John* in the estuary of the Liffey. He bore a typical English racial contempt for the Irish and to him the situation was a black and white one—innocent, honest English colonists had been slaughtered by the treacherous, uncivilised Irish. His knowledge of the Irish insurrection was taken from the propaganda pamphlet histories with all their distortions of Irish atrocities against the colonists. According to Cromwell:

> ...Englishmen had good inheritances which many of them purchased with their money, they or their ancestors from many of you and your ancestors. They had good leases from Irishmen for a long time to come; great stocks therefrom; houses and plantations created at their cost and charge. They lived peaceably and honestly among you; you had equal benefit of the protection of England with them, and equal justice from the laws—saving what was necessary for the State, for reasons of State, to put upon some few people apt to rebel upon the imaginations of such as you. You broke the union. You, unprovoked, put the English to the most unheard of and most barbarous massacre without respect of sex or age, that ever the sun beheld, and at a time when Ireland was in perfect peace, and when, through the example of English industry, through commerce and traffic, that which was in the natives' hands was better to them than if all Ireland had been in their possession and not an Englishman in it; and yet then I

say, was this unheard of villainy perpetrated by your instigation who boast of peacemaking and unity against the common enemy . . .

It was a ludicrous farrago but it represented Cromwell's sincere belief and made his actions during the terrible military campaign that proceeded more understandable.

The campaign opened with the siege of Drogheda. On September 10, 1649, he called upon the town to surrender and Sir John Aston, the Royalist commander, refused. The Cromwellian artillery opened up a bombardment. The next day the town fell and Cromwell reported: 'Our men getting up to them, were ordered by me to put them all to the sword . . . I forbade them to spare any that were in arms in the town.' Cromwell let his troops plunder the town and seek out, in particular, Catholic priests and execute them. The pillage went on all through the night of the 11th/12th and by next morning only two strong points remained. These pockets of resistance were soon overcome. 'When they submitted,' wrote Cromwell, 'their officers were knocked on the head; and every tenth man of the soldiers killed; and the rest were shipped for Barbados. The soldiers in the other Tower were all spared, as to their lives only; and shipped likewise for the Barbados.' Some 3,500 men, women and children had been killed. Cromwell felt it was a 'righteous judgement of God upon these barbarous wretches, who have imbrued their hands in so much innocent blood'. Ironically, well over half the Drogheda garrison were English Catholics and Royalists and the others were mainly Anglo-Irish Royalists. It was highly improbable that any man in Drogheda had a hand in the 1641 insurrection. But Cromwell believed the lesson of Drogheda 'will tend to prevent the effusion of blood for the future, which are the satisfactory grounds to such actions, which otherwise cannot but work remorse and regret'.

In this Cromwell was right. The Royalist-Confederate alliance evacuated Trim and Dundalk and Colonel Robert Venables was despatched to Ulster to support Sir Charles Coote. Carlingford and Newry surrendered, leaving Cromwell to advance on Wexford, which he reached on October 1. After unsatisfactory parleys Cromwell's artillery opened up on October 11. Wexford was defended by Colonel David Sinnott and 3,000 men. After a barricade defence in the town's market place, Cromwell's forces smashed resistance and slaughtered over 1,500 soldiers and civilians.

A small garrison was left in Wexford and Cromwell turned on New Ross, defended by Lucas Taafe, brother of Lord Taafe. After an artillery bombardment Taafe agreed to vacate the town. The English under his command decided to join the Commonwealth army.

Malaria and dysentery, as well as plague, the spotted fever, were taking its toll of the Commonwealth army. Oliver himself fell ill with malaria and his second in command Michael Jones died in Dublin of the plague in December. Ireton was immediately appointed Cromwell's deputy. Illness also took its toll of the Irish leaders. On November 6 at Cloughoughter in Co. Cavan, Eoin Ruadh O'Neill died. It was a terrible blow to the Irish for O'Neill was perhaps the only Irish commander with personality and competence to inspire his ill-clad and ill-fed troops to face Cromwell. The Lord Lieutenant, meanwhile, spent Christmas resting at Youghal, Co. Cork, and on January 29, 1650, began an early spring campaign by marching on Kilkenny. During the spring months the Commonwealth army broke down Irish resistance throughout the country. Kilkenny fell in March.

The English Parliament now required Cromwell's presence in London and Ireton was appointed commander in his place. Lieutenant General Ludlow was to arrive in January, 1651, to be Ireton's second in command. He brought with him a female relative of his who had been a colonist and had been driven out of Ireland in 1641 with her children during the early days of the uprising. Ludlow took his views from her and her family, who were wiped out by the plague within days of returning to Ireland. Ludlow accepted all the tales of Irish barbarism, even 'that they roasted men and ate them to supply their necessities'.

On May 26, 1650, Cromwell embarked on the frigate *President Bradshaw* and, after a rough passage, arrived at Bristol five days later. He was received as a conquering hero; in Ireland he had become the devil personified.

The forty-year-old Major General Ireton now faced renewed activity by the Irish in Ulster. Bishop Emer MacMahon had gathered an army of 4,000 infantry and 400 cavalry. Sir Charles Coote's forces could not get to grips with MacMahon who was displaying a considerable flair for military strategy. Finally, in the middle of June, 1650, the two armies clashed at Scarrifhollis, on a hillside overlooking the western shore of Lough Swilly. Coote managed to break the Irish and the bulk of the Irish leaders were hunted down and executed, including Henry O'Neill, the only son of Eoin Ruadh. Sir Phelim O'Neill managed to escape but MacMahon was caught and executed. The last sizeable field army that the Irish possessed was gone, although a small army of 2,000 foot and 700 horse, commanded by Lord Clanricarde, held Tyrrells pass.

Ireton had turned on Carlow and was mopping up isolated garrisons. He took command of the siege of Waterford, which was still holding out, and at the end of July the city asked for terms. It surrendered on August 10. Ireton reported: 'There marched out about 700 men, well armed, and townsmen more numerous than we believed, and the town better fortified in all parts and more difficult to attempt than our forces conceived, there being many stores sufficient to have maintained them a longer time.' On August 17 Duncannon surrendered and Waterford harbour was now open to the English navy.

The end of resistance by the Royalist-Confederate alliance was in sight and Ormonde decided it was time to quit the country. He issued a commission to Lord Clanricarde to act as his deputy and left in a fast sloop of four guns on December 11 from Geneinagh, a little port in Co. Clare. Twelve years were to pass before Ormonde returned to Ireland. In the spring of 1651 Clanricarde tried to reconstitute the Irish armies but the offensive was entirely with the Commonwealth forces.

In June Ireton was before Limerick, where, supported by the navy, which landed stores and artillery at the Shannon Estuary, he set up several artillery pieces. On June 19 he summoned the commander Hugh O'Neill to surrender. When his terms were refused, twenty-eight field guns opened up on the Castle, which covered Thomond Bridge, and Ireton's mortars harassed the town. On June 20 the Castle was destroyed. Limerick doggedly held out, hoping that winter would come. Some Irish boasted that while the English 'laboured to beat them out with bomb shells . . . they would beat them away with snow balls'. A few civilians tried to leave town but Ireton had them hanged as examples; they included a young girl whose father tried to redeem her life for his own.

Fresh English troops were pouring into the country as reinforcements. On April 18, 1651, the English Parliament had passed 'An Act for the Imprestment of Soldiers for the Service of the Commonwealth in Ireland'. The Act was made because 'of great necessity, considering the great preparation now making by the malignant Papish and ill affected party to this Commonwealth'. It provided for the conscription of 10,000 men and those who refused to serve would be punished by three months' imprisonment. On October 27 Limerick, weakened by death, by bombardment and plague, not to mention hunger, surrendered. The original garrison of 2,000 was reduced to 1,200 and over 5,000 townspeople had lost their lives. The Irish garrison began to march out of the town to surrender. 'As they were marching out,' observed Ludlow, 'two or three of them fell down dead of the plague. Several of them also lay unburied in the churchyard.' Some of the Irish leaders, including Major General Purcell, were immediately executed, although Ireton spared the life of the commanding officer, Hugh O'Neill. Ireton's attitude was clear. According to Ludlow, he stated 'that Ireland being a conquered country, the English nation might with justice assert their right of conquest . . .'

Ireton decided to cross into Co. Clare and subdue the Irish garrisons there, at the same time offering Galway, the sole remaining city in the hands of the Irish, identical terms to those offered to Limerick on November 7. Ludlow had captured Clare Castle but soon after had fallen ill with a cold. Ireton also caught the cold and returned to Limerick to recuperate. Oliver's youngest son, Henry, now twenty-three years old and serving as a Captain with Sir Hardress Waller against Lord Muskerry in Cork and Kerry, had arrived in Limerick to report to Ireton. He found the Commander-in-Chief ill with 'a very great cold' but refusing to go to bed until he had heard a case 'touching an officer of the army who was accused of some violence done to the Irish'. Weakened by his condition, Ireton caught the plague and by November 27 he was dead. Ludlow, the staunch republican, wrote:

Some of General Cromwell's relations who were not ignorant of his vast designs now on foot, caused the body to be transported to England and solemnly interred at Westminster in a magnificent monument at public charge ...

Ludlow was now acting commander-in-chief in Ireland and began to make preparations for the final phase of the conquest.

'the Gaels are being wasted'

Ireland's economy now lay in ruins. In the early years of the Confederate Government there had been a growth towards prosperity. The old impoverished landowning classes had mortgaged their property to the growing Irish middle class who, precluded from practising the 'professions of the gentry' by English law, found themselves in an equivalent situation to European Jews, indulging in trade and moneylending. They had thus become a strong factor in building up a stable Irish economy.

The most serious loss to Ireland was the decrease of her population. According to Petty's reckoning the population of Ireland in 1641 had been 1,448,000 of which 616,000 had perished by 1652. Of these 504,000 were natives and 112,000 were colonists and English troops. Within another few years Petty was to reckon that a further 40,000 young Irishmen, remnants of the Irish armies, had sought service in other European countries and that another 100,000 Irish men, women and children had been transported to the colonies in the Americas.

Ordinary agriculture had been suspended. Naas, the centre of a rich farming country with access to the great market of Dublin, could not boast one tilled field in 1652. Within a decade the diet of the Irish had changed drastically. Before the insurrection they had had an abundance of milk, butter, sour curds, oatmeal, oaten bread, and plenty of meat. They were also addicted to meat puddings. Potatoes had been introduced into Ireland about the turn of the century by people returning from voyages to the Americas. The first written reference to the potato was made in 1606 at Comber, Co. Down. Dr. Petty reported that by 1660 the potato had become the staple diet of the Irish. 'Their food is bread and cakes, whereof a penny serves a week for each—potatoes from August till May . . . as for flesh they seldom eat it.' The change over to the potato had been made out of necessity. The destruction of agriculture was a deliberate policy of the Commonwealth Army and had been deliberately conceived by Cromwell as part of his campaign. It was strikingly illustrated by the lists of 'military weapons' issued from the army stores at Waterford. They included eighteen dozen scythes with handles and wings, forty reaping hooks and whetstones and rub stones. In 1651 the Governor of Dublin, Colonel John Hewson, wrote to the Commissioners saying that his soldiers 'doth now intend to make use of scythes and sickles that were sent over in 1649, with which they intend to cut down the corn growing in these parts'. With their crops being cut down and burnt, as Ludlow had done throughout the Wicklow mountains, the Irish were forced to rely on the potato which, lying hidden underground, could be harvested only when it was wanted for eating while the rest could stay hidden from the soldiers' wanton destruction.

Badly hit also were the cattle. As the English soldiers destroyed the Irish herds, the Irish retaliated by destroying English herds. So great was the cattle slaughter that Dr. Petty reported that in 1652 cattle had to be imported into Ireland from Wales. He calculated the Irish herds to be worth £4 million in 1641 while in 1652 they had decreased to £$\frac{1}{2}$ million. That same year of 1652 a proclamation was published prohibiting the slaying of sheep and lambs, and which referred to the country being rife with starvation and plague. Birds were killed and eaten when possible and even the traditional Irish belief in misfortune coming to those who killed swans was ignored.

For those who had money, even money had become a

problem. The Confederacy had issued its own coins of silver and copper. Much coinage was carried abroad by exiles and by 1651 there was a great shortage of money in Ireland. In 1652 a number of London merchants were circulating worthless money in the country—some of them were caught and executed for fraud. Neither was Ireland in a position now to produce her own coin for the once valuable silver and lead mines, especially the one at Dunally, Co. Tipperary, the success of which had been a project that Charles I had kept a close eye on, had been devastated and were no longer operating.

As for Irish shipping, during the years of the Confederacy it had been expanding and was becoming a thriving business; now there were no Irish ships to speak of. Ireland was not allowed free trade with England, although, in 1652, it was allowed this with Scotland and the Isle of Man. The situation became worse than it was for merchants in the colonies. The 'Act for the increase of Shipping and encouragement of the Navigation of this Nation' passed in the English Parliament on October 9, 1651, provided that goods from the Plantations be imported into Ireland only in English ships. Within a year Irish shipping had disappeared from the seas. Even the fishing industry was destroyed as the fish could only be imported to England in English ships.

The vast woods, which had always been a feature of the Irish landscape and a safe retreat for many hard-pressed men fighting an incessant guerilla warfare with the colonists, were beginning to thin drastically. They began to suffer under the Elizabethan colonisation when they were systematically destroyed as affording places of refuge to Irish insurgents. In 1609 an inducement offered to the citizens of London to colonise Ulster was the great store of timber promised for ship-building there. By 1610 the colonists found the forests of Ulster were mainly wasted and turned to Munster. Most ships at the time were built from Irish wood. The dangers of this policy were seen as early as 1611 when an 'Act for the Preservation of Timber' was put before Parliament but not passed. The chief offender was "The Great Earl of Cork', Richard Boyle, an adventurer from Canterbury, who had arrived in Ireland in June, 1588, aged twenty-two years old, with the clothes on his back and the sum of £27 3s, as well as a diamond ring and a gold bracelet given to him by his mother. He had secured a post as deputy to Sir John Crofton, Escheater General of Ireland, and begun to enrich himself in the process of carrying out his official duties of investigating forfeited lands and lapsed titles. He was twice imprisoned for embezzlement before the Irish uprising of 1598 forced him to flee to England. He was soon back in Ireland as owner of the 42,000-acre estate previously owned by Walter Ralegh. By the time the Irish uprising of 1642 broke out Boyle, who had been rewarded with the title Earl of Cork, had iron foundries in the Blackwater Valley exporting bar iron and artillery, smelted lead at Minehead, worked silver at Ardmore, engaged in woollen weaving at Clonakilty and Capoquin, and linen production at Youghal as well as the reckless felling of forests for timber to keep his industries running.

To make matters worse, soldiers deliberately destroyed as much of the woods as they could. Gerard Boate, who published a book entitled *Ireland's Natural History* in London in 1652, dedicated to Oliver Cromwell and Charles Fleetwood, wrote:

... the English, having settled themselves in the land, did by degrees greatly diminish the woods in all the places where they were masters, partly to deprive the thieves and rogues, who used to lurk in the woods in great numbers, of their refuge and starting holes and partly to gain the greater scope of profitable lands. For the trees being cut down, the roots stubbed up, and the land used and tilled according to exigency, the woods in most parts of Ireland may be reduced not only to very good pasture, but also to excellent arable and meadow [lands].

Whole shiploads sent into foreign countries yearly: which as it brought great profit to the proprietaries, so the felling of so many thousands of trees every year as were employed that way, did make a great destruction of the woods in tract of time. As for Charcoal, it is incredible what quantity thereof is consumed by one iron works in a year, and whereas there was never an iron works in Ireland before, there hath been a very great number of them erected since the last Peace in sundry parishes of every province, the which to furnish constantly with charcoals, it was necessary from time to time to fell an infinite number of trees all the lopings and windfalls being not sufficient nor in the least manner.

As well as sickness, disease and starvation, yet another danger threatened. The war conditions had proved favourable to the existence, and increase in numbers, of wolf-packs, which could even be found on the outskirts of Dublin. In December, 1652, a public wolf hunt was organised in Castleknock and rewards were posted ranging up to £6 per head for a bitch. The export of wolf hounds with those leaving Ireland to go into exile was now strictly forbidden on account of their usefulness. Lady Marion Clotworthy, wife of Sir Hugh, a Presbyterian colonist, recounted a story that while walking alone along the shores of Lough Neagh she was attacked by a wolf. She had given herself up as lost when a wolf hound leapt from the forest and attacked the wolf, killing it after a fierce struggle. The hound was wounded in the affair and Lady Marion took it home and cared for it.

While the Confederate government had demanded freedom of religious worship, particularly the freedom of Catholics from the penal laws, the religious situation now worsened. Until 1641 the Catholics had been mainly tolerated in spite of the penal laws. On December 8, 1641, the English Parliament had issued a declaration saying it would not tolerate Catholicism in Ireland or in any of the English dominions. In 1650 the Protestant Bishop of Clogher, Dr. Henry Jones, ordered all Catholics to quit the city on pain of death, they were not to be found within two miles of its walls nor were they to harbour priests. In a reply to an Irish petition Oliver Cromwell issued a declaration 'in Answer to the Acts of the Popish Clergy at Clonmacnoise', printed in Cork in 1650. He declared that while Parliament held power the Mass (Catholicism) would not be tolerated. Priests were killed on many occasions when they surrendered and £20 was offered to any who would capture them. On October 4, 1650, the Commissioners issued orders for the suppression of Catholicism and on December 25 of that year all the English statutes against Catholics were brought into force. A general reward of £5 per priest was agreed upon. During 1651 there were fifteen recorded executions of Franciscans, Augustinians and Dominicans. Many priests went into hiding or exile. Father Nugent, a Capuchin, wrote on June 30, 1651, from Waterford, that he passed freely about the city, in disguise, being the gardener to the chief Protestant there, Colonel Richard Lawrence, the governor of the city.

One of the friars driven into exile wrote a lament between June, 1650, and February, 1653, in Rome, which he entitled *An Síogaí Rómhánach,* or the Irish Vision at Rome. He says that he is writing the poem by the graves of Rory O'Donnell, Earl of Tyrconnell, and Hugh O'Neill, Earl of Tyrone, in the cemetery of the Franciscan Convent of San Pietro, in Montario, Rome, the supposed site of St. Peter's martyrdom. The poet describes a beautiful young girl lamenting over the graves of the two great Irish heroes, lamenting what has befallen her country.

> The Gaels are being wasted and deeply wounded
> Subjugated, slain, extirpated,
> by plague, by famine, by war, by persecution ...

After a long lamentation the poet seems to raise his hopes for he says there will come a day when the Irish will rise up again.

> Then shall Erin be freed from settlers.
> Then shall perish the English tongue.
> The Gaels in arms shall triumph
> Over the crafty, thieving false set of Calvin ...

The Catholics were not the only religious sect to be persecuted following the conquest. The Presbyterian ministers in Ulster were now hunted by the authorities. One of the few ministers to remain in Ulster during this period was Patrick Adair, who had arrived in Ireland as a preacher from Scotland in 1646. He was given the pastorship of Cairncastle, near Larne, Co. Antrim. Before his death in 1694, he wrote a book entitled *A True Narrative of the Rise and Progress of the Presbyterian Church in Ireland.* He recalled how Colonel Robert Venables, the Commonwealth commander in Ulster, had tried to make the Presbyterians swear allegiance to the new order. Adair had replied:

First, that though Ireland was subject to the King of England, yet they had a parliament of their own by which the subjects of Ireland were governed and Ireland's parliament had made no such acts against the King and Lords. It was further urged that now they were a conquered people under England and this party. It was answered a conquest might draw from them [the Presbyterians] a passive obedience out of necessity but no acknowledgement of their lawful power.

Venables decided to remove the more troublesome of the Presbyterian leaders and an order to that effect was signed by him, with Sir Charles Coote, Chidley Coote and Colonel Robert Barrow, Governor of Co. Down. 'However', wrote Adair,

those that stayed in the country, though they could not exercise their ministry orderly as formerly, and though their stipends were sequested. yet changing their apparel to the habit of countrymen, they frequently travelled in their own parishes, and sometimes in other places, taking what opportunities they could to preach in the fields or in barns and glens and were seldom in their own houses.

The hunting of Presbyterian ministers continued into the summer of 1651. Those who were caught were imprisoned in Carrickfergus jail and were then transported to Scotland. By the end of the year there were only six ministers in Ulster. These were Patrick Adair, in Co. Antrim; Anthony Kennedy in Templepatrick; Robert Cunningham in Ballycarry; and James Gordon, Thomas Peebles and Gilbert Ramsey in Co. Down. These resolute men were put to even greater difficulties.

Yet [wrote Adair] they continued preaching in remote or private places, where the people willingly met them. They had frequent meetings amongst themselves in order to strengthen one another, and consult about their present carriage; and they drew up causes of fasts and humiliation to be kept among the people in a private way in several little societies, as the times permitted. Some time the minister would, in his parish, call all together a part of the day, and preach and pray with them; and thereafter, the people would repair to their several societies for prayers the rest of the day, the minister always joining with one of these little societies after another. This continued for another year, during 1652, at which time the people were discouraged through want of public ordinances. The ministers also wearied, and ceased this manner of living and preaching, yet indeed, it appeared that these small endeavours of an oppressed people, and remnant of the ministry, were not in vain, for after this, matters began to grow more encouraging.

Some ministers of the Anglican Church also suffered. The Reverend Pádraig Ó Duincín, the vicar of Domhnach Mór, in Co. Down, was forced to go into exile in the Isle of Man. A graduate of Trinity College, Dublin, he had been appointed vicar of Domhnach Mór about 1640. In the Isle of Man he wrote a moving fourteen-verse lament entitled

Truagh mo thuras ó mo thir—Sad my voyage from my country—which began:

> Sad my voyage from my country
>   to the boundaries of the Ocean God [Isle of Man]
> three sharp faced Puritans
>   have shortened my life, if they can.

The Irish had been encouraged to keep fighting in order to effect a diversion favourable to Charles Stuart's attempt to re-cover England with the aid of the Scots. The scheme ended with the battle of Worcester on September 3, 1651, and Charles now advised the Irish to seek terms for themselves. Many of the Irish had seen the alliance with the Royalists merely as a good piece of political strategy. Their main aim was still to re-establish the Confederate government. They were fighting for freedom, not for the English monarchy. Father Christopher Plunkett observed in 1650:

> So far the spirit of ambition and dissension invaded the hearts of that nation that they will sooner pull God out of His throne or throw themselves headlong into the sea than become loyal to the Crown of England.

When Royalist officers started to surrender, many Irish soldiers dispersed into the woods and mountains and formed guerilla bands. These had long been a feature of the Irish struggle against the colonists. The name Tories (from the Irish word *toiridhe*—a pursued person) was first given to such bands in 1647, and was first officially used when, on September 25, 1650, Lord Ormonde ordered all partisan bands 'as are termed Toryes or Idle Boys' to enlist in the Royalist army or be deemed and treated as traitors. The Tories were to spearhead the struggle against the Commonwealth for the next decade and soon a song, *Eamonn an chnoic*—Eamonn of the Hill, was to become popular, sung often in defiance, as the soldiers of the Commonwealth tried to track down the Tories and kill them. It was the song of a Tory who chose the hunted life among the mountains rather than leave Ireland and go into exile. It was sorrowful in cadence like the wind in the glen in winter. Eamonn is seen knocking at the door of a croft and gaining succour from one personified as Ireland who can give him nothing but a fold of her gown as shelter.

'Long am I wandering,' cries the Tory, 'under the snow and frost, my plough unloosed, my fields unsown.'

As 1651 drew to a close and the news spread through the country of the fall of Limerick and the death of Ireton, the Irish wavered between desperation and hope. The poet Daíbhí Cundún identified Ireland's enemies as 'English people, English churls, wild English, English rabble.' He wrote:

> *Is buartha an cás so dtárlaig Éire*
>
> It is a grievous situation that has befallen Ireland
> Wild blows heaped on her by ruffians
> Her nobility struck to the ground, unable to rise,
> Her heroes now heaps of bones.

But he has hopes for the future; after all, he says, 'God is stronger than the English speaking churls.' In the future 'Foreigners will have no living in Ireland'.

The hope was forlorn.

'war dogs who yielded naught to their opponents'

Six days after the death of Henry Ireton, Lieutenant General Edmund Ludlow was officially confirmed as Acting Commander-in-Chief of the English forces until such time as Parliament made a permanent appointment. The situation he took over on December 2, 1651, was a worrying one. The passing, on October 9, 1651, of the Navigation Act, which had destroyed the remnants of Irish shipping, had hit mainly at the profitable carrying trade of the Dutch (the Act demanded that English men-of-war could stop and search Dutch ships on the high seas for cargo deemed by them as contraband, particularly French cargoes). The Anglo-Dutch war was to break out in the summer of 1652 as this intolerable situation continued. With the passing of the Act, Holland's States-General had issued orders to equip a hundred ships of war to protect the merchant fleet. Ludlow wrote:

This alarm awakened us to a diligent performance of our duty in Ireland, fearing that the Hollanders might transport some foreign forces by their fleet, to the assistance of the Irish, who were not only still numerous in the field, but had also divers places of strength to retreat to.

Rumour had it that Theobald, Viscount Taafe, and the Duke of Lorraine had signed an agreement to bring an army into Ireland 'to restore the Irish to their possessions'. Such an agreement was, in fact, signed by Ulick, Marquess of Clanricarde, Ormonde's deputy, and Stephen de Henin, Lorraine's ambassador, on April 4, 1651, and a second document was signed by Taafe, Nicholas Plunkett and Geoffrey Brown, 'deputies authorised on behalf of the Kingdom of Ireland', and Henin.

Ludlow did not fancy the prospect of a protracted war against the Irish and their foreign allies. Irish resistance had to be smashed within a few months to prevent such an alliance. On December 20 he convened a meeting at Kilkenny with his fellow Commissioners and senior army officers. Among those who attended was Henry Cromwell who noted: 'We had been eight days considering of business in which time I believe we have had a more true light and sense of the want and worth of our task of our late dear lord [Ireton] than ever we had before and shall daily see now.'

The main problem, as Ludlow reported to the Council of State, was the Tories and their guerilla tactics. The remnants of the Irish field armies and isolated garrisons Ludlow was confident of overcoming. The Tories were a different matter, the chief difficulty being the great bogs which were their sanctuaries. In these wastes were many dry islands, generally wooded, with causeways along which horses could only go in single file. From these islands the Tories could sally out at any time, harrying and destroying and thus depriving the army of its resources. The Irish guerillas were used to living in such conditions, but the English soldiers were prey to the wet and cold and dysentery (Ireton had successfully used rice to combat dysentery and large quantities were provided by Parliament). As in all guerilla warfare, the ordinary people acted as scouts and look-outs, being, according to Ludlow, 'possessed of an opinion that the Parliament intend them no terms of mercy and therefore endeavour to preserve them [the Tories] as those that stand between them and danger'.

In Ulster that December, it was reported that 140 Tories had been killed. But the council at Kilkenny were told that there were 50,000 Irish still in arms against the Commonwealth and many of these were in guerilla groups. A plan was adopted to subdue the Tories by seeking to destroy their means of subsistence. No smiths, harness-makers or armourers would be allowed to ply their trade outside the English garrisons. No beer, wine or spirits were to be sold, nor fairs or markets held, beyond garrison limits. A new Pale, the district within which the English held power, was to be formed from the Boyne river to the Barrow river. The counties of Wicklow, parts of Dublin, Kildare and Carlow, where the Tories were particularly active, were to be excluded from 'protection' so that anyone found in arms in those areas after February 28, 1652, was to be killed.

The council now turned their attention to Galway, the last city to remain in the hands of the Royalist-Confederate alliance under the command of General Thomas Preston. Sir Charles Coote was in command of operations against the city and had offered Preston, as Ireton had in November, the same terms as those given to Limerick on condition that these were accepted by January 9, 1652. The council decided to wait until that date. Finally, before the meeting ended, Commissary-General Sir John Reynolds, the Governor of Athlone, just recovered after being dangerously ill with a fever, was ordered by Ludlow 'to lie with a nimble army of near 3,000 horse and foot at Athlone to answer all alarms'. Reynolds was further ordered on February 11 to offer rewards to any person 'that shall bring in the person or head of any rebel in arms against the Commonwealth and under the command of Colonel Donnough O'Connor'. £40 was to be given for O'Connor and 40s. each for soldiers. An officer would entitle the soldier to a month's pay 'according to the quality of the officers'. While Ludlow trusted Reynolds' qualities as a soldier, he did not like his political leanings. The third son of Sir James Reynolds of Castle Camps, Cambridgeshire, he had, after studying law, become an officer in Cromwell's regiment, and Cromwell's 'greatest favourite'. Reynolds had been given his own regiment on October 24, 1648, and ordered to Ireland, but half of the regiment had mutinied with the

Levellers. He had been active in suppressing the Levellers and was therefore hated by them and anyone leaning towards republicanism. In 1650 John Maylier had attacked Reynolds in a pamphlet in the form of an abusive life story entitled *The Newmade Colonel or Ireland's Jugling Pretended Reliever.* Ireton had appointed him Commissary-General of the army in 1651 and Governor of Athlone.

While Ludlow was preparing his troops for a sweep against the Tories he heard that a new Lord Deputy and Commander-in-Chief had been appointed by Parliament on January 30. This was thirty-two-year-old Major General John Lambert, who had made a reputation for himself in northern England during the civil war as one of the most efficient Commonwealth generals. No sooner had Lambert been appointed Lord Deputy and hurried to London to indulge himself in his new position than it was announced that Parliament had decided to abolish Cromwell's Lord Lieutenant's office and with it the Deputyship. Lambert's pride was too great to permit him to accept a lesser situation and when it was suggested he go to Ireland merely as Commander-in-Chief he refused. The choice of commander then fell on Charles Fleetwood who was appointed on July 8, shortly after he married Bridget Ireton. On August 24 he was appointed as a member of the Commissioners for the civil government. Lucy Hutchinson told a malicious story about Lambert's loss of position and Fleetwood's appointment.

There went a story that as my Lady Ireton was walking in St. James Park, the Lady Lambert, as proud of her husband, came by where she was, and as the present princess always hath preceeding of the relict of the dead prince, so she put my Lady Ireton below; who, notwithstanding her piety and humility, was a little grieved at the affront. Colonel Fleetwood being then present, in mourning for his wife, who died at the same time as her lord died, took occasion to introduce himself, and was immediately accepted by the lady and her father, who designed this to restore his daughter to the honour she had fallen from.

On February 28, 1652, Ludlow went to Talbotstown personally to take command of 4,000 horse and foot with which to search the Wicklow mountains for guerillas. It was an area dominated by the O'Byrnes, O'Tooles and Kavanaghs. According to Ludlow:

I marched with a party of horse and foot into the fastness of Wicklow, as well to make example of such as had not obeyed the proclamation, as to place a garrison there, to prevent the excursion of the enemy ... We scoured by different ways the passes and retreats of the Irish, but met not with many of them; our parties being so big that the Irish, who had sentinels placed on every hill, gave notice of our march to their friends, so that upon our approach, they still fled to their bogs and woods.

Colonel George Cooke, the Governor of Wexford, reporting on the result of his sorties into the area on March 17, said:

In searching the woods and bogs we found great store of corn, which we burnt, also all the houses and cabins we could find; in all of which we found plenty of corn: we continued burning and destroying for four days, in which time we wanted no provision for horse or man to lie in, though we burnt our quarters every morning and continued burning all day. He was an idle soldier that had not a fat lamb, veal, pig, poultry or all of them, every night to his supper. The enemy in these parts chiefly depended upon this country for provision. I believe we have destroyed as much as would have served some thousands of them until next harvest.

Cooke was a returned emigrant from the New England colony. He had gone to America in 1635 and been elected to the Massachusetts Assembly, becoming its Speaker in 1646. As a captain in the colony's artillery company he had won a degree of fame by capturing nine Indians single-handed. He returned to England to take part in the second civil war, before accepting a command in Ireland. Archbishop John Lynch said:

In 1652 the same General [sic] Cooke shut up 300 men and many infants in a house in the county of Wexford and then setting fire to the house, all were burned in the flames.

A few weeks after his sorties into the mountains, Cooke was killed in an encounter with a band of partisans led by a Captain Nash in Kilkenny. Colonel Thomas Sadler was confirmed as Governor of Wexford in November to replace him.

Among the important captures by Ludlow's troops was that of Father Brían Mac Giolla Phádraig, who in 1651 had been appointed Vicar-General and Apostolic Vicar of the diocese of Ossory, an area in which the Tories were most active. Mac Giolla Phádraig had been ordained in 1610 and was a poet and scholar in his native language. He had made several copies of Irish manuscripts such as *Leabhar Branach*, the Book of the O'Byrnes. In a poem entitled *Ábhar deargtha leacan do mnaoi chuinn é*, Ireland's cause for shame, he condemned Ireland for acting as a whore to foreigners and neglecting her rightful progeny. In another poem *Faiscan chláir Éibhir*, the Irish Fashion, he notes that some Irishmen were adopting the use of English and using English-style clothing. The soldiers gave Mac Giolla Phádraig a drum head court-martial and executed him by beheading.

The activity of the Commonwealth forces in the area forced the surrender, on March 23, of Colonel Eamonn O'Dwyer who commanded the Irish regulars from Waterford and to Tipperary. He agreed to terms of surrender under which he would leave the country, taking with him the Irish soldiers under his command to serve the King of France. Soon a new song had become popular with the people.

Ar m'éiri dhom ar maidin,
> *grian an tsamhra ag taitneamh*

Rising in the morning, when the summer sun was shining
I heard the bugle crying, and the sweet song of the bird.
Hares and badgers running, long-beaked woodcocks calling,
loudly rang the echoes, and the strong noise of guns;
The red fox rockward speeding, horsemen all hallooing,
the woman in the roadway, lamenting her lost fowl,
but now the woods are falling, overseas we'll travel
and Sheáin Uí Dhuibhir an Ghleanna, you have lost your game.

Galway had not surrendered on January 9. But now it was a city divided. In spite of the persecution of the Catholic clergy, those of the Hierarchy in Galway were anxious for a peace settlement with the Commonwealth, believing that this measure would obtain for them a degree of religious tolerance. Such thinking was led by John Bourke, Bishop of Clonfert and titular Archbishop of Tuam, and Nicholas French, Bishop of Ferns. Lord Clanricarde opposed them but was pressed into writing a letter to Ludlow proposing terms for a general surrender on February 16. If such terms were not met, declared Lord Clanricarde, Galway would sell its life dearly. Ludlow answered ten days later from Dublin that it was for the forces of the Commonwealth to grant terms. Clanricarde did his best to prolong the resistance of Galway but when he saw the inhabitants were not prepared to endure the siege much longer he left the town.

Galway surrendered to Sir Charles Coote on April 5. Clanricarde announced that 'Galway, having basely and perfidiously yielded' he would resist to the end. He ordered Lord Westmeath from Leinster, Lord Muskerry from Munster and Philip Mac Hugh O'Reilly from Ulster to meet him with their forces in Sligo or Leitrim and 'unite in one clear score for God, our King and country'. But the month of April was a month of surrenders for the Royalist-Confederate alliance. On April 2 Tadhg O'Connor Ruadh drew his regiment into Tully in the barony of Ballytubber, and delivered all his arms to Commissary-General Reynolds. He was then allowed liberty to transport his regiment, excepting any of his men involved in the massacres of 1641–42, to Spain. The next day Eamonn Daly surrendered Roscommon to Colonel Francis Gore. Then came the surrender of Galway, Jamestown and Drumrushe. On April 19 Captain Walter Welsh handed over his command to Sir Hardress Waller at Limerick; two days later Murtagh O'Brien surrendered the remnants of the Clare Brigade of the Irish army to Waller.

In spite of the hopes of the Hierarchy at Galway for tolerance for Catholicism, the Commonwealth forces continued their persecution of priests. During the year five secular priests and nine regular priests—among whom were three Dominicans—were executed. Many others decided to go underground, like Father Mark Baidhtuín of Cashel, who in the disguise of a herdsman, looked after cattle for three years, ministering to his flock by night until he went blind. Even then he assumed the disguise of a beggar going from place to place, hearing confessions and administering the sacraments. Others, like Father James Finaghty, Vicar-General of the diocese of Elphin, was arrested and 'suffered many tortures and cruel afflictions from the common enemy for the faith of Christ'. At one time he was tied to a horse's tail and dragged naked through the streets, then thrown into a dungeon. On August 24 the clergy sheltering on one of the few remaining Irish strongholds, in the Aran islands, appealed to Pope Innocent X for help expressing the hopelessness of their position.

On May 12 the Leinster division of the Irish army, commanded by Lord Westmeath, surrendered. By agreement, eleven regiments of foot and six regiments of horse would lay down their arms on June 1 at Mullingar, Maryborough, Carlow and Kildare. The officers would retain their horses and arms, and the non-commissioned officers, whose horses were confiscated, would receive compensation. The officers would be allowed to leave the country and serve any foreign state in amity with the Commonwealth. Of the Leinster division permission was given for 6,000 to leave the country and the same permission was sought for a further 6,000. Life and personal estate were declared to be 'secured' and owners of the land were promised 'equal benefit with others in the like qualifications with themselves' when the Commonwealth decided on what settlement to make. Priests would be excepted and also persons guilty of murder or robbery were to be dealt with 'according to due course of the law'.

Despite such a large-scale surrender, Clanricarde tried to keep active, capturing the fortress at Ballyshannon, garrisoning it with 300 of his own men under Brian O'Rourke, before securing Donegal. But O'Rourke surrendered to Colonel William Reeves on May 26. The surrenders continued with that of Newtown, Co. Leitrim, by Donogh O'Hart to Major Robert Ormesby.

In the province of Munster the Irish were still extremely active. Murtough O'Brien, who had surrendered the Clare Brigade, had second thoughts and slipped away to join Donogh MacCarthy, Lord Muskerry, who commanded the area. The Munster division was now a strong threat to Ludlow as a field force numbering several thousands. The headquarters of Muskerry's army was at the fifteenth-century Castle of Ross, which stood on Ross Island, which in fact was a peninsula—the Irish word *ros* meaning a promontory—on the lower lake of Killarney.

The approach to the castle was by a narrow causeway through a bog. Ludlow decided that the castle must be reduced to effect the surrender of the Munster army. He took personal command, with Lord Broghill and Sir Hardress Waller acting as divisional commanders, and assembled a force of 4,000 foot and 2,600 horse. Hugh O'Keefe had already surrendered Dromagh so that the dangers of a rear attack on the Commonwealth forces were slight. However, the area was alive with Tories who supplied Ross with provisions. Ludlow realised that boats were needed to effect a successful attack on the castle and so he ordered them to be brought up from the harbour of Castlemaine on June 13; some were dragged from Castlemaine to the River Laune and then rowed into Lough Leane. At the same time Ludlow had to disperse a strong force of Irish soldiers from Killagh Abbey, near the mouth of the Laune. Other diversionary actions, scouring the woods to prevent guerilla attacks, were also ordered, and two heavier ships, designed to carry cannon, were sent up the Laune; they took two days to assemble. On June 18 the boats were brought to Ludlow's entrenchments round the castle. On June 20 he was ready to begin his assault. But there was no need.

A local legend, embodied in a poem, said:

> Ross may all assault disdain
> Till strange ships sail on Lough Laune.

Strange ships were on the lough. An anonymous eye-witness in Ludlow's forces wrote down his recollection of what happened.

They sent to some of the adjoining seaports for boats one whereof was so large they were forced to draw it on sledges by oxen from the Abbey of Killaugh. The merrily disposed soldiers that attended the boat in its land passage had adorned her pageant like with streamers, sail and waste clothes, so that to the enemy in the castle of Ross at a distance it appeared most terrible but [being] above, seeing it in that place upon dry land, and not being able to well view the oxen that drew it, did wonderfully astonish them, for now they thought most certainly it was impossible any longer to retain Ross, which was then taken, when ships sailed on land, which saying was now most surely verified so that before the boat could come nigh the castle, as to betray the fallacy, the Irish beat their drums for a parley.

The castle officially surrendered on June 22. Some 960 men marched out of the castle and 3,000 more men came in from the surrounding countryside. On the same day Muskerry formally surrendered the Munster division while Colonel Florence MacCarthy surrendered his command to Lord Broghill. Murtough O'Brien escaped into the Kerry mountains with 200 men to continue the resistance. Muskerry, meanwhile, secured an agreement to take 3,000 foot and 600 horse abroad. Many of his officers feared that they would be held liable for the murder of English colonists, 'which', says Ludlow, 'was an exception we never failed to make'.

With the Commonwealth forces more or less in control of the Kerry area several prominent local leaders were immediately executed. Among the first to be hanged and then beheaded was Seán an Fhíona O Conchubhair Chiarrai (Seán of the Wine O'Connor of Kerry). The O'Connors were prominent in leading resistance in Kerry, and Seán an Fhíona's uncle Seán of the Battles had taken a leading part in the insurrection. Seán an Fhíona himself, who had a reputation as a poet, had defended his castle at Carraig an Phoill but Ludlow's troops had taken it by storm, hanging its occupants, five men, six women and a child.

Colonel Richard Grace, who had a price of £300 on his head, remained in command of a considerable Irish force at Birr. He now crossed the Shannon with 3,000 men but was surprised by Colonel Henry Ingoldsby near Loughrea and his cavalry was routed while his infantry was driven into a bog. Grace escaped, but his followers were either hacked down, or managed to disperse and reform as Tories, or sought terms for themselves. By June 20 Grace had gathered another force and crossed into Leinster where he took refuge in a strongly fortified island in Lough Cowa, near Birr. Sir Hierome Sankey surrounded the lake and prepared to starve him out. Grace, realising the helplessness of his position, sued for peace and was allowed to leave for Spain taking 1,200 of his men. At the end of June Lord Clanricarde, cut off in the Isle of Carrick, and realising the futility of continuing the war, made terms for himself. He was allowed to go abroad with not more than twenty servants, in return for which he was required to divest himself of his vice-regal authority, and promise to undertake no more hostile acts against the Commonwealth. He was further allowed to enlist 3,000 men for foreign service. Clanricarde preferred to go to England, accepting a pardon and a small estate at Somerhill in Kent, where he died in 1657. He was buried in Tonbridge Church.

Disaster for the Irish continued during the summer months

of 1652, with many more surrenders. Part of the Ulster army surrendered to Venables at Ballynacargie on July 8, and five days later Lord Mayo surrendered his command in Connaught to Colonel Richard Coote, Sir Charles's brother.

Within a short space of time 40,000 Irish soldiers were allowed to leave the country to seek service under the colours of France, Austria, Spain and other European states 'in amity with the Commonwealth'. It was a brilliant move from Ludlow's point of view for it prevented the experienced soldiers remaining in the country and joining the Tory bands. There was bitterness in the eyes of the young Cork poet, Dáibhí Ó Bruadair, as he watched the lines of Irish soldiers marching down to the ships, their pipes playing laments as they left their homeland, never to return. He wrote:

> Not a foot of land hath been left in their possession,
> not even the makings of a bed. As state doled pittance
> they will grant them now the favour and the pleasure
> of letting them go safe to Spain by proclamation.

With the leaving of the Irish soldiers people were now trying to ingratiate themselves with the victors.

> Hundreds now are proclaiming themselves as English
> by kinship welded to the war successful faction.
> They who opened oft a breach in thriving districts
> while guarding her estates, maintaining her dominions.

An anonymous Irish officer, serving with the French army, was to write a few years later of the soldiers who had left their homeland:

> *Nach léir duite Gaoidhil bhocta na glan-áille*

> See you not the kindly countenanced, unhappy Gaels,
> the war dogs who yielded naught to their opponents,
> scattered in troops through Europe?
> Wealth they lack, raiment and retinue.

> A share of them are serving men to Spaniards,
> a gallant heroic host of them serve the Germans,
> nor can I count at all those of them
> now in Italy, afar off.

> Though he is mighty and in battle victorious,
> the King of Versailles, fortunate lord of cities,

I'd rather from him in glad exchange for victuals
to grant me once again to see my homeland.

For daily now I rise up sadly, look forth
in hope to see grass growing in Hy-Maine.
But now my course is curbed, my fortune waning,
no more I see Ireland's king among his people.

Ludlow decided that a final push was needed to clear up
the few remaining pockets of resistance. Hugh Mac Phelim
O'Byrne of Ballinecar, Co. Wicklow, still controlled most of
Wicklow and Wexford. With him was his brother Brian
O'Byrne. They were sons of Phelim Mac Feagh O'Byrne, an
'ancient rebel', and Hugh had served as a soldier for the
Spanish in Flanders and in the wars against Catalonia. He
had been chosen by Sir Phelim O'Neill, the organiser of the
'41 insurrection, to lead the attack on Dublin Castle, and had
become Governor of Wicklow in 1649. Ludlow decided, for
the second time in a year, that an operation must be mounted
to flush out the Irish in the Wicklow mountains. Before com-
mencing this campaign, however, he published a declaration
stating that all who surrendered would enjoy the protection
of the Kilkenny Articles, the peace terms which allowed
officers and men to leave the country. Many of the Catholic
clergy in the mountains with the O'Byrnes decided to surrender, including the Vicar-General of Dublin, Eamonn
O'Reilly. O'Reilly had been a strong supporter of Eoin
Ruadh O'Neill and was the cousin of Philip Mac Hugh
O'Reilly, the principal commander in Ulster. Hugh Mac
Phelim O'Byrne saw many of his men influenced by the decision of the clergy and felt that resistance was useless under
such circumstances. He left the country secretly while his
brother, Brian, went to join the Ulster forces. After the surrenders Ludlow moved against those who still held out, conducting what was to be his last field campaign. Resistance
was minimal and among those captured was Colonel Luke
O'Toole. Ludlow placed garrisons in the country, cut and
burnt the green corn and then set off for Ulster, the last
stronghold of the Irish.

'By beat of drum and sound of trumpet'

In Ulster moves were being made by the Independent ministers to contact Patrick Adair and his fellow Presbyterians. An Independent army chaplain named Timothy Taylor, who had himself been a Presbyterian until their ejection from the House of Commons, met Adair together with Hugh Vesey, the Anglican minister at Coleraine. Taylor proposed a conference to discuss the differences between them. The Presbyterian minister pointed out that he and his colleagues would need a safe conduct from the military authorities and Taylor approached Colonel Robert Venables. This safe conduct was sent, with an accompanying letter, to Arthur Kennedy, the Templepatrick minister. It was taken by Jeremiah O'Quinn of Templepatrick, a graduate from Edinburgh University, who had been ordained Presbyterian minister of Billy, near Bushmellin, in 1646, but had become an Independent. O'Quinn was to aid the Commonwealth authorities by preaching in Irish to the natives to try to convert them to Protestantism. When O'Quinn arrived in Templepatrick, according to Adair, 'the place where he was bred, where before he had been in great reputation, and where he had much acquaintance' he found that no one would reveal where the minister, Kennedy, was, such being their distrust of the Commonwealth authorities. O'Quinn left the letter with some citizens who eventually passed it on to Kennedy. In reply the Presbyterian ministers pointed out that, while in conscience they could not meet other denominations in a day of fasting and prayer, as had been suggested, they were willing to meet Taylor and an Anabaptist called Weeks at a private meeting to see if some unity could be resolved.

On the day agreed, a Thursday in March, 1652, they had arrived at the appointed place to find that the meeting had been extensively advertised. In the local church the Anabaptist Weeks was preaching about the Presbyterians and, says Adair 'indirectly reflected on them as troubles of the country and dividers of God's people'. The Presbyterians were challenged to debate their beliefs in public, in direct contradiction to the agreement which had been made. A crowd had gathered and were waiting in the hall of the local castle. Taylor opened the debate, saying that it was the Independents who represented the religion of the common people, that they cared about the freedom of God's people without anything like tyranny over their consciences. Independents did not measure their congregations by measures of land and tithes but by Godliness. Adair in turn pointed out that they had come in response to a private invitation by Taylor and Weeks and that they had been forced into a public debate without their consent. He then went on to argue theological principles between their faiths and apparently worsted Taylor who finally turned to Weeks, who was not supporting him, and remarked in exasperation 'What has become of your argument, brother?' Weeks did not reply.

The response by the public to the debate was encouraging for the Presbyterians, who now returned to their parishes and began to preach openly again. This encouraged the exiled ministers in Scotland and soon Archibald Ferguson returned to his ministry in Antrim and Andrew Stewart returned to Donaghadee. The authorities in Ulster called a meeting with them on October 21 to discuss how they might preach the gospel without disturbing the peace. They wanted each minister to swear an oath.

I—do hereby declare that I do renounce the pretended title of Charles Stuart and the whole line of King James, and every other person, as a single person, pretending to the government of these nations of England, Scotland and Ireland, and the dominions and territories thereunto, and that I will, by grace of the Almighty God, be true, faithful, and constant of this Commonwealth, against any king, single person or House of Peers, and every of them, and thereunto I subscribe my name.

The ministers immediately refused and whereas the authorities made threats, no attempt was made to arrest them and they continued to preach openly.

Jeremiah O'Quinn and several other Ulster ministers were employed by the Commissioners to convert the Irish to Protestantism. As early as January, 1651, Colonel John Hewson, the governor of Dublin, reported that there were

750 Catholics in the city who now embraced the Protestant faith and a Mr. Robert Chambers was appointed to minister to them. The need to proselytise in the Irish language also pressed the Commissioners to provide literature for the work. William Perkins' *The Christian Doctrine or the Foundation of Christ's Religion gathered into Six Principles necessary for every ignorant man to learn* was translated into Irish by Geoffrey Daniel and printed in double columns in Irish and English by William Bloden, a Dublin printer, during 1652. To it was appended a series of brief rules for learning Irish. The Commissioners also wrote to Colonel Venables in November asking that O'Quinn be sent to preach in Irish in Dublin, Limerick and Kilkenny and other places where the Irish spoke no English. Provost Winter of Trinity College took a practical interest in the conversion work and among the books he took on his tour of Ulster was a *Catechism* in Irish.

Ludlow had little trouble in clearing up the small pockets of resistance presented by the remnants of the Ulster army under Lieutenant General O'Farrell and Philip Mac Hugh O'Reilly, who nevertheless managed to avoid a major engagement with him. Ludlow garrisoned Carrickmacross and began to move south to Dundalk. On the way he came across some caves where some Irish had taken shelter. The soldiers tried to smoke them out and when it was supposed they had suffocated, the soldiers tried to enter the cave. A shot rang out and a soldier was killed. On Ludlow's orders the area was searched and a ventilation hole was discovered and blocked up. The cave was smoked again. Ludlow recalled:

The passage being cleared, the soldiers entered, and, having put about 15 to the sword, brought four or five out alive with priests robes, a crucifix, chalice and other furniture of that kind. Those within preserved themselves by laying their heads close to water that ran through the rick. We found two rooms in the place, one of which was large enough to turn a pike ...

Ludlow now received an urgent despatch from his fellow Commissioners, dated August 30 at Drogheda. They had received a copy of the legislation passed by the English Parliament on August 12 for the confiscation of Irish land and its redistribution to those who had financed the English army in Ireland and to the soldiers who were to receive the land in

lieu of their pay arrears. There were two separate Acts, the
'Act for the Settling of Ireland' and an Act for determining
how much the officers and soldiers were owed in back pay. It
was the first Act which worried the Commissioners and they
wrote to Ludlow expressing their apprehension that its publication might provoke a major uprising against the army and
strengthen those still holding out.

The Commissioners also wanted to consult with Ludlow as
to how the Act should be published, how it should be imple-
mented, what time to give those who were to be banished
from Ireland and how long to give those still in arms to surrender. Ludlow was inclined to agree with the Commissioners
that the publishing of the Act might cause Irish resistance to
stiffen for a while—after all, by a conservative estimate some
100,000 landowners would be liable for execution under the
terms of the Act. But Ludlow was confident that any resistance could easily be suppressed by his troops. The army
musters of July, 1652, had shown that there were 7,365 horse,
1,447 dragoons, and 25,316 foot, a total of 34,128 men spread
among the fifteen military precincts into which Ireland had
been divided. But Ludlow was a cautious soldier and he
wrote a letter on September 6 advising the commanders of
the precincts as to the provision of the Act, telling them to
prepare for possible disturbances. He did not order the Act
to be published immediately, however, as he wanted first to
force the surrender of the Ulster army of O'Farrell and
O'Reilly.

The legislation was not unexpected. The scheme for the
conquest and colonisation had existed since February, 1641,
four months after the insurrection had broken out, when a
group of London merchants had approached the English
Parliament with a scheme whereby they would finance the
army to crush the Irish at the end of which 'they may have
such satisfaction out of the rebels' estates ... as shall be
reasonable'. The rights of those who would 'adventure money'
for this cause were drawn up in an Act 17 Charles 1 (1642)
known as the 'Adventurers' Act' and which was subsequently
endorsed by further Acts and Ordinances. Ten million acres
of land were to be confiscated out of all four Irish provinces
and given to the speculators.

Towards the end of 1651 the Commissioners had found that they were being hard pressed by the financiers for a settlement and by the soldiers for back pay. On January 1, 1652, they suggested to the Council of State that the financiers should cast lots for the land in four allotments, one in each province. The first allotment was to be the Cos. of Limerick, Kerry and Clare in Munster, and Galway in Connaught; the second allotment would be Cos. Kilkenny, Wexford, Wicklow and Carlow in Leinster; the third allotment would be Cos. Westmeath and Longford in Leinster, and Cavan and Monaghan in Ulster. The last and fourth allotment would be Co. Donegal in Ulster and Cos. Sligo and Leitrim in Connaught. The Commissioners at the same time proposed that the problem of the soldiers' back pay could be settled by giving the soldiers land in lieu of pay out of the confiscations as well. They would thus be encouraged to follow husbandry and maintain their own interests as well as that of the Commonwealth.

On January 30 the financiers attended a meeting in the Speakers' Chamber at Westminster to listen to the proposals. They disliked the plan to scatter the homesteads amongst a hostile population. They made a counter proposal that the area they were to settle should be entirely cleared of natives and settled by colonists. They put this proposal in a more concrete form on April 5. They asked if the lands allotted to them might be contiguous. They also implied that all labour should be brought directly from England. The plan necessitated the removal of at least the greater part of the native population. On April 20 Parliament referred the matter to the Council of State, directing it to 'prepare something for the judgement of Parliament for the settling of the affairs of Ireland' to 'give way for transporting out of Ireland into foreign parts such of the Irish as they shall think fit for the advantage of the Commonwealth'. They added 'that, in qualification, they do make provision touching the transporting of persons from one part of the nation to another, as shall be most for the benefit and advantage of this Commonwealth, and report their opinion to the House'.

John Weaver was sent to London on April 30 to 'hasten the Parliament's resolutions' and to suggest that the financiers might agree to colonise the land within a fixed number of years. On May 12, Weaver found himself chairman of the Committee of Parliament for the Planting of Ireland. The Committee suggested that the financiers be given land in the provinces of Leinster and Munster provided they, on their part, undertook to colonise it within three years from September 29, 1653, with Protestants of any nation, except Ireland, in a manner to be directed by Parliament. The financiers would also be entitled to forfeited houses in walled towns at easy rates on long leases. A further meeting was fixed for Thursday, May 20, at 3 p.m. in the Speakers' Chamber. The financiers were still not happy with the proposals. They feared attacks by Tories and also pointed out that labour was scarce. They also observed that it would take 40,000 labourers and families to make the colonisation effective and that no housing had been provided nor guards against Tory raids. To attempt colonisation under the conditions suggested by the Committee would destroy the scheme before it had a chance of success.

In spite of the lengthy series of meetings and disagreements, the general principle of confiscation was never in doubt. The Committee of Parliament for the Planting of Ireland felt the first step to take was to draw up a bill listing the offences which would 'qualify' for confiscation of property or even loss of life. The bill was presented to Parliament and passed on August 12 as *An Act for the Settling of Ireland*. The preamble to the Act stated:

WHEREAS the Parliament of England, after the expense of much blood and treasure for the suppression of the horrid rebellion in Ireland, have by the good hand of God upon their undertaking, brought that affair to such an issue, as that a total reducement and settlement of that nation may win God's blessing be speedily effected, to the end therefore that the people of that nation may know that *it is not the intention of the Parliament to extirpate that whole nation,* but that mercy and pardon both as to life and estate, may be extended to all husbandmen, ploughmen, artificers and others of the inferior sort, in manner as is hereafter declared, the submitting themselves to the Parliament of the Commonwealth of England and living peaceably and obediently under their government, and that others also of higher rank and guilty may know the Parliament's intention concerning them, according to the respective demerits and considerations under which they fall, be it enacted . . .

The Act listed ten categories. Those people who fell under the first five could expect no mercy—they were to be hanged with the confiscation of all their property. These were: persons who had 'contrived, advised, counselled, promoted and acted in the rebellion, murders or massacres' and those who had assisted 'by bearing arms or contributing men, arms, horses, plate, money, victuals or other furniture or habiliments of war' unless such things were taken by force; priests, particularly Jesuits, who had abetted the war; 106 prominent persons mentioned by name; those who had killed Englishmen, and their accessories, except those who had enlisted in the Irish Army and killed enlisted men on the opposing side; those persons who did not surrender within 28 days of the publication of the Act. It was estimated that at least 100,000 people fell under these first five categories.

Those who fell under the final five categories were subject to confiscation of their property but no loss of life. These were: those who held high civil or military office but were too young to take part in the beginning of the insurrection. These were to be banished and estates forfeited, though a third of the value of their estates would be granted to their wives and children 'in such places in Ireland as the Parliament, in order to the more effectual settlement of the peace of this nation, shall think fit for the purpose'. The seventh category listed those not covered by former categories who had borne arms against the Commonwealth, and those who had borne arms after November 10, 1642, as regular soldiers, would, if they surrendered within 28 days, receive one third of the value of their estates in a place in Ireland to be nominated by the Parliament. Category 8 referred to those who, between October 1, 1641, and March 1, 1650, had not maintained 'constant good affection' to Parliament. These were to receive two-thirds of the value of their estates also in an area to be nominated later. Protestants who failed to show 'good affection', 'constant good affection' not being required, would forfeit only one-fifth of their property but could retain the remainder wherever it was situated. Category 9 referred to persons who had no estate or personal property above £10. These could be pardoned provided they did not qualify in the first five clauses. The tenth and final category stipulated that estates inherited by 'delinquents' since March 25, 1639, were to be forfeited. A final proviso gave the Commissioners power to transplant people 'to any such place in Ireland as should be judged most consistent with public safety'. The way was now clear for the passing of future legislation for the colonisation of the country. On August 25 'An act for determining the accompts of such officers and soldiers as are or have been employed in the service of the Commonwealth in Ireland' was passed. This laid out a means for officers and soldiers, who were owed back pay, to receive debentures for grants 'out of rebel lands, houses, tenements and hereditament in Ireland or other lands, houses, tenements and hereditaments there in dispose of the Commonwealth of England'.

While Ludlow was waiting for a sign that the Ulster army was prepared to surrender the new Commander-in-Chief, Charles Fleetwood, arrived in Wexford on September 11. The Commissioners arranged to meet Fleetwood in Kilkenny, the former capital of the Irish Confederacy, within a few weeks. Ludlow was able to travel to the meeting in a buoyant mood because, on September 21, Lieutenant General O'Farrell signed the surrender document with Commissary-General Reynolds and Colonel Robert Venables.

Fleetwood arrived at Kilkenny at about the time of the surrender of O'Farrell's Ulstermen. The old town, situated on both banks of the River Nore, with its winding streets and ancient buildings was agreeably pleasant to the new Commander-in-Chief. Kilkenny had been the capital of the ancient kingdom of Ossory and the venue of many Irish parliaments from 1293 until 1408. Some of the older buildings were now ruins, like the Dominican Abbey and the Franciscan Friary. St. Canice's Cathedral was also in disrepair since the Commonwealth soldiers used it as a stable for their horses. Fleetwood took up residence in the thirteenth-century Castle standing at the south eastern end of the town.

A court martial was taking place there on September 23 under the presidency of Colonel Arnop. The Advocate-General, Dudley Loftus, was prosecuting a man named Murtagh Cullen, and his wife, who were alleged to have sheltered 'Blind Donnogh' O'Derrick, a notorious Tory commander who had plagued the English colonists for some years. Both Cullen and his wife were sentenced to death but were allowed to cast lots that only one of them might die. The lot of life was thrown by Murtagh and it was his wife who cast the lot of death. The sentence was deferred on account of Mrs. Cullen's pregnancy.

The Commissioners, Ludlow, Corbet, Jones and Weaver, arrived in Kilkenny shortly after Fleetwood. 'I gave him,' recalled Ludlow, 'an account of the army with my assurance of my resolution to obey his orders'. Fleetwood was delighted with the news of the surrender of O'Farrell and confident, as was Ludlow, that the few remaining isolated garrisons could soon be overcome. On September 24 he issued a proclamation declaring the Irish insurrection to be officially over. Dr. Petty wrote that 'it was hoped that it would be possible to regulate, replant and reduce the country to its former flourishing conditions'. Certainly, Fleetwood felt, it was time to 'ask account of the innocent blood that hath been shed', as Cromwell himself had phrased it. Those who had been responsible for the slaughter of colonists during the winter of 1641/42 were to be brought to trial. A meeting of the Commissioners and officers had discussed the subject as early as April 17 that year at Kilkenny and sent a letter to Parliament on May 5.

The Commissioners had enclosed some depositions concerning certain of the massacres. Indeed, the stories stirred up the emotions of some people so much that Justice John Cook declared from the bench that all Irishmen and women living on October 23, 1641, or born in Ireland since were traitors and as such should be punished.

Fleetwood decided that High Courts of Justice should be established to try those who were alleged to have taken part in the massacres. From the start the insurrection had been vicious and bloody. Hatred of the colonists lent a ruthlessness to the Irish and, in spite of the efforts of the Irish leaders to safeguard the lives of civilians and prisoners, many were killed. The terrible cold and hunger of the long winter of 1641/42 killed many more fleeing colonists than the Irish killed, either in battle or cold blood. Survivors began to tell tales of ghastly atrocities some of which were undoubtedly true, though others were dramatised to the point of fiction.

The English public began to read lurid tales of colonists burnt alive, or crucified outside their farmsteads and children spitted on long knives before their parents. The appetite for such tales grew as Parliament authorised the publication of such reports. It was commonly believed in England that 200,000 colonists had been murdered and Justice Gerard Lowther increased the figure to 300,000 when giving a judgement in the Dublin High Court. It was certainly true that when the northern clans turned on the colonists, they remembered that a scant thirty years before they had been hunted and killed by those self same colonists like animals and they paid off old scores. But a figure of 5,000 slain in Ireland during the first year of the insurrection was far more reasonable than 300,000. The historian Ruairí Ó Flaithearta, banished to Connaught in 1653, dryly commented that there were not that many Protestant colonists in the length and breadth of Ireland, let alone Ulster where the majority of the massacres were reported to have happened. In all 15,000 had lost their lives on both sides during the insurrection, of whom a third lost their lives in the actual fighting, while the rest died of privations.

It was probable that a seventh of the colonists in Ulster lost their lives. Dr. Henry Jones, the Scoutmaster-General, had been the first to take depositions concerning the massacres. He had published *A Perfect Narrative of the Beginning and the Continuation of the Rebellion* as early as 1642. Seven Protestant ministers formed a Commission to investigate the allegations and when their report was published in London in 1642 they found there had been no general massacre. Yet four years later Sir John Temple, in his *History of the Horrid Rebellion in Ireland*, had claimed 100,000 people had been slaughtered. The Commissioners had appointed Henry Jones and a clerk to gather evidence in August, 1652, for which he was to receive a salary of £85 for compiling the material as *A Narrative of the Late Bloody Rebellion in this Nation*.

Fleetwood felt a committee was now needed to undertake the work of compiling evidence for presentation before the courts. He appointed a thirteen man commission, including four judges, Sir Gerard Lowther, Sir Edward Bolton, James

Donnellan and Thomas Dongan. They were to employ clerks and interpreters to travel the country seeking evidence. The trials, however, were to begin immediately, opening at Kilkenny that October. A High Court of Justice would be convened under the presidency of Justice James Donnellan, who had become a Judge of the Common Pleas in 1637 and had once represented Dublin University in Parliament.

The High Court began its sittings in mid October and the first person to be brought before it was Colonel Walter Bagenal, a descendant of Sir Nicholas Bagenal, Knight Marshall in the army of Elizabeth I. He had signed the execution warrant for one William Stone, as a spy, in May, 1642, before the date of the official recognition by England of a state of war in Ireland. For this he was found guilty and shot. Fifteen others passed through the High Court to their execution. *Mercurius Politicus* of October 21–28 reported:

> The Court sits in much pomp and the President is attended with the same ceremonies that were used in England having 24 halberdiers continually to wait on him, as also the Serjeant of Arms with the great mace and other officers of the Court, with their staves tipt with silver which formalities, though of themselves of little or no value, yet have much influence upon the spirit of the natives who generally seem to be much daunted at the solemn proceedings, especially those who know themselves guilty of blood.

Later in the year Hight Courts were set up at Clonmel, (where six men were tried and executed in November) and at Cork (where thirty-two were condemned and twenty-four were acquitted).

Not only members of the Royalist-Confederate alliance went through these courts but some officers and soldiers of the Commonwealth Army. Captain Henry Sankey, the nephew of Hierome Sankey, was charged with the murder of one Rory alias James MacCann. H. Stopford, having heard the evidence, wrote to Thomas Herbert:

> I pray, sir, that this gentleman may have all the civil respect that may be, for I am confident there is nothing against him ... and by examination of several witnesses it appears he hath been very kind to several of the English and deserves much respect for it. I know, sir, you may serve in getting his discharge with all convenient speed ...

Colonel Herbert obviously did use his influence for Sankey was acquitted.

In October the Act for the Settling of Ireland was finally published. The four Commissioners signed the order at Kilkenny Castle for the publication. Fleetwood went up to Dublin in November. At the same time Henry Cromwell was recalled to England. He was now twenty-five years old, a handsome young man and an able soldier. He had found it strange to bid goodbye to his sister one year as the widow of Henry Ireton, whom he respected and admired, and welcome her back within the year as the wife of Charles Fleetwood, of whom he was suspicious. When Henry arrived back in England his sister, Mary, tried to make him marry the daughter of Lord Wharton but he was in love with the beautiful Dorothy Osborne. Rejected by her, it was not long before he married, happily, Elizabeth Russell on May 10, 1653. He kept in close contact with Irish affairs and became one of a fifteen man Committee on the Affairs of Ireland and, in November, a member of the Council of State.

Ludlow was already in Dublin to welcome Fleetwood to the old capital. But there was a sickness about and he was ill, though he confessed to being 'pretty well recovered' when Fleetwood arrived. There was still much to be done in organising the administration. The problem of wolves, for example, had to be dealt with. They were still on the increase and reports of packs of wolves destroying and maiming cattle were frequent. On April 27, 1652, the Commissioners had noticed that 'some of the enemy's party, who have laid down arms, and have liberty to go beyond the sea, and others, do attempt to carry away several such great dogs as are commonly called wolf dogs, whereby the breed of them, which are useful for destroying of wolves, would, if not prevented, speedily decay'.

The Commissioners therefore prohibited 'all persons whatsoever from exporting any of the said dogs out of this dominion, and searches by other officers of the customs in the several parts and crecks of this dominion are hereby strictly required to seize and make stop of all such dogs and deliver them either to the common huntsman appointed for the precinct where they are seized upon, or the governor of the said precinct'.

On November 1 Richard Toole and his servant Morris

MacWilliam, with their two fowling pieces and half a pound of powder and bullets, were given passes to permit them to go from Dublin into the counties of Kildare, Wicklow and Dublin to kill wolves. They were given permission to pursue this occupation for two months from the date of the order.

On December 21 Fleetwood decided to tighten up army security. He issued orders that no precinct commander or governor of a garrison was to be absent a night out of his precinct or garrison unless upon specific public service; no junior officer must likewise be absent and no private soldier should go more than a mile from his garrison or colours. The penalty was loss of rank or cashiering. Commanders, when granting leave of absence, were to take into account the circumstances of the time 'so as the public work may not suffer'. Strict care was to be taken to disarm all the Irish, and all guards on sentry duty were to carry lighted matches for their firelocks at all times. No more than two Irish at a time were to be allowed into any fort and the commanders were to see to the frequent exercise of troops on defensive manoeuvres.

The Royalists were watching the proceedings with interest. On April 1 Dean John King had written to Charles Stuart's Council in Paris of his confidence that the Irish would continue the war against the Commonwealth.

The great love the generality of the Irish seems to have of your Majesty's regal government, [wrote King, conveniently forgetting the 1641 insurrection and the near defeat of Charles I by the Confederates], the present dislike of the (Catholic) clergy, the most violent of which, excepting those named, are either extinct or have quitted the kingdom, the known perfidy, breach of faith and ill usage of the parliamentary power, inclines them, if supplied, to continue the war.

Now that Irish resistance had collapsed the Royalists still found satisfaction in the state of the country. Captain William Heald, writing from Brest on December 12, to Thomas Holder, said 'as to the present state of Ireland, in my opinion it stands more easily reduceable into entirety for his majesty than it did at any time'. There were also 'dissensions between the English forces and those of Sir Charles Coote (who are called by the former Tame Tories)'. Sir Charles Coote, representing the conservative old colonists, disliked the radicalism brought in by the new colonists. A Captain Potter of the Munster forces had written, after the collapse of Galway, that there was now little to do but 'fall on Sir Charles Coote and his Tame Rebels'. Coote had intercepted the letter and thrown the offending officer into prison. Captain Potter was released on the orders of Ludlow, who had no love for Coote, whom he suspected of Royalist sympathies. Ludlow rebuked Coote for exercising authority over an officer not belonging to the army of his province. William Heald commented: 'It is hard for the officers or soldiers in Coote's army to contain themselves from fighting with the other upon such bitter provokements from them, calling them Tame Tories, and these again provoking the other with terms of Round Heads . . .'

Coote was therefore seen as a likely ally for the Royalist cause. Heald added:

Thus much touching the occasion of their discontents which every day augments and are ready to fall into action, did not the good success of the Catholic party in Ulster tie them to attend their motions and waive their own intestine discontents till Coote shall be settled in agreement with the King's party.

Heald tried to estimate the strength of the Commonwealth forces in Ireland, which he did with wild inaccuracy, allowing only 15,000 foot, 1,7000 horse and no dragoons. Thomas Holder forwarded his report to Charles Stuart pointing out the advantage of contacting Coote.

In Ireland an Anglo-Irish Royalist was just beginning to write, in the English style used by the older colonists, a mammoth history of the war from 1641–1653 under the title of *An Aphorismical Discovery of Treasonable Faction*. He described 1652 as a year of '. . . executions, contributions, transportations and persecution of the clergy'; he condemned the conduct of the partial judges at the High Courts and the 'cruel and bloody tragedies acted on the sanguinean theatre of this languishing kingdom'. Of the people that had brought the country to this sorry state he wrote:

Their bones and their posterity (if the Divine clemency will permit them to have any) shall be subject to all deep censure of infamy and reproach, and to God's severe and just indignation with the indelible character of deform and ugly stain of both murder, treason and per-

jury, their further trial we remit into the All Seeing Power to be dealt with according to their deserts.

'The barbarians are in the beds of the Irish'

Organised Irish military resistance to the Army of the Commonwealth was now minimal. Those isolated garrisons still holding out were cut off from each other and short of supplies, with no alternative but to surrender.

On January 6, 1653, the Commissioners in Dublin shocked the Catholic clergy, who were hoping that the Commonwealth administration would tolerate the practice of their religion. In spite of the fact that on October 4, 1650, the Commissioners were ordered to suppress the Catholic priesthood, and had announced that all the English statutes against Catholicism were to be brought into force, the clergy harboured the delusion that freedom of religious worship would be granted them. After all, on March 18, 1651, Reynolds, Vernon, Allen, Sankey and Henry Jones had issued a declaration stating: 'moreover, we declare that it is the will of the officers of Parliament in Ireland that none of the Irish rescusant should be compelled to attend any religious worship or divine service contrary to his conscience.' Now the Commissioners announced that the Catholic priesthood had twenty days to leave Ireland before the 27th Act of Elizabeth I c. 2, 1587, was brought into force. The Act declared that any priest who was caught was to be hanged, cut down while yet alive, disembowelled and burnt. From his hiding place in the vicinity of Galway, Francis Kirwan protested to the Commissioners and pleaded for 'liberty of worship'. The Commissioners answered him curtly, refusing the plea on the grounds that Catholics held allegiance to a foreign power in Rome.

Many priests now began to apply for state protection to allow them to leave the country. On February 1 the Commissioners had decided that 'the priests now in the several prisons of Dublin be forthwith shipped with the party going for Spain'. A Jesuit Father named Quinn, reporting to the

Vatican on 'The State and Condition of the Catholics in Ireland from the year 1652–1656' recalled:

> ... in that year the last Superior of our Society in Ireland, who was then lying in fever in the house of a certain Catholic citizen, was reduced so much he could neither move nor ride on horseback, nor by any other conveyance.

In the depth of 'a very severe winter, amid storms of wind and snow, the sick man was carried forty leagues to a seaport' where ten Jesuits and forty secular priests were waiting to be transported to Spain. Whether the priests arrived safely at the seaports was a matter of luck for, observed Father Quinn, 'what one soldier spares today is devoured by another to-morrow'.

With the Ulster division of the Irish army now surrendered and awaiting ships for service in Europe, the Commissioners had to deal with the problem of what they called 'keraghts' or 'creaghts'. The Irish word *creach*, meaning plunder, spoil, booty, and more specifically used in terms of cattle or horses, was the name applied to many homeless families who wandered from place to place behind the Irish field armies with their herds or flocks, in order to maintain themselves by the victualling of the army. Ludlow had pleasant memories of the *creach* he came across on June 5, 1651.

> ... about ten in the morning our forlorn (company) perceived a creaght, as the country people call it, where half a dozen families with all their cattle were got together. Some of those who saw them first, presuming all the Irish in that country to be enemies, began to kill them, of which, having noticed, I put a stop to it, and took a share with them of a pot of sour milk, which seemed to me the most pleasant liquid that I ever drank.

Now, on January 25, the Commissioners gave orders for all *creachaí* to be broken up and their members dispersed 'upon serious consideration of the inconvenience of permitting the Irish to live in creaghts after a loose disorderly manner whereby the enemy comes to be relieved and sustained. . . .'

News was received that the Irish garrisons of Inishbofin, Clare Island and Turk had surrendered to Commissary General Reynolds. The Governor of Inishbofin, Colonel George Cusack, whom, it was said, had been holding out with the help of arms supplied by the Duke of Lorraine, had signed the surrender on behalf of all three garrisons. A Dominican Father named O'Canon, who had been prior at the Dominican Abbey of Kilkenny, said that the decision to surrender had come when seven warships had surrounded the island and threatened bombardment. O'Canon, who was eventually transported to Spain, had only recently made his way to the island in a skiff, accompanied by a young boy following an attack on Burrishoole Abbey, in Co. Mayo. O'Canon had been in the Abbey when Commonwealth troops had attacked it. They had been repulsed twice but had succeeded in storming it and killing those friars who, unlike Father O'Canon, did not escape into the mountains. Reynolds had made it quite clear to Cusack that he had little mind to spare the garrison if surrender was not immediate. He had just lost 270 troopers who had been on their way to attack Inishbofin, when Tories had successfully ambushed them near Rinvyle Castle and the entire command had been wiped out. With Cusack on the island was Rory O'More, one of the leaders of the 1641 insurrection, who had done more than most to bring it about. He managed to reach the mainland and disappeared. It was rumoured that he lived in the guise of a fisherman in Ulster for a while before he eventually died.

Ten days after the surrender of Inishbofin, the Irish garrison at Ballyleague surrendered to Reynolds and, finally, Philip MacHugh O'Reilly, Eamonn O'Reilly's cousin, surrendered the last garrison in a castle on Lough Oughter on April 27. Under the terms of this final surrender, priests were given a further month to leave the country, which was again extended by one month on June 10 and again on July 18. From now on the Irish were to pursue a more vicious policy of guerilla warfare in Tory bands which would sweep down on isolated settlements or patrols of soldiers. It was a form of warfare the armies of England in Ireland were to grow uncomfortably familiar with for many centuries to come. The most active area in the February of 1653 was in West Cork and Co. Kerry where the fighting was led by the O'Sullivans and O'Driscolls.

The most active leader of the Irish in the area was Piaras Feiritéar, called Pierce Ferriter by the English. He was a chieftain whose family, which was of Norman origin, con-

trolled much of Corcha Dhuibhne in Co. Kerry, ruling from
Baile an Fheirtearaigh (Ballyferriter) or Ferriter's town.
Piaras Feiritéar was not only a soldier but a scholar, a poet
and musician. He was an expert at writing *dánta grádha*,
love verses of the courtly kind in the old bardic metre. 'Hard
is it to escape the malady of love' he sings in a poem about
his love for *Inghean an Ghaill,* the Englishman's daughter.
In another poem he wrote

> *Léig Diot t'airm, a mhacaoimh mná ...*
>
> Gentlest of women, put your weapons by
> Unless you want to ruin all mankind:
> Leave the assault, or I must make reply
> Proclaiming that you're murderously inclined
> Put by your armour, lay your dart to rest
> Hide your soft hair and all its devious ways.
> To see it lie in curls on your breast
> Poisons all hope and mercilessly slays.

Feiritéar was on good terms with the English colonists in
his area and was apparently non-political until the insurrection broke out in the north. Then he found himself facing an
agonising choice of loyalties. One of his English friends,
Patrick Fitzmaurice, Lord Kerry, governor of the county,
asked Feiritéar to fight against the Irish insurgents and gave
him arms to equip 150 to 200 of his followers to fight with
the colonists. But Feiritéar came to the realisation that his
loyalties lay with his own countrymen and not with the
English. On the last day of June, 1642, Honora, Lady Kerry,
wrote to 'my very loving friend Mr. Pierce Ferriter at
Ferriter's Town in Kerry'. She began: 'Honest Pierce, and I
hope in God I shall never call you otherwise.' She had heard
from Florence MacFineen Carthy of Castlelough, that
Feiritéar was joining the insurgents and planning to attack
Tralee Castle, where her husband was in command. '. . . but
I hope in God it is far from your thoughts . . . I cannot believe any such thing of you and therefore will not take much
pains to persuade you, knowing that you want not wit and
understanding enough to conceive and apprehend the danger
and punishment justly due to such offences . . .' Feiritéar
knew well the dangers but nevertheless he was one of the
group that seized Tralee Castle in the autumn of that year.

He was wounded in the action. Feiritéar gave not only his sword but his pen to the Irish cause, giving his full support to Eoin Ruadh O'Neill and addressing him as the stout hearted lion which would rule the clean earth of Fodhla (Ireland). When O'Neill died in 1649 he poured out his grief in a *caoine*, a wrathful lamentation: 'The barbarians are in the beds of the Irish.'

As the Irish armies began to collapse before the troops of the Commonwealth, Feiritéar took his men into the Kerry mountains and continued the war with a series of lightning raids on troops, supply routes and settlements. In 1652, having watched the fall of Ross Castle to Ludlow, he began to realise the hopelessness of the Irish situation. Grimly he watched the English troops swarming through Kerry, killing priests, arresting people and burning Irish homesteads. From his hideout in the mountains he wrote:

> *Is biogadh báis liom cás mo chomharsan ...*
>
> I am startled by death, the death of my neighbours,
> untroubled, happy sages,
> in a land where their importance was recognised,
> Ite, Vade is now said to them.

He expressed the despair the Irish were now feeling at the success of the English; they attributed it to divine wrath against Ireland. There was no hope against God's wrath.

> Alas it was not the power of their army,
>   Nor the fierceness of the English (crew from Dover)
> Nor the strength of the enemy that quenched our hope
>   But the retribution of God in pursuit of His justice.

In 1653 Feiritéar had come to the decision that resistance was useless and, under a safe conduct, he went into the town of Kilmallock, Co. Limerick, to discuss terms of surrender for himself and his men with the governor, Colonel John Nelson. The town was sparsely populated and lay in ruins, its fortifications demolished by the soldiers and the fourteenth-century castle converted into a hospital. Perhaps Feiritéar chose Kilmallock for his surrender in memory of James Mac Thomas, known as the *sugán* (straw) Earl of Desmond, who had been compelled to make his submission there to the English fifty-three years before. Having discussed terms,

Feiritéar said he would return to his men to organise their surrender. Nelson agreed but ordered a troop to follow Feiritéar at a distance and arrest him the moment he met up with his men. Feiritéar went as far as Castlemaine before the troops, suspecting Feiritéar was leading them on a wild goose chase (Castlemaine being forty miles from Kilmallock) seized him.

He was taken to Killarney, with Bishop Egan, and Father Tadhg O'Connor. From there the three men were taken out to Cnocán na gCaorach, the Hill of Sheep, in front of the ruins of the Franciscan Friary, where they were hanged. 'Our term of life is not too long,' Feiritéar had written less than a year before his death. A fellow poet, Seán Ó Conaill, lamented in a poem entitled *Tuireadh na hÉirinn* (Dirge of Ireland):

> Who would not mourn the soul of generosity?
> Piaras Feiritéar, of much erudition,
> Tadhg O'Connor and Bishop MacEgan (who)
> were hanged on the Hill of Sheep.
> The head of O'Connor was put on a spike ...
> others they transported and transplanted to Jamaica.

'not being bred anything of a soldier'

On February 4, 1653, Colonel Robert Venables reported news to the Commissioners that both surprised and pleased them. 'It hath pleased God', he wrote, 'to deliver into your hands the ringleader in the late bloody massacres and rebellions, Sir Phelim O'Neill'. With Rory O'More, Sir Phelim Mac Tirlogh O'Neill of Kinard, Co. Tyrone, had been the main leader of the insurrection and he, himself, confessed the plan had been fermenting six years in his mind before he led the Ulster clans out on October 25, 1641. He had initially commanded the Ulster army before handing over command to his better qualified kinsman, Eoin Ruadh O'Neill the following year. According to an anonymous British officer of Sir John Clotworthy's regiment, in his *History of the Warr*, Sir Phelim 'was a well bred gentleman, three years at court, as free and generous as could be desired, and very complacent; stout in his person, but not being bred anything of a soldier, wanted the main art, that is policy in war and good conduct'.

It was commonly rumoured that Sir Phelim had fled abroad in 1650, after the disastrous battle at Scarrifhollis. His wife, Lady Jean Gordon, the daughter of the Marquis of Huntley, had lived in Charlemont since it surrendered to Colonel Venables' troops. Lord Caulfield, whose father had been killed when in Sir Phelim's custody, had suspected that Sir Phelim was still in Co. Tyrone and was keeping in touch with his wife. Caulfield's vigilance was rewarded when, at the end of January, 1653, he discovered O'Neill with Tirlogh Groom O'Quinn and twenty followers, hiding on an island called MacHugh's Island in Lough Catherine, Co. Tyrone. They escorted O'Neill and O'Quinn to Marshalsea prison in Dublin where, on February 23, O'Neill made a statement. He was told he was to be arraigned for High Treason and murder. Having studied law at Lincoln's Inn, Sir Phelim decided to defend himself. Sixty-four-year-old Sir Gerard Lowther was to be president of the court.

The trial opened in Dublin on March 3 amidst a great clamouring from the colonists and soldiers for O'Neill's blood. While he denied the murder charges, Sir Phelim openly admitted the general charge of High Treason. A point which the judges questioned O'Neill closely about was the fact that O'Neill had claimed in 1641 that he had orders from King Charles to seize the houses and property of the colonists. He had displayed a Charter to that effect with the King's great seal on it 'witnessed Ourself at Edinburgh, the first day of October in the seventeenth year of our reign'. Had this commission really come from Charles I, asked Sir Gerard Lowther. The British Officer of Clotworthy's regiment said 'he made manly answer that the King was so far from giving them the commission that he did not know anything of the rising'. Sir Phelim had seen with satisfaction the growing split between King Charles and his Parliament and when he had discovered a charter with the King's seal on it in Charlemont Castle he had altered the wording accordingly and published the commission in order to help to widen the split between the two English factions, who had not yet come to open warfare. O'Neill, quite rightly, reasoned that with the English administration split and quarrelling within itself, there would be little likelihood of a strong English army arriving to oppose the Irish until the affair between Charles and his Parliament had been resolved. By that time the Irish insurgents would be in a strong position. Sir Edward Bolton pressed the matter further and asked O'Neill why he had deceived the people by forging the commission. Sir Phelim replied that no man could condemn him for using all means whatsoever to promote the cause he had so engaged in. The judges were not satisfied on this point for, while it had been politically expedient for Sir Phelim to pretend the commission genuine in 1641, it was now equally expedient and advantageous for the administration of the young English republic to maintain its authenticity, pointing out that it had been the monarchy who had instigated the bloody war and was responsible for the deaths of the English colonists.

After three days, on March 5, the court made its judgement. Sir Phelim was found guilty of all the murder charges and 'for the general charge: testified out of your own mouth, you were heard to say that the plot was for six years in your head before you could bring it to maturity'.

Lowther now with great sarcasm began to describe O'Neill's career in the insurrection and alleged that the Pope had made him Prince of Ulster.

Are we yet at an end? No, yet is there one more title wanting— Phelim Totane, the last and most affecting, as sung by your bards, none of them singing of any other title but Phelim Totane.

The nickname, Phelim a Thotane, derived from the Irish word *tóiteán* meaning a fire or conflagration, was given to O'Neill in the insurrection and he became widely known as 'Phelim the Firebrand'.

Repeating the charges, Sir Gerard commented 'all this is truely sustained according to the evidence, and upon all and singular you are found guilty...' The sentence was that O'Neill be hanged, drawn and quartered. The same day the Commissioners told the governor of Marshalsea prison that O'Neill was to be allowed visitors while awaiting execution but, lest an attempt at rescue be made, he was to receive only one at a time. On March 10 he was taken to the public place of execution. Dean John Ker of Ardagh, who witnessed the event, recalled that the rope was being fastened round O'Neill's neck when Peake, the marshal of the Four Courts, galloped up and cried 'Stop!' He whispered urgently to Sir Phelim at the end of which Sir Phelim replied in a loud voice:

I thank the Lt. General for his intended mercy but I declare good people, before God and His holy angels, and all of you that hear me, that I never had any commission from the King for what I have done in levying or prosecution of this war, and do heartily beg your prayers, all good Catholics and Christians, that God be merciful to me and forgive my sins.

'More of his speech', wrote Dean Ker, 'I could not hear, which continued not long, the guards beating off those that stood near the place of execution.'

A last minute attempt, perhaps with a promise of a reprieve, had been made by Fleetwood to get O'Neill to claim his commission from King Charles as genuine in order to use it as a propaganda weapon against the Royalists. O'Neill refused and was executed. After the sentence had been carried out, and O'Neill's body quartered by the axeman, one quarter was sent to Lisburn, a town which O'Neill had burnt; another went to Dundalk, which he had captured; a third went to Drogheda, which he had besieged, and the fourth remained in Dublin, which he had failed to capture.

In late February, Theobald Bourke, Viscount Mayo, was charged in Dublin with the 'Shrule massacre', when over sixty colonists were killed while in the custody of himself and his father, the late Lord Mayo, in 1642. Lord Mayo had surrendered the Connaught division of the Irish army on July 14, 1652, since when he had been held in custody while evidence was collected against him. Mayo pointed out that under the terms of his surrender he was entitled to be tried in Galway and his trial now opened under the presidency of Sir Charles Coote, sitting with ten other judges, including Colonel Peter Stubber, whom, it was rumoured, was the actual executioner of Charles I.

Lord Mayo said that after the surrender of Castlebar, in Co. Mayo in February, 1642, a group of English and Scottish colonists led by Sir Henry Bingham elected to go to Galway for safety. They asked to be escorted under the protection of his father with a troop of Irish horse as escort. Theobald Bourke had accompanied his father. It took them four days to reach the border of Co. Galway at Shrule for there were a number of women and children in the company. The company arrived at Shrule on the evening of February 16. The late Viscount Mayo decided to spend the night on the Mayo side of the border, in Kinlaug, Walter Burke's town. The next morning, said the young Lord Mayo, they saw seven or eight score men on the Galway side of the border who they identified as two companies of O'Flaherties led by Eamonn of the Hills. The Bishop of Killala's horse had been stolen from him and the old Viscount had given him his own horse and procured horses from his own men for the Bishop's daughters. The custody of the prisoners had been given to Eamonn Bourke who marched the prisoners across the bridge which lay over the river which runs through Shrule. Here he halted the prisoners. As old Lord Mayo and his son were left behind in Kinlaug, Eamonn seized the opportunity to loot what few valuables the prisoners had. The O'Flaherties now marched up and joined in the looting. Several of the prisoners began to complain whereupon, according to a witness named John Hussey, the Irish commenced to murder them 'some with clubs knocking them down, others shooting at them, others running them through with swords, and stabbing them with skeans'. A *scian* is a knife or dagger.

The commotion was heard by old Mayo and his son, Theobald. The young man said he had immediately drawn his sword and run across the bridge to protect the prisoners but the O'Flaherties had fired some shots at him and John Garvey, the local sheriff, 'conveyed him away for the safety of his life'.

Four of the judges did not think that Mayo could be held responsible for the massacre but the other seven judges disagreed and Mayo was found guilty. He was executed before a firing squad. On March 29, 1654, Fleetwood granted his mother, Elizabeth, the Dowager Lady Mayo, 'being English and old and decrepit' the sum of £25 to help her return to England.

The number of people convicted and executed by the

High Court trials was now nearing the one hundred mark and 'all not inconsiderable people'. Many people became the victims of informers on whose solitary word their lives became forfeit, informers who used the opportunity to settle old scores. There were many more still awaiting trial including Donogh MacCarthy, Earl of Muskerry. After the surrender of Ross and the Munster division of the Irish army, Muskerry had been allowed to go to Spain. He had spent some time in Spain and Portugal but, because of his opposition to Rinuccini in the days of the Confederacy, he found the clergy and many fellow exiles did not welcome his presence. He decided to return to Ireland with Colonel Callaghan O'Callaghan and place himself at the mercy of the Commonwealth.

In late February, Muskerry and O'Callaghan were lodged in Marshalsea prison and inquiries made. After due deliberation, Muskerry was informed that he would be charged with committing several murders in 1642 and that his trial would take place in December. Unlike others accused, Muskerry, due to his influential friends, was told the prosecution's line of attack and given ample opportunity to find witnesses and prepare a defence.

'the transplantation of popular men'

Next to the native Irish, the people most disliked by the English Commonwealth administration were the Scottish Presbyterian colonists in Ulster. The Presbyterians refused to give assent to the trial of King Charles I and, after Colonel Pride had forcibly ejected them from the House of Commons, the Ulster Scots, under General Monro, had thrown in their lot with the native Irish to fight against the forces of the English Parliament. The question of how to deal with the Scottish colonists fell to Colonel Venables and the Commissioners of Revenue in Carrickfergus. They had, at first, sought to come to some understanding with the Presbyterian ministers, asking them to swear an oath of allegiance to the

Commonwealth. This the Presbyterians had refused to do. It was proposed that two of the ministers, Patrick Adair and Archibald Ferguson, go to Dublin to discuss the situation with Fleetwood himself. Adair said that they were in no mind for insurrection but only desired to preach the gospels to a poor, afflicted people. Venables gave them a safe conduct to go to Dublin. Nothing, however, was obtained from Fleetwood by way of an understanding and the matter was referred to a meeting of officers in Dublin Castle.

The officers asked Adair and Ferguson why the Scottish colonists should expect protection from the Commonwealth while refusing to swear loyalty to it. Ferguson said they refused on grounds of conscience 'and that withal they were men insignificant for insurrection and not dangerous'. The Adjutant General, William Allen, an ardent Anabaptist, observed that 'Papists would and might say as much for themselves and pretend conscience as well as they'. To this Adair replied: 'Sir, under favour, it's a mistake to compare our conscience with those of Papists for Papists' conscience could digest to kill Protestant kings, but so would not ours, to which our principles are contrary.' This was greeted in grim silence as most of the officers present were either regicides or approved wholeheartedly the trial and execution of Charles I.

The two Presbyterian ministers returned to Ulster and it was decided to try to suppress them and any who followed their teachings. Colonel Arthur Hill, the governor of Carrickfergus, Major Anthony Morgan, and Dr. Henry Jones met with Colonel Venables in Carrickfergus to discuss the best way of dealing with the situation. It was felt that it would be impossible to deduct a fifth of the land of the determined Scottish colonists in Cos. Antrim and Down, under the Act of Settlement in which Protestants who had not shown good affection to Parliament were liable to have that amount of their estates forfeited. They therefore proposed, on April 9, 'the transplantation of popular men . . . of whose dutiful and peaceful demeanours' they 'had not assurance'. The idea was welcomed by Fleetwood. In the meantime Venables sent out troops to search houses of leading Scottish Presbyterians, seeking evidence of disaffection. Some sixteen soldiers arrived at Patrick Adair's house and gathered up all his papers, which

James Butler, 12th Earl of Ormonde and and later 1st Duke. Royalist Lord Lieutenant in Ireland from 1643 until the Cromwellian conquest of 1649. He returned to office on the Restoration in 1660.

Edmund Ludlow Esq.
Lieu.ᵗ Gen.ˡ

Lieutenant-General Edmund Ludlow, an unrepentant republican, who became Acting Commander-in-Chief of the Army in Ireland 1651–2 and Commander-in-Chief 1659–60.

Charles Fleetwood, Oliver Cromwell's son-in-law. He became
Commander-in-Chief in Ireland 1652–5, and was appointed Lord
Deputy of Ireland in 1654, but returned to England in September 1655.

Henry Cromwell, Oliver's youngest son. He became Commander-in-Chief in Ireland in 1655, Lord Deputy in 1657 and Lord Lieutenant in 1659.

Photograph: Courtauld Institute of Art

they bundled in an old cloak. It was obvious that the sergeant in charge could not read and the soldiers did not know precisely what papers they were taking. Adair was absent from his house at the time but his maid followed the soldiers to an inn, two miles away, where they prepared to spend the night. Thinking the papers might be incriminating the maid 'went in the night, when the sergeant and the soldiers were asleep, and quietly brought a bundle of papers out of the cloak not knowing what they were'. By luck, they happened to be documents concerning the Presbytery's resolution expressing the 'horridness of the murder of Charles I'.

Venables had several Scottish colonists in jail at Carrickfergus on charges of participating in a massacre of native Irish on the Island of Magee, east of Carrickfergus, which was a promontory of land and not really an island at all. The promontory enclosed Lough Larne. On January 8, 1642, Scottish colonists had killed about sixty men, women and children of the native Irish population. As with the Irish massacres of the colonists, the figure rose each time the affair was retold until it was commonly accepted by contemporary historians that 3,000 had been slaughtered. During the summer of 1653 Venables had taken steps to trace the survivors of the massacre and to take depositions for use against the colonists.

From a previous deposition Venables decided that he had enough evidence to arrest one John Weyley or Willy, who had been a captain in Monro's army. He had been named by several witnesses as one of those who had led the colonists on the night of the killings. Troopers William Bayley and Patrick Kelly were despatched to the Island of Magee where Willy had his farmstead. Bayley swore out a statement of arrest on February 7. The troopers had arrived at Willy's farm and had seen what they took to be Willy standing on a ladder thatching a stack of corn. A woman, however, had seen the troopers approaching and cried out a warning to the man, who had jumped down from the ladder and run in among the haystacks. Willy's son appeared and told the soldiers that the man was merely a hired hand, and that his father had gone to Portdarvy for the day. The two troopers pushed past the boy and started to search the corn stacks, poking about with their swords until Kelly cried: 'I have found the rogue and here he is!' Willy emerged from a stack with blood running from his thigh where Kelly's sword had stabbed him. Bayley told Willy that he was under arrest, and advised him to bring a change of clothes with him. At that moment a neighbour, Thomas Eaton, rode up and demanded to know on what authority they were arresting Willy.

'I do so by virtue of a warrant,' answered Bayley.

'Show it to me', demanded Eaton.

Bayley showed him the warrant and, having glanced at it, Eaton rode abruptly away.

The prisoner and escort set out for Carrickfergus but, as it was now late at night and Tory bands still roamed the area, they decided to stop at the house of John MacCallow, who ran an inn in Ballycarry. There were a number of colonists drinking there who greeted Willy and wanted to know what he was doing there.

'He spoke softly to them' recalled Bayley 'whereupon they became very still and quiet, the said MacCallow beating his hands on his thigh and others of them seeming very sad in the room.' Several of them offered the troopers money to let Willy go. Thomas Eaton then arrived in the company of Patrick Crossan, the constable of Kilroot, who suggested that the troopers might stand to receive as much as £10 to share between them if they let the man go. Eaton even pressed 24s. 6d. into Bayley's hands there and then. The two troopers, however, presented their guns and took their prisoner outside, pressing on to Carrickfergus lest the mood of the colonists turn to thought of armed rescue.

Carrickfergus prison was filled with a considerable number of colonists awaiting trial by late summer, 1653. The trials were held in the Town Hall, Carrickfergus, about September. The basis of the evidence from the survivors of the massacre was that the colonists had descended on their homes one night in a party, maintaining they had a warrant from King Charles to kill all the Irish and any who tried to protect them. They then killed men, women and children. The survivors identified many of their neighbours among the attackers. When the survivors had fled to Carrickfergus for protection, the soldiers of the garrison there had killed several more. The colonists did not deny that the massacre had taken place but they denied that any colonist who lived in the Island of Magee had taken part. They maintained that the massacre had been conducted by men from Ballymena.

In September the defendants went before the High Court, many of them to pay the supreme penalty.

By mid May the Presbyterian ministers were ordered into Carrickfergus and told not to leave the town. A little while later they were told that a frigate was to transport them out of the country. In the meantime the authorities were clarifying plans to transplant the Scots. On April 24 Venables had written to Fleetwood that they were planning 'transplanting some of the Scotch inhabitants into some of the towns of the south, if we can fit grounds to hold out for this removal, their number being at present almost equal with the English, which we judge very dangerous to be allowed . . .' Later in May, the ministers were informed that they were to be transplanted with their flocks to Co. Tipperary 'where they promised to give them who had estates here, a proportional value in land there'. A list of transplantees was drawn up headed by Sir Robert Adair and Mr. Shaw of Ballygelly. On June 30 a meeting was held in Dublin, after which a letter was sent to Venables signed by Fleetwood, Ludlow, Corbet and Jones to the effect that:

. . . the time for the persons named in the list for to be moved out of Ulster into the places before mentioned shall be at or before the First of November next. And that the respective families of those persons so removed as aforesaid shall also remove out of Ulster to the places chosen by them—Munster as aforesaid at or before the 16th of April now next ensuing.

Although Oliver Cromwell personally intervened on March 22, 1654, on behalf of Sir Robert Adair for exemption, the transplantation of the Scottish colonists generally never took place. On April 20 the Lord-General, Oliver Cromwell, had abolished Parliament and exerted a temporary dictatorship. A new and far more drastic policy of land confiscation and transplantation was to be announced which made the proposed transplantation of the Ulster Presbyterian Scots superfluous. The Presbyterian ministers began to enjoy a greater liberty to preach among their old parishes and from a scant half dozen ministers in early 1653, their numbers had risen to twenty-four by the end of the year.

'they had been rather ghosts than men'

Galway had always been a frontier town so far as the English colonists were concerned. It had been colonised at an early date by such Anglo-Norman families as the Blakes, Bodkins, Brownes, D'Arcys, ffrenches, Kirwans, Joyces, Lynches, Morrises, Martins and Skerrets. Hence the Irish had named the town *Gaillimh*. The township of colonists had guarded itself against intercourse with the native Irish and a bye-law of 1518 specifically stated 'that neither O nor Mac shall strutte through the streets of Galway'. In 1520 the city decreed that the English language should be used and that 'no judge or lawyer shall plead in no man's cause nor matter within this our court in Irish, for it agreeth not with the King's laws'. For many years the colonists in the town had lived in a state of virtual siege, especially from the raids of the O'Flaherty clan, the biggest clan in the west of Connaught. So harassing and successful were the O'Flaherties in their raids against the township that the colonists had inscribed on the West Gate the prayer: 'From the fury of the O'Flaherties good Lord deliver us.' But the Lord had not delivered the settlers during the grim struggle of 1641. Now that the troubles were over, there was a public outcry from the Galway settlers for the authorities to track down the leading members of the O'Flaherties for punishment.

Early in May, 1653, the Lord President of Connaught, Sir Charles Coote, despatched a troop of soldiers to search the province. The soldiers were particularly to seek Eamonn Mac-Morogh na Maor of Bunowen, whose brother Morogh na Mart, Morogh of the Beeves or cattle, had been knighted by Lord Deputy Stafford in 1637. Morogh na Mart had inherited Castle Bunowen and an estate of 1,300 acres from his father Morogh na Moore. He was chieftain of the O'Flaherties but it had been his brother Eamonn MacMorogh na Maor who had led the clan into battle, with his cousin Morogh na Doe of Aghnenure as his lieutenant. Lord Clanricarde had disparagingly called the fighting O'Flaherties 'the rude kearns of Irr-Conght' (Iar-Connachta or West Connaught). At the start of the insurrection Eamonn had led 1,800 men to besiege Galway. They took the town after a few days and afterwards Eamonn had taken one hundred of his men to secure the Isles of Aran. From Aran he had made a raid on the coast of Co. Clare where he laid siege, with local insurgents, to the Castle of Tromra at Ibrickan. It was owned by an English settler named Peter Ward. The castle was taken after four days and the Ward family were slain. For the past few months, Sir Charles Coote had collected depositions swearing out a murder charge against Eamonn.

The soldiers, led by Colonel Brayfield, had a fruitless search through Connaught. But as a troop commanded by Lieutenant John Bolton were returning to Galway, and nearing Rinvyle, they came to a wood to which their attention was drawn by a number of ravens croaking in alarm. The soldiers dismounted and entered the wood. After a search they found a cave in which were a man and a woman huddled in beggars' clothing. The woman looked emaciated and the man was in a state of advanced fatigue. A soldier identified them as Eamonn MacMorogh na Maor and his wife. 'And truely,' observed Francis Lynch of the island of Omey, near Rinvyle, who was one of the troopers, 'who had seen them would have said they had been rather ghosts than men, for pitifully they pined away for want of food and altogether ghastly with fear.'

Lieutenant Bolton, who was rewarded with £20 on December 5 that year for the capture, set off to Galway with his prisoners. On May 24 Eamonn was brought before the High Court.

The court first dealt with the behaviour of the O'Flaherties during the capture of Galway. Thomas Scott swore that when the city fell he had seen Morogh O'Flaherty, who was styled Colonel of West Connaught, in the street with 300 Irish troops. They had broken into a house and five of them had stabbed to death a Mrs. Collins with their *scians* or knives. John Turner swore that the Irish troops had robbed the English inhabitants and killed several of them. They had cut off the heads of one John Fox and his wife and killed Mrs. Collins while she was kneeling at her prayers. They had, added Turner, even used the head of Fox as a ball which they kicked about the streets, yet the mayor and aldermen of the city made no move to punish them, which forced him to the conclusion that they had planned to hand over the city to the O'Flaherties. A baker, John Sheehy, said that the Irish had threatened him with their knives and shouted: 'You English jocks or dogs, we will cut your throats!' Lieutenant John Gill insisted that the O'Flaherties were brought into town to kill all the English colonists 'and he believeth they would have murdered all accordingly had not some priests hindered them by going out in their vestments with tapers and a crucifix carried before them and commanding the said murderers to cease.'

The court then heard the specific charge of the murder of Ward and his family. John Browne of Aran gave a general statement. The principal accuser was John Ward, the son of the murdered man. He accused Eamonn of having 'murdered or caused or consented to murder' his father, mother, brothers and sisters on April 25, 1643.

Replying to the charge Eamonn told the court that he had been in charge of the attack on Tromra Castle on May 1, 1643, 'which was possessed by one Mr. Ward whom he heard was an honest gentleman and never heard of him before, and neither doth know of what religion or nation he was of'. Eamonn said that his main accuser, John Ward, had made terms for himself and left the rest of his family to escape as best they could.

Eamonn said that Ward's wife, Alison, was killed by a shot fired through a window of the castle, and that Peter Ward had been slain in fair fight by Tadhg MacDonell MacOwen MacEnrya 'who is now living as is supposed' and by Downdarra Óg MacEnrya 'now dead'.

There was no question of an acquittal. The cry for the blood of the O'Flaherties was too strong. Eamonn Mac Morogh na Maor was found guilty and he was taken to the same spot where his kinsman Lord Mayo was executed for the massacre at Shrule, and there hanged. Eamonn left three sons,

Domhnall, Morogh and Eamonn. The younger two fled to England where Morogh soon fell into trouble for killing a Captain Vernor in a duel because he insulted the Irish. His brother Eamonn Laidir (often called 'Strong Ned' O'Flaherty) returned to Ireland as a soldier under Charles Stuart. Eamonn's brother, Morogh na Mart, was granted his life but had his lands confiscated.

Another member of the clan, Ruairí O'Flaithearta, known to the English as Roderick O'Flaherty, son of Aodh O'Flaherty of Moycullen, also had his estate confiscated. Ruairí had been born in Galway and had gone to school in St. Nicholas' College, which had been founded in 1501 by Donogh O'Murray, the Archbishop of Tuam. It was the school where such famous Irish scholars as Mac Firbisigh, Terence Mac Donogh of Creevagh, Co. Sligo and Francis Browne, had been sent for their education. Finding his lands under confiscation, Ruairí appealed to the Commissioners of Revenue at Athlone but his appeal was dismissed. On the lands allocated him in Connaught he began to work on scholastic projects such as *A Chorographical Description of West or H-Iarr Connaught*, which was published in 1684. *A Chronology of Irish History* and *Ogygia*. In his work O'Flaherty attacked Sir John Temple's account of the Irish insurrection which gave substance to the myth of the massacres of the colonists. But O'Flaherty swung to the other extreme. He wrote:

140,000 souls in a few weeks dislodged by the authority of Sir John Temple's Irish Rebellion is by many thousands further from truth than the relation of 17 persons only massacred, as appears by the straight enquiries made in Cromwell's time; and yet but few of these many thousands could be found to have been really murdered. For there were not so many thousands of Protestants living then in all Ireland much less in Ulster, where most of these murders were said to have been committed.

Many of the petty chiefs of the O'Flaherty clan were executed, while all had their lands confiscated. The O'Flaherties never recovered from the vengeance of the colonists and henceforth the settlers of Galway had no cause to pray for deliverance from the fury of the clan.

Throughout mid 1653 the trials continued; by autumn

nearly 200 executions had taken place, some of these in answer for the 'Cashel massacre'. In 1643 a force of Irish had captured Cashel, Co. Tipperary and had taken the castle, which stood on a remarkable outcrop of limestone which rises 200 feet above the plain. The name of the township took its name from Caiseal Mumhan, the stone fort of Munster, which had once been the seat of the Munster kings, the hub of civil and ecclesiastical life. There had been a fierce resistance from the colonists holding the town and many were killed, while the survivors were expelled to make their way as best they could to Cork, a journey of sixty miles through wasteland, teeming with hostile forces. The executed men, claimed the authorities, were also responsible for a massacre at Sir George Hamilton's nearby silver mine, where workers had been slain.

An anonymous Irish report, written just after the trial, claimed that the sons of Dermot O'Kennedy of Dounarieke were responsible. O'Kennedy had seven sons: John who 'bore the name of a colonel to uphold himself' but which 'could not maintain him in any decency, so debasely addicted was he to swearing, tippling and plundering, that with a party of thieves and Tories he wasted his native country and cruelly oppressed Upper Ormonde, and at last was killed in action and beheaded, his head left put on a spike and his body left to the fowls of the air'. His second son, Henry, following the massacre, was 'troubled in conscience, for he ran headlong into the Shannon and drowned'. Kenny O'Kennedy, a third son, had been jailed in Limerick charged with the murder, but had escaped; Donogh, a Franciscan, had been killed; Eamonn, another Franciscan, was also killed, while Tadhg and William had disappeared.

As early as February 10, 1643, Anna Skerring, whose husband had been killed at the silver mine, signed a deposition naming the O'Kennedy brothers as the killers. On May 26, 1645, William Timms confirmed Mrs. Skerring's account, adding that the Irish Confederate government had set up an inquiry into the murders and ordered John O'Kennedy to arrest those he thought responsible, not realising that he was the culprit himself. O'Kennedy arrested a few people who were then allowed to escape or were set at liberty. These stories were confirmed by a third deposition made by John Powell on July 15, 1645.

'there is no hope of accommodation of liberty of conscience'

On April 20, 1653, Henry Scobell, the clerk of the House of Commons, wrote the following entry in the Commons' journal: 'This day his Excellency the Lord-General dissolved this Parliament: Which was done without consent of Parliament.' For some years now there had been a growing division between Parliament, the Army and the people. The Army was becoming increasingly restive that nothing was being done to dissolve the inadequate remnant of Parliament which had sat for over eleven years. As early as August 15, 1652, the Army had presented a petition for a speedy solution to their own and the country's grievances. They asked that the inequalities of the law be reformed but, moreover, they demanded that a time limit be put on the Parliamentary session and a nation-wide election be held immediately. But the Parliament did not make any moves in that direction. The majority group in Parliament, led by Sir Henry Vane, feared the effects of a new election. Pressed on by an opposition from a group of Army officers, some Parliamentarians agreed to bring in a bill to keep the Parliament in being and fill the empty seats with local elections. In fact, Vane pressed that Parliament be kept in permanent session without general elections and, as seats fell vacant, by death or resignation, they should be filled by local election. The bill was put forward in April, 1653, in spite of the protest of the Army and of the Lord-General Oliver Cromwell, who sat on the Council of State and several other parliamentary committees. Cromwell had discussed the matter with Vane and thought he had procured a postponement of the bill. On the morning of April 20, when Cromwell was absent from the House, the bill was suddenly presented for a vote. Colonel Thomas Harrison slipped out of the House and brought the incredulous Lord General hurrying to the chamber.

The Lord General listened with growing annoyance as the

bill was debated until the Speaker, William Lenthall, rose to put it to a vote. Then the Lord General said softly to Harrison: 'This is the time. I must do it.' He stood up and began to address the House recalling its early heroic history in the struggle against the Royalists. Now their heroism was dead. He berated their injustices, their corruption, petty jealousies, their private sins, their drunkenness, embezzlement, uncleanness. 'It is not fit that you sit as a Parliament any longer,' he cried, clapping his hat on his head. Sir Peter Wentworth, an Oxfordshire member, rose to complain of the scandalous language of the Lord General, 'their servant whom they had so highly trusted and obliged'. This was the final straw for Cromwell, who cried: 'I will put an end to your prating. You are no Parliament. I say you are no Parliament.' A file of thirty musketeers under Lieutenant-Colonel Charles Worsley entered and on Cromwell's instructions cleared the House. That night a Cockney wit scribbled on the door of St. Stephen's 'This House to be let unfurnished.'

The dissolution of Parliament by Cromwell was greeted with wild enthusiasm, even by Royalists. Sir Edward Hyde, later Lord Clarendon, called it a 'glorious action' in that it had rid England of 'an accursed assembly of rogues'. The radical preachers, Anabaptists, Fifth Monarchists and others, saluted Cromwell for 'grubbing up the wicked Parliament, not leaving a rotten root thereof'. Within ten days the Lord General had signed a declaration that a 'new representative' of 'persons of approved fidelity and honesty' would be called. In the meantime Cromwell set himself up as the principal officer of government of the Commonwealth. To help him he appointed a Council of State of seven army officers and three civilians. These were to govern the three nations while plans went ahead to nominate a parliament of 140 members, 129 for England, 5 for Scotland and 6 for Ireland—the Irish representatives were to be Henry Cromwell, John Hewson, John Clark, Sir Robert King, Daniel Hutchinson and, as the only civilian representative for Ireland, Vincent Gookin. The parliament was to become known as the 'nominated parliament' which was more popularly referred to as 'Barebones parliament' after one of its more colourful members, Praisegod Barebones, a London Anabaptist preacher.

When the new Parliament opened on July 4. 1653, Cromwell made no specific reference to the colonisation of Ireland. He had, however, already commenced work on the project. On June 1 he appointed a Committee which would examine the claims of the financiers, and preside over a lottery to be held by the financiers for their land. At the same time a London linen draper, Methusaleh Turner, and eight other merchants, were asked to meet in the Grocer's Hall at 8 a.m. on June 20 to decide, by lottery, where each land allocation should be made. The value of one single lot was not to exceed the sum of £10,000 and the province of Connaught together with Co. Clare was to be exempted from colonisation. The total value of the lands in the three provinces of Munster, Leinster and Ulster, was to be £360,000 of which the government would deduct 1d. in the pound for expenses. This, however, did not please the officers of the Army in Ireland who felt that their case for receiving land in lieu of pay was far more pressing than the claims of the financiers because there were several regiments now due for disbandment. On June 9 the officers of the Army asked that soldiers whose service was no longer needed should be put in immediate possession of the land. The dissatisfaction of the officers had already cost John Weaver, the Lincolnshire lawyer, his job as a Commissioner in Ireland. Dissatisfied with the way Weaver had represented their interests in drawing up the scheme of colonisation, they had petitioned for his removal on February 18. Four days later Weaver resigned and left Ireland, to receive a reward from Parliament of an estate in Scotland on April 14.

On June 22 a new set of Commissioners for the Administration of the Affairs of the Commonwealth of England in Ireland were appointed. The new Commission consisted merely of the reappointed of the previous Commissioners, Fleetwood, Ludlow, Corbet and Jones. They now received specific instructions from Cromwell to take the ten counties of Limerick, Tipperary, Waterford, King and Queen's counties (Offaly and Leix), Meath, Westmeath, Down, Antrim and Armagh 'and to divide all the forfeited lands, meadow, arable and profitable pastures with the woods and bogs and barren mountains thereunto respectively belonging, into two equal moieties' of which one was intended for the financiers and the other for the soldiers' arrears. Co. Louth was to be surveyed separately and the Cos. of Dublin, Cork, Kildare and Carlow were to be specially reserved for the government. The Commissioners were also authorised to assign any five counties not previously named to pay soldiers' arrears only to those soldiers who had served from June 5, 1649. The Army officers were less than happy to learn that their arrears allotment was limited to only five counties and to those who had served since June, 1649.

The Surveyor-General appointed by the Commissioners was Dr. Benjamin Worsley, who began his survey in August. He decided to survey the confiscated estates without regard to the establishment of divisions such as baronies, parishes and townlands or to the physical features of the country. He was to be paid for the profitable land that he surveyed and so he tended to include entirely worthless plots of land as being 'profitable'. Moreover, subdivision would still have to be made either at a greater charge to the state or at the expense of those who were granted the land. Sir William Petty, the Physician-General, immediately pointed out the defects in Worsley's scheme. The rate of pay to Worsley was excessive, said Petty, and the men he employed were not skilled artists used to map making. The whole scheme appeared to be carried out for the benefit of a few powerful individuals. Also, added Petty, Worsley had not taken the responsibility of the scheme upon himself but had set up a committee to absolve himself of blame should his scheme fail. Worsley's greater objective 'was so to frame a committee of conceited persons, intermixing some of credit and bulk amongst them as whereby he might screen himself in case of miscarriage'.

Lists of people whose lands were to be confiscated were drawn up. Many people like Garratt Kinsellagh, who owned a large estate of 1,420 acres in Kynogh, Kilechmond and Kilcoursey, as well as other estates in Co. Carlow, refused to leave their property quietly. Kinsellagh took to the nearby forests and mountains, to become a famous Tory leader.

In the meantime wolf packs were still menacing the countryside. On June 29 the commanders of the fifteen military precincts of Ireland were asked to appoint various times for public wolf hunts in their areas. Some lands, nine miles north of Dublin, were leased to Captain Edward Piers, the former commander of the frigate *Primrose*, on condition that he paid part of his rent in wolves' heads. Under the terms of the lease he was to have all the lands in the barony of Dunboyne, Co. Meath, valued at £543 8s. 8d. per annum, on terms of maintaining, at Dublin and Dunboyne, three wolf dogs, two English mastiffs and a pack of hounds consisting of sixteen couples, plus an expert huntsman, two men and a boy. He was to bring the Commissioners of Revenue a stipulated number of wolves' heads each year. But for every wolf head he fell short of, £5 was to be deducted from the credit of his rent.

There were, of course, many other problems worrying the Commissioners, such as the great number of homeless in the country. On July 1 the Commissioners issued the following order:

Upon consideration had of the multitude of persons, especially women and children wandering up and down the country, that daily perish in ditches, and are starved for want of relief: it is thought fit that such women as have able bodies to work, and such children of about twelve years, whose husbands or parents are dead or gone beyond the seas, or friends to maintain them, or means of their own to preserve them from starving, maybe taken up by the overseer of the poor, and that to prevent the said persons from starving, the overseers are hereby authorised to treat with merchants for the transplanting the said persons into some English plantation in America.

The solution of shipping unwanted people, suspected criminals or political opponents, to the plantations in the Americas had been popularised by Cromwell following the defeat at Drogheda. On April 1, 1653, the Commissioners had given a licence to the Presbyterian leader, Sir John Clotworthy, 'to transport to America 500 natural Irishmen'. But the main body of Irish political malcontents were still being allowed to leave for exile on the continent. On July 19 Captain Antipas Kelly of *The Cardiff*, out of Kinsale, reported to the Navy Commissioners that his ship had victualled in Dublin and was now bound for Waterford to meet a Captain Walters 'who is employed for raising certain companies of Tories for the King of Spain, and to convey them to St. Sebastian in Biscay'. Captain Kelly added: 'We shall get them off as soon as we can.'

Nor were the Commissioners free from intrigue and plots. On July 25 a spy reported to the Council of State that Murrough O'Brien, Lord Inchiquin, was trying to raise a revolt in Munster. The spy added: 'Let the Lord General take notice that, when all interests are ripe, his life will be attempted. . . .'

The Catholic clergy had finally given up hope of concessions for Irish Catholics under the new regime. Father Edward Barry, who had escaped from Limerick after its surrender to Ireton, wrote to the Congregation of the Mission during that July:

> The news I hear from Ireland is that there is no hope of accommodation of liberty of conscience for the poor Catholics there. Those of the Irish army who forced us to surrender the city of Limerick to the enemy, upon so base conditions, were hanged at Cork. viz. Colonel Edward Fennell and Lt. Col. William Bourke of Brittas. All the clergy were banished except very few. As I am informed there are three scores of priests for the present at Nantes.

The Irish guerillas, the Tories, after several months of quiet were suddenly active again. On July 21 they raided a colonist settlement in Co. Cork and carried off a herd of cattle. On December 26 that year, the governor of Cork, Colonel Robert Phayre, gave permission to John Percival, a leading colonist, to make up the losses from the English settlement by conducting cattle raids against the Irish living in the surrounding areas.

On July 2, two days before the nominated Parliament was due to meet in London, the Lord General sent the Commissioners 'Further Instructions' to the Act for Settling Ireland. The Commissioners were told to announce publicly in each of the precincts that the country would be colonised with English Protestants. All those in Ireland who owned land which was due for confiscation under the various clauses of the Act were to remove themselves into the province of Connaught and Co. Clare, west of the River Shannon, which formed a natural boundary. All those who were found east of the river after a date prescribed would suffer death. All those who removed themselves before the date would be pardoned for any crime except murder; they were not to possess arms nor reside in any town without licence on the penalty of death. The transplanted persons were to receive free from the authorities appointed for the purpose land in such proportion to the value of their original property as set out by the Act. They 'or others', the only indication that non-landed people were to be transplanted, might take leases on terms not exceeding twenty-one years or three lives under the Commonwealth. Catholic priests, however, were not to be 'pardoned, tolerated or admitted'. Boys under fourteen years of age and girls under twelve years of age would be allowed to remain among the colonists as servants provided their masters undertook to train them as Protestants. Protestant colonists, specifically the Ulster Presbyterians, who had not joined the native Irish until after September 15, 1643, and any woman who married an English Protestant before December 2, 1650, were to be exempted from transplantation, the latter on condition of renouncing Catholicism. Protestants living in Connaught and Co. Clare who had shown 'good affection' and adhered to the English Parliamentary forces might, on application to the authorities, receive grants of lands in the provinces marked for colonisation.

The new plan for the colonisation was, for financiers and soldiers alike, a distinctly better proposition than that which the old Parliament had granted. Cromwell's simple soldier-like mind had seen the logic of the colonists' suggestion of contiguous land allotment by moving the native Irish land-owners into one area of the country and colonising the de-populated areas. The soldiers were no longer threatened with the prospect of having to take their land from a mere five counties. Most of the soldiers were already in possession of the land they wanted for, wherever they had bivouacked on lands belonging to native landowners, they had simply taken over the running of it and there they had stayed. Cromwell promised that his new Parliament would soon pass a bill incorporating the points he proposed. In the mean-time the Army in Ireland was to start the first of its dis-bandments.

This Army had a total strength of 34,128 men, of which there were 7,365 horse, 1,447 dragoons and 25,316 foot. It was felt that the Army should be reduced by 10,000 men to a peacetime strength of 5,000 horse, 1,000 dragoons and 18,000 foot. Four regiments of horse, nine regiments of foot and five companies of dragoons were disbanded in August.

By the end of August, 1653, well over 10,000 soldiers had been disbanded and were drifting round Ireland waiting to be allocated land in lieu of their back pay. Many had already seized land and chased the owners, if owners there still were, off the estates. In England hundreds of land hungry merchants and others who had speculated sums of capital to back the army, waited with eagerness to be allocated their proportion of the confiscated estates.

'wound follows wound'

By September, 1653, Ireland was in a state of expectation. Most people waited with dread to see whether Cromwell's plan for the colonisation of the country would be passed into an Act of Parliament and become law. In the meantime the Catholic clergy, facing up to the realities of the situation, tried to reorganise the shattered remnants of their church. At the beginning of the summer a Jesuit Father, Peter Talbot, arrived secretly in the country. He was thirty-two years old and a member of a prominent Anglo-Irish Royalist family. His younger brother Richard, for his services to the Stuarts, would, after the restoration, become the Earl of Tyrconnell. Peter Talbot had joined the Jesuits in Portugal in 1635 but had returned to Ireland during the rise of the Confederates. As a Royalist he vehemently opposed Rinuccini's separatist policies. After the Cromwellian conquest he fled the country. Now he was back again 'undergoing the same dangers as others' and arranging a system of Royalist spies and an underground network of priests. By November, 1654, he was safely back in Cologne. At the same time another priest was in Ireland, this time more openly, on different business. The Franciscan, Father Peter Walsh, who signed himself as Valesius, had been allowed to return at the

end of May, as agent for the Spanish King, in order to recruit and transport 4,000 Irish soldiers for Spain's service.

By the autumn it had become a standard procedure for
the Commissioners to imprison captured priests with a view
to transporting them, those under forty years of age to the
American colonies, and those over forty years of age to
France or Spain. Those Irish, such as the Tories, who re-
belled against the new order were also transported, usually
to the Barbados but sometimes to the American mainland.
On September 6 David Selleck, a Boston merchant, was given
a licence to use his ship *Goodfellow*, out of Boston, and the
Providence, out of London, 'to sail to Ireland and, within
two months, to take in 400 Irish children and to transport
them to those plantations' of New England and Virginia. On
September 24 a Bristol merchant named Richard Netherway
was given permission to transport 100 Irishmen to Virginia.
Such penalties, rather than decrease Tory activity, seemed to
intensify Irish attacks on settlements. Lord Broghill's elder
brother, the Royalist Earl of Cork, wrote in his diary for
September that he had met a Captain Maynard while stag
hunting near his estates by Fermoy. The stag ran off towards Castlelyons, where Barrymore Castle stood near the
fourteenth-century Franciscan friary. The Earl decided not
to pursue it being 'somewhat fatigued'. The Earl's fatigue
saved his life. 'I was told afterwards that there were Tories
who did be in wait for me, who the next day in those woods
did kill Antient (Sergeant) Leech and took young Mr. Gerard
as they were hunting. God make me thankful for this preservation.'

In Dublin the trials were continuing and although many
people had been publicly executed—well over two hundred
—the trial which opened in the Dublin High Court of Justice
on September 6 attracted considerable attention. It was the
trial of the Vicar-General of Dublin, Eamonn O'Reilly. The
specific charge of murder brought against him was the
slaughter of the colonist garrison at the Black Castle of
Wicklow on December 29, 1642. The Irish insurgents, having made the garrison prisoners, had slaughtered them and
demolished the castle. O'Reilly was jointly charged with this
act with Eamonn Dubh O'Byrne. There were over twenty

witnesses for the prosecution. Even O'Reilly's fellow prisoner in the dock, Eamonn Dubh, decided to give evidence against the Vicar-General in an effort to save his own life. He told the court that after the castle had been captured and the garrison made prisoners he and his men were resting and drinking when he heard noises. Going to investigate he found John Joyce, the Vice-Constable of the Castle, and the rest of the prisoners slain. He went and told O'Reilly what had happened and said he was much afraid that Lieutenant General Phelim MacHugh O'Byrne, who commanded the area, would arrest and punish him for it. O'Reilly, claimed Eamonn Dubh, replied 'You need not fear, I warrant you'. The prosecution's evidence ended with several other witnesses who presented various ambiguous statements, attributed to O'Reilly, as proof of his guilt. One witness, Simon Archpole, O'Reilly's former clerk and registrar, told the court that he had heard O'Reilly say that he had given £3 towards the cost of demolishing the castle a month after it was taken.

It did not take Sir Gerard Lowther long to pronounce a verdict of guilty on both men. Eamonn Dubh was executed almost immediately but O'Reilly was kept languishing in Marshalsea prison for twenty-one months before the Irish Council decided to grant him a pardon provided he went into exile in Europe. Pressure had been brought to bear on Fleetwood by Henry and Theophilus Jones because O'Reilly had acted as the negotiator between Eoin Ruadh O'Neill and their brother Michael, when he commanded the Parliamentary forces in 1648. At the beginning of 1655 O'Reilly left Ireland for Flanders. It was not long, however, before he was to return, this time as the Catholic Primate of all Ireland.

Towards the end of September John Ufflet arrived in Ireland bearing a copy of 'An Act for the speedy and effectual Satisfaction of the Adventurers for lands in Ireland, and of the Arrears due to the Soldiery there and of other public debts and for the Encouragement of Protestants to Plant and Inhabit Ireland.' The Act had been approved by the nominated Parliament on September 26. Following Cromwell's orders of July 2, a Standing Committee was appointed in Ire-

land, on August 1, to consider ways and means by which the
colonisation could be carried out, specifically in regard to
the removal of the Irish landowners west of the River Shannon. The committee consisted of thirteen men, including
Lord Broghill, who, according to his chaplain Thomas Morrice—in a biography of Broghill published in 1742—was the
man who suggested to Cromwell the scheme of transplanting
the Irish into Connaught. Broghill was also behind the
moves to depose Fleetwood, whose Anabaptist leanings were
now obvious. He suggested that Henry Cromwell should be
appointed as Lord Lieutenant of Ireland. Broghill was a
close intimate of the Lord General. On September 8 Parliament had given the title of Blarney Castle and an estate to
the annual value of £1,000, to him and his heirs in perpetuity
as 'a mark of the Parliament's favour to him for his eminent
and faithful service to the Commonwealth'.

The Act of September 26 followed closely the Lord
General's proposals of July 2. Connaught and Co. Clare were
to be set aside for 'the habitation of the Irish nation' where
they must transplant themselves with wives, children and
such servants as would volunteer to go with them before May
1, 1654. If they were found on the eastern side of the River
Shannon after that date the penalty would be death. It was
made clear that the transplantation order was confined to
proprietors of land and their families, specifically those
persons who had contributed to, or abetted the Irish insurgents, or had actually been in arms with them. The landless,
those whose goods were valued £10 or less, could either go
with the landowners as tenants into the new areas, or as
servants, or they could remain behind as hewers of wood and
drawers of water to the new landowners.

Connaught and Co. Clare was chosen as the area 'for the
habitation of the Irish nation' by reason of its being surrounded by sea and the River Shannon except for a stretch
of land ten miles wide which the authorities decided could
be closed up by a line of forts, thus imprisoning the troublesome Irish in a reservation. The order for the transplantation
caused tremendous panic among the people. Farmers, in the
middle of the winter season, were alarmed at the thought of
having to leave their land at such a time, and were deprived

of all motive to go on with their tillage. Apart from this, Connaught was the most wasted province in Ireland and the authorities reported 'the said county of Clare housing in it nine baronies containing above 1,300 ploughlands is now totally ruinated and deserted by the inhabitants thereof; there not being above 40 ploughlands at the most of the whole country, and lying in the barony of Bunratty, at present inhabited, excepting some few persons who, for their own safety live in garrisons'.

The financiers, now pleased that an agreement had been reached, had set up a committee at the Grocers' Hall to establish what lands were to be allocated to them. The chairman of the committee was the Cheapside linen draper, Methusaleh Turner. All claims were to be examined by the committee, which was empowered by the Council of State. The main list of financiers who had 'adventured money' for the Irish wars bore 1,360 names. Number 72 on the list was the Lord General himself who had at first given £300. Most members of Parliament, starting with John Pym, who was the first to subscribe with a donation of £600, had given £100 or more. Richard Wade, a London carpenter, had given £6,100, while Richard Warring and Thomas Turgis, two London grocers, had given £2,001 each. The Presbyterian leader, Clotworthy, had given £1,000 and George Powell, the Mayor of Taunton, had given £1,360. Merchants, booksellers, stationers, grocers, carpenters had all rushed to buy debentures which, they hoped, would result in raising them into the new landed aristocracy of Ireland. Financiers and soldiers alike saw themselves as the future feudal lords of the country. For the Irish it was a different matter.

The poet Fear Dorcha Ó Mealláin of Co. Down wrote in *An díbirt go Connachta*—The Banishment to Connaught—about the

> fine rich land divided
> where strong and weak are both laid low.

He wrote of the faint hope his people still had; God had delivered Jonah and the Israelites, so also would he deliver the Irish on their long winter trip to Connaught. He bade the Irish have Jonah's patience and entreated them to have

strong faith, hope and charity. The poet reminded the
people that they would have a rich land in heaven without
rent or boundaries. More realistically he added:

> Long from them is this now—
> We're being deprived of land:
> But Lazarus once was cured;
> From sorrow we're all be released

Another poet, who remained anonymous, was more bitter:

> The worst of all evils has come to us
> But we refuse to be sad,
> Since we have been spared no evil
> Let us be merry and glad.

The Jesuit Father Quinn, writing to the Vatican from his
hiding place in the mountains, lamented:

Wound follows wound that nothing be wanting to fill up the cup
of sufferings. The few Catholic families that remain were lately deprived by Cromwell of all their immovable property, and are all
compelled to abandon their native estates, and retire into the province
of Connaught.

He adds:

... the design, obviously, is to extirpate gradually the whole nation,
since no plan can succeed in shaking the attachment to the Roman
Catholic faith. Some of our Protestant garrisons lately told the
Catholics that nothing could stay these persecutions, save the abjuration of the Pope's authority and Mass, but vain was their labour,
their labour now is vain.

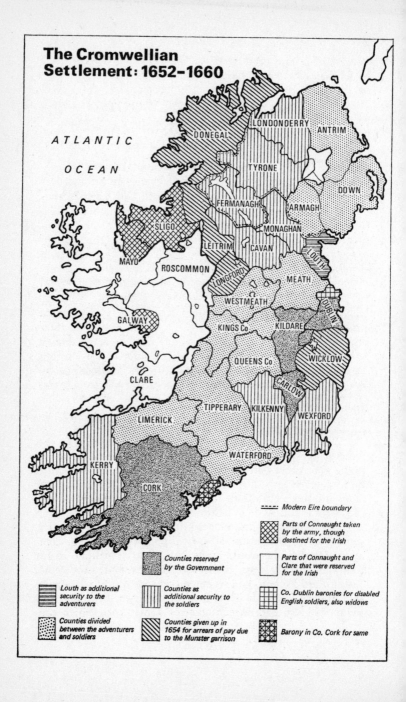

The Cromwellian Settlement: 1652–1660

ATLANTIC

OCEAN

DONEGAL

LONDONDERRY ANTRIM

TYRONE

DOWN

FERMANAGH

ARMAGH

MONAGHAN

SLIGO

LEITRIM CAVAN

MAYO

ROSCOMMON

LONGFORD MEATH

WESTMEATH

DUBLIN

GALWAY

KINGS Co KILDARE

QUEENS Co WICKLOW

CLARE

CARLOW

TIPPERARY KILKENNY WEXFORD

LIMERICK

KERRY WATERFORD

CORK

===== Modern Eire boundary

Parts of Connaught taken by the army, though destined for the Irish

Counties reserved by the Government

Parts of Connaught and Clare that were reserved for the Irish

Louth as additional security to the adventurers

Counties as additional security to the soldiers

Co. Dublin baronies for disabled English soldiers, also widows

Counties divided between the adventurers and soldiers

Counties given up in 1654 for arrears of pay due to the Munster garrison

Barony in Co. Cork for same

CHAPTER 2

CHARLES FLEETWOOD

'power over the three nations'

The reaction to the publication of the transplantation orders was immediate. All over Ireland Irish and Old English landowners began to apply for exemption. On October 14 the Commissioners issued their 'final directions for the transplantation'. Heads of families liable to transplant were to proceed before January 20, 1654, to the Commissioners of Revenue in the precinct where they lived. The fifteen precincts into which Ireland was divided were Dublin, Trim (Tredath or Drogheda), Athy, Kilkenny Waterford, Wexford, Clonmel, Cork, Kerry, Limerick, Athlone, Galway, Belturbet, Belfast and Derry. They were to give the names of their families, particulars of tenants and others who were prepared to accompany them voluntarily. Ages, colour of hair, height and distinguishing marks were to be listed by the Commissioners plus an account of cattle and tillage, 'for which they pay contribution in the place from whence they remove'. After satisfying themselves as to the accuracy of the information, the Commissioners of Revenue were to issue Transplantation Certificates which, when presented to the authorities in the reserved area, would entitle the holder to land proportioned under the Act of Settlement. The heads of the families were then to travel to Connaught or Clare, claim their allocated land, and there build huts to house their families and tenants who were to follow them before May 1, 1654.

Some landowners protested while others resignedly obeyed. James, Lord Dunboyne of Co. Tipperary, told the Commissioners that he would transplant with twenty-one of his followers, taking four cows, ten garrans and two swine. Pierce Lord Ikerrin, said seventeen persons would accompany him and he had four cows, five garrans, two sheep and two swine. He also had sixteen acres of winter corn which con-

siderably increased the value of his property. Lesser landowners like Pádraig Mac Giollaiasachta, whom the colonists
called Patrick Lysaght, had an estate in South Ballynanty,
Co. Limerick, which he also had to leave. Pádraig had played
no part in the insurrection but he had been busy building
up a profitable business in Limerick city and, a year later,
had married Margaret Browne of Camus. He had left
Limerick just before Ireton started his siege and he spent
the time farming with a very depleted stock on his farm at
Ballynanty. The year after his first son William was born
Pádraig received, in December, 1653, his Certificate of
Transplantation, the twentieth to be issued by the Commissioners of Limerick Precinct.

That Patrick Lysaght of Camasse in Small County barony in
Limerick has appeared before Commissioners of Transplantation.
The said Patrick Lysaght aged 40 years, middle stature, brown hair.
   Margaret, his wife, aged 27 years, middle stature, brown hair, and
their two small children. Cathleen White, sister to the said Patrick,
aged 30, tall stature, black hair, and her two small children.
   Their substance
   16 cows, 16 sheep, 6 pigs and piggeens, 12 garrans, and mares, 12
acres of winter corn for which they pay contribution and 7 servants.

Pádraig did not complete his final removal until 1657 and,
unlike most of the transplantees, he was to rebuild his
business interests again. He lived on his Co. Clare property
at Shandagan, in Kilkerry, and from there still ran a business
in Limerick. His two daughters Margaret and Slane were
born there. He was not the only one of his family to transplant—his cousins James of Killonierkan and John of
Athdare, Co. Kerry, who had actually fought in the war, were
likewise removed.

From the confiscations in December, Ludlow managed to
secure a comfortable estate for his own use. On December 16
Walter Cheevers, who owned property in Dublin and in
Kingstown (Dun Laoghaire) was ordered to present himself
before the Commissioners for the Dublin precinct. Cheevers
was of an old Anglo-Norman family who had settled in Ireland in the twelfth century. He had taken no part in the
insurrection but he was a Catholic. Three days later a certificate was given to Cheevers to transplant to Connaught.

His confiscated estate was given to Ludlow, who asked the Athlone Commissioners to allocate Cheevers a good house in Connaught, perhaps because of feelings of guilt. In August, 1656, however, Cheevers was complaining bitterly that he had not been allocated a good house.

While the work of the transplantation was getting under way, there were other pressing problems to be seen to. Following the disbandment of many regiments, a council of officers met in Dublin to consider organising new rates of pay for the army. On October 19 they agreed that Colonels should receive £4 4s. a week with £2 9s. for Lieutenant Colonels. Regimental strengths were also clarified. Foot regiments were to have a strength of 1,000 men divided into ten companies. Horse regiments were to have 480 men divided into six troops and dragoon regiments were to have 600 men divided into six companies.

Many Catholic priests had now fled the country while others awaited transportation to the American colonies. Several merchants were making a growing business out of transportations of the wretched Irish. On October 25 David Selleck of Boston and a Bristol merchant called Leader were given permission to transport 250 Irishwomen between the ages of 15 and 50 to the New England colony while, on December 28, Selleck and Leader were given another licence to transport all 'rogues and vagabonds' to Virginia. Some leading priests were still executed as it was not deemed conducive to the public good of the Commonwealth merely to transport them. On October 15, 1653, Father Tadhg Moriarty was executed. He was described by Father Dominick de Rossario O'Daly, in his book *The Fall of the Geraldines*, published in Lisbon in 1655, as 'the last friar of the Dominican Convent of Tralee. Well skilled in moral and dogmatic theology...'

Moriarty had studied in Toledo and was in the General Chapter of Dominicans held in Rome in 1644. With Father Albert O'Brien he was appointed a judge to decide the boundaries of the Dominican Order in the province of Munster. 'Never,' commented Father O'Daly, 'did the bride more joyously go forth to the marriage altar than he did to death, and never did the starveling more eagerly desire food than did this glorious champion the scaffold and martyrdom.'

Father Moriarty had been well liked and respected in Tralee where he was now brought to be hanged.

... from the scaffold he exhorted the spectators not to be dismayed, but to cling with tenacity to their hallowed creed and to be ever mindful of the vicissitudes and transitoriness of this life; he more over described martyrdom as the secure as well as the shortest path to the heavenly crown, and was then immediately executed.

Father Moriarty was the fifteenth member of the Dominican Order to die under the rule of the Commonwealth.

The trials were still dragging on, though they were not as frequent and attracted less attention than they had earlier in the year. The trial of Donogh MacCarthy, Lord Muskerry, one of the early leaders of the insurrection, was, however, the centre of attraction in Dublin during December. Muskerry had actually been dining with Richard Boyle, the first 'Great Earl of Cork' at Castlelyons when the news of the insurrection reached Munster. At the table were Cork's eldest son, the Lord Burlington, and his son Lord Broghill. The earl wondered whether the news from Ulster could be true and Muskerry had laughed scornfully at the idea. A few days later it was Muskerry who was leading his MacCarthy clan against the colonists and pushing them back to the garrison town of Kilkenny. Muskerry was now charged with the murder of Mrs. Hussey, Mrs. Crocker and her daughter, George, a miller and his wife, Ellen Coman and her child, Charles Vavasour, his wife and two children and two persons unknown near Blarney on August 1, 1642. Having considered the evidence Sir Gerard Lowther pronounced a 'not guilty' verdict. Dismissing Muskerry from the court, Lowther reminded Muskerry of the Sicilian Vespers when, in 1282, the Sicilians turned on the French settlers and slaughtered them, and of the St. Bartholomew's Day Massacre in Paris 'but it and others are short of it... here in a short time above 300,000 British and Protestants murdered or lost in cold blood, so as that number far exceed Paris or Sicily, no torment, no burying alive there, only death, but here death was a mercy!' Lowther paused and said sternly: 'Go! Expiate it by repentance!'

Muskerry thanked the court for its verdict and added:

I met many crosses in Spain and Portugal. I could get no rest till I came thither and the crosses I met here are much affliction to me. But when I consider that in this court I come clear out of that blackness of blood by being so sifted, it is more to me than my estates. I can live without my estate but not without my credit.

It was not until May, 1654, following another trial on a further murder charge on which he was again found 'not guilty' that he was finally allowed to go into exile in Poland.

There was news also from England which caused great dissension in the Commonwealth administration in Ireland. The nominated Parliament had fallen into the hands of extremists who disagreed with the Lord General's conservative views. Fifth Monarchists and Anabaptists seemed to dominate the assembly. Measures to amend the laws of the state were being blocked again. The crunch came when a proposal was placed before the House on the abolition of tithes, by which ministers were supported. This was urgently demanded by the Fifth Monarchists, Anabaptists and other sects but strenuously resisted by landowners and the parochial clergy as an onslaught on the rights of property. The Lord General, despairing of the bickering assembly, wrote to his son-in-law, Fleetwood, 'Truly, I never more needed all help from my Christian friends than now!'

The matter of the tithes was due for a vote on December 21, 1653. Before it was brought forward Sir Charles Worsley was on his feet attacking the assembly and denouncing the tithe question as a bid to abolish private property. He moved the dissolution of the nominated Parliament, confident that his group had a sufficient majority at that time in the House. The House, deciding that it would not be for 'the good of the Commonwealth' that they should sit any longer, 'it was requisite to deliver up to the Lord General Cromwell the powers they had received from him'. After much discussion among the leaders, both civil and military, it was decided that Cromwell should be handed 'power over the three nations, without bound or limit set'. An Instrument of Government was drawn up, by which Oliver Cromwell was to be installed in Whitehall and known as His Highness the Lord Protector. The office was to be elective, not hereditary.

Legislative authority was a 'reside in one person and parliament'; the parliament was to be called every third year and was to sit for not less than five months. But executive authority was to be solely with the Lord Protector and his Council. The Parliament was to consist of 400 members, including thirty each from Scotland and Ireland.

On Friday, December 16, 1653, at 1 p.m. the Lord General, Oliver Cromwell, at the age of fifty-four, was installed as His Highness the Lord Protector of England, Scotland and Ireland.

Lieutenant General Ludlow commented: 'the news of this great alteration of affairs was very unwelcome to us in Ireland.'

'The Lieutenant General behaves himself most childishly'

The strongest section of colonists to voice their indignation at Cromwell's new title were the Anabaptists who were particularly angered. They pointed out that the title Protector should only apply to God Himself. The Fifth Monarchists raged that only Christ should rule the government. On grounds of practical politics rather than theology, the Commonwealth Party, the republicans, aided by the Levellers, also lined up with the Anabaptists and Fifth Monarchists. The most influential man in Ireland to throw his weight firmly against the declaration of the Protectorate was Lieutenant General Edmund Ludlow.

He used his position on the Commission of the Parliament of the Commonwealth of England for Ordering and Settling the Affairs of Ireland, to argue that they should refuse to recognise Cromwell as Lord Protector. Fleetwood, despite his Anabaptist leanings, fully supported his father-in-law; perhaps it was his influence which had stirred William Kiffyn, John Spilsbury and Joseph Fansom, the Anabaptist leaders in England, to write to the Anabaptists in Ireland asking them to accept the new government. Miles Corbet supported Fleetwood and John Jones supported Ludlow. The Commissioners were therefore in deadlock. Ludlow recalled that Fleetwood spent five hours at one meeting trying to break the deadlock in favour of recognition of the Protector. Finally, Edmund Roberts, the Auditor-General, arrived to discuss some army matters with the Commissioners, and Fleetwood, seizing the opportunity, asked him to voice an opinion. Roberts was in favour of the Protectorship. Undemocratically, Fleetwood co-opted Roberts to temporary membership of the Commission and declared in favour of the recognition of the new government. Ludlow refused to sign the declaration. Fleetwood, to get round the dissension among the Commissioners, ordered that the declaration be published over the signature of John Hughes, the secretary of the Commissioners 'which way was taken', observed Ludlow, bitterly, 'that it might not appear that any of the Commissioners hands were wanting to the proclamation'.

A few weeks later Jenkyn Lloyd wrote to the secretary to the Council of State, John Thurloe:

The order for proclaiming His Highness was signed only by their secretary, whereas others usually signed by themselves. The reason whereof I understand to be, that three Commissioners having signed it, it was tendered to the Lt. General also, who refusing used this expression, that he would rather cut off his hand, and then the three others blotted out their names.

Ludlow decided to have no further part in the civil administration of the country and fell back on his military office. He wrote:

Having done what I could to obstruct the proclamation of that, which was called an Instrument of Government, imposed upon the people by the military sword, contrary to many oaths and solemn engagements, as well as to the interest and expectation of the people, I thought myself obliged in duty to act no further in my civil capacity as a Commissioner of Parliament lest I should seem by acting with them to acknowledge this as lawful authority, to that end I forebore to go to the Cork House which was the usual place where the Commissioners sat.

I was unwilling to decline the exercise of my military authority as Lt. General of the Horse, having received my commission from the Parliament, which I resolved to keep till it should be forced from me, and to act by it in order to attain those ends for which I received it, the principal whereof were to bring those to justice who had been guilty of the blood of many thousands of English Protestants and to restore the English who remained alive to lands which had been taken from them by the Irish.

The proclamation announcing that Oliver Cromwell was now Lord Protector of the three nations was finally published on January 30, 1654, in Dublin. Ludlow says that not many people turned out to hear the publication of the news. The artillery batteries in Dublin 'wasted some of the powder belonging to the public, the report of which was very unwelcome music to me, who desiring to be as far from this pageantry as I could, rode out of town that afternoon'. In fact, apart from Fleetwood himself, the only other high ranking officer to attend was Sir Hardress Waller. In spite of the fact that most of the army hierarchy did not support Cromwell's Protectorship, either from religious or political grounds, Ludlow was the only officer who practised open rebellion. He refused to surrender his military commission, saying that it had been given to him by the Parliament of the Commonwealth of England and only that Parliament could take it away; he refused to carry out the functions of a Commissioner for civil administration and, above all, he refused to recognise the establishment of the Protectorate. He even began to distribute anti-Cromwellian literature.

Jenkyn Lloyd wrote to Thurloe on March 13:

The Lt. General behaves himself most childishly, not refraining from very poisonous and bitter expressions in public meetings, for which I conceive it is that he is so much cried up by the Anabaptists of late, and ever since admitted to the private weekly meetings which before was denied him. He refuses to act as Commissioner and only acts as Lt. General. The riddle can be resolved no otherwise than by this distinction, that the one is more beneficial than the other ...

Among the literature that was soon to flourish was a twenty-three page pamphlet, dated at Waterford on June 24, 1654, written by 'R.G.' and entitled *A Copy of a letter from an Officer of the Army in Ireland to His Highness the Lord Protector, concerning his changing of Government*. The writer warned the Lord Protector

... nothing can be more pernicious to these Nations at this present time than for you to govern well, for it would palliate the assumed power and so hide it from the just indignation of this age and prove like the guilding of poisonous pills, or painting of sepulchres and be a bribing us out of our rights and liberties with a seeming justice; nothing but this can lull asleep so many patriots, who have been often awakened with drums and trumpets to adventure their lives against a tyrant, neither indeed could any other thing than a just and happy reign of Augustus Caesar have given the last defeat to Roman Liberty or made way for those Monsters who succeed. You see, my Lord, what a business you have undertaken, when you have made it the interest of honest men to wish that you may commit all excesses and use more violence, break more laws and ties in carrying on this arbitrary sovereignty than you have done in the assuming of it.

Naturally the antagonism in Ireland was worrying to the Lord Protector, who decided that someone should be sent over to Dublin to check opinion there. He could find no better person to undertake the task than his twenty-six year-old son, Colonel Henry Cromwell. Henry knew Ireland, was on the Council for Irish Affairs and could be entrusted to return with an accurate report on how matters stood. Secrecy as to the purpose of the visit would have to cloak the trip. The journal *Several Proceedings* for February 16–23 records: 'The Lord Henry Cromwell with divers officers are despatched for Ireland for filling up of the regiment and settling the nation.' Even Edmund Ludlow, who constituted one of the main reasons for the trip, was left in doubt, and thought that Henry Cromwell had come 'to feel the pulse of the officers there touching his coming over to command in that nation'. Indeed, Henry's arrival prompted a spate of rumours that the Lord Protector was sending him over to replace Fleetwood. *Several Proceedings* reported: 'All people here are at a stand not knowing the end of my lord Henry's coming over: most imagining he hath a commission in his pocket to be Lord Deputy.' Fleetwood wrote to know the truth of the matter and Cromwell replied on June 22 that:

It is reported that you are to be sent for and Harry to be Deputy: which truly never entered my heart. The Lord knows, my desire was for him and his brother to have lived private lives in the country and Henry knows this very well and how difficult I was persuaded to give him his commission for his present place. This I say from a simple and sincere heart. The noise of my being crowned etc. are like malicious figments.

Henry left Holyhead in the frigate *Fox*, leaving the Welsh port at about three or four in the morning and arriving off Dublin at about twelve noon. Ludlow was in his house, the one confiscated from the unfortunate Walter Cheevers, called Monkstown Castle. The 'castle' overlooked the old

Bullock harbour, nearly five miles from the city. Ludlow could hear the boom of a cannon announcing Henry's arrival. He naturally wished to see Henry before Fleetwood did, and to advise him on his viewpoint. He immediately sent a coach to the harbour with an invitation to visit him but Fleetwood, his wife, and a party of 'divers officers, civil and military and other gentlemen of quality' had already arrived at the harbour to greet the Protector's son.

It was a few weeks before Ludlow had the opportunity to entertain Henry at his home at Monkstown. After the two men had dined together Ludlow took Henry round the stables, where he kept twenty horses ready for service. Then they strolled round the gardens, which Ludlow was redesigning.

> ...after a short collation in the garden [recalled Ludlow], I acquainted him with the grounds of my dissatisfaction with the present state of affairs in England, which I assured him was in no sort personal but would be the same were my own father alive and in the place of his.

Why, Ludlow asked Henry, had Oliver Cromwell left 'his former station wherein his power was as great, and his wealth as much as any rational man could wish, to procure himself nothing but envy and trouble?'

Henry replied: 'You that are here may think he had power but they made a very kickshaw of him at London.'

Ludlow felt 'the extraordinary remedy is not to be used till the ordinary fail its proper effect, so ought it to be continued no longer than the necessity of using it subsists: whereas this that they call a Government had no other means to preserve itself but such as were violent which not being natural could not be lasting.'

Henry demanded 'would you then have the sword laid down? I cannot think but you believe it to be as much your interest to have it kept up as any man.'

Having honestly confessed why he could not support Cromwell's government, Ludlow was assured by Henry that no one would interfere with him provided he confined himself to carrying out his military duties only. However, Henry immediately despatched a secret report to Thurloe dated March 8, in cipher, in which he stated: 'To offer my poor thought I would take advantage by Ludlow's forwardness to put him out of the army and put General Desborough in his place.' John Desborough was the Lord Protector's brother-in-law. Henry also warned Thurloe of John Jones, the Commissioner who suported Ludlow. Jones was 'endeavouring to render the government unacceptable' but was 'more cunning and close' in his opposition than was Ludlow. As for Fleetwood, Henry thought he was 'a little too deeply engaged in a political affection to the persons of the Anabaptists ... though I believe it rather to proceed from tenderness than love to their principles'.

Before Henry left Ireland, having completed his father's mission, he was approached by the Physician-General, Dr. William Petty, who complained about the way his medical colleague, Benjamin Worsley, was conducting the surveying of the confiscated lands. Petty said that not only were Worsley's methods those of an incompetent but he was corrupt and surveying purely for selfish gains. Henry liked Petty and decided to support his plea about the survey. He wrote to Thurloe, having investigated some of Petty's allegations, 'I know three men that took 18,000 acres of the Commonwealth's land in the County Meath for £600 per annum and let it out again for £1,800, and these were commissioners instructed with letting your lands!'

On March 29 the *Mercurius Politicus* reported: 'The Lord Henry Cromwell is returned from Ireland and is (blessed be God) safely arrived at the Cockpit.'

The Protector's Council of State was much impressed with Henry's reports from Ireland and felt that Henry himself should replace Ludlow as second-in-command to Fleetwood, with the rank of Major General. The Lord Protector prevaricated over this recommendation but certainly Ludlow would have to go. Orders were sent to Fleetwood asking him to demand that Ludlow surrender his military commission. This Ludlow point blank refused to do.

'The Tories fly out and increase'

Father William Tirry, an Augustinian, and Prior of Fethard, Co. Tipperary, was captured in January, 1654 and taken to Clonmel where he was publicly executed on April 22 of that year. His death caused a fellow Augustinian, Father James O'Mahoney, to write to the Prior-General of the order, Philip Visconti, in Milan, on September 4, giving some details of Father Tirry's death. O'Mahoney had fled into exile in Brussels sometime after July, 1653. The Prior-General was interested to learn about the sufferings of the members of his order in Ireland and felt something should be done to gain world wide sympathy for the state of affairs existing in that country. He wrote asking for further details. O'Mahoney sent them on November 7 and on December 5 Visconti wrote back suggesting O'Mahoney publish a full account of the sufferings of the Irish priesthood. By April 10, 1655, O'Mahoney had published anonymously a work entitled *Sanguinea Eremus Martyrum Hiberniae Ord. Eremit S. P. Augustini*, which contained details of the fate of twenty-seven Augustinians who had either been executed, jailed or deported.

It was obvious, however, that the attitude of Fleetwood and his Commissioners was beginning to change. On January 26 he had allowed 'Colonel Teele, who has licence to transplant 1,000 Irish for the service of the King of Spain, to have liberty to take away all the priests in Ireland and send in their names'. The older priests were now mostly transported to the continent while the younger priests were sent to the American colonies.

Due to the organisational work of Father Peter Talbot, who had spent some time reorganising the shattered priesthood in Ireland, a number of priests had gone underground. Father Barnabus Barnewall, writing in Dublin on October 4, 1669, recalled how a Capuchin, Father Anselm Ball, had worked in disguise among the people in the city of Dublin itself, ministering the sacraments 'so much so, that he did often pass two successive days and nights without an interval for repose'. As the danger of discovery increased he went into the Dublin mountains. Because 'none were allowed to receive him into their homes under penalty of death and of the confiscation of their property, he built for himself a little hut of brambles in a rocky district'. Disguised as a beggar he more than once came close to arrest and was forced to find shelter deeper in the mountains and in caves. During the plague years in the city he attended the sick 'being often obliged to enter, creeping on hands and feet, the fetid huts of the persecuted poor'. On one occasion a cavalry trooper recognised him but Father Ball managed to unhorse and disarm the man. He was finally caught, ordered to be transported to the Barbados, but was still in jail when Charles II was restored.

Father Quinn, reporting on the state of the Jesuits in 1656, recalled that in 1654 Father James Ford dwelt on an island in a large bog teaching students who had gone there with him, building crude shelters to live in. Another Jesuit, Father Stephen Gelosse, also continued the Jesuit practice of teaching, disguising himself at various times as a dealer of fagots, a servant, a thatcher, a porter, a beggar, gardener, a miller and a carpenter. He was arrested four times on suspicion of being a priest but managed to persuade his captors to let him go, surviving until the Restoration when he opened a school at Ross.

Priests donned various disguises. Jesuits could usually be found among peasants or beggars; Franciscans and Capuchins lived as shepherds, herdsmen or ploughmen, while others merely hid in remote spots. According to Father Quinn:

Father Christopher Netterville, like St. Athanasius, for an entire year and more, lay hid in his father's sepulchre, and even there with difficulty escaping the pursuit of the enemy, he had to fly to a still more incommodious retreat. One was concealed in a deep pit, from which he at intervals went forth on some mission of charity. The heretics having received information as to his hiding place, rushed to it, and throwing down immense blocks of rock, exulted in his destruction, but Providence watched over the good Father, and he was absent, engaged in some pious work of his sacred ministry, when his retreat was thus assailed. As the Holy Sacrifice cannot be offered up in these receptacles of beasts rather of men, all the clergy carry with them a sufficient number of consecrated hosts, that thus they themselves may be comforted by this Holy Sacrament and may be able to administer it to the sick and to others.

Other priests were caught and died in jail, like Father Bonaventure Carew of Killarney, a Capuchin, who had gone into exile in 1650. He had decided to return on a mission and was arrested, 'cast headlong into a subterraneous dungeon, so small that he could not stand erect nor lie down, and there without one ray of light he was detained for eighteen months in a lengthened martyrdom'.

Leniency was shown in some individual cases. In August, Father Roger Begs, in prison in Dublin, told the Commissioners that he had been nine months in jail and was ill. He desired liberty to go to his friends who would help him so that he would not be a burden on the authorities. He was released 'upon giving sufficient security that within four months he do transport himself to foreign parts, beyond the seas, never to return, and that during that time he do not exercise any of his priestly function, nor move from where he shall choose to reside in above five miles without permission'. At the same time Father William Sheil 'being old, lame and weak and not able to travel without crutches' was granted permission to live in Connaught.

Other priests were shipped directly to France or Spain. On July 24 Lieutenant Colonel Hewson, the governor of Dublin, ordered that all priests in the jails of Dublin 'as are not under suspicion of murder' be delivered to Captain William Hazlewood's ship *Globe* to be transported to Cadiz or Malaga.

Two bishops took advantage of the change in attitude by the authorities to surrender themselves. These were John Patrick de Burgo, the Archbishop of Tuam, and Francis Kirwan, Bishop of Killala. Kirwan had been persuaded to give himself up to the governor of Galway, Colonel Peter Stubber, because he was ill after being constantly on the run since the fall of Galway in 1652. Kirwan, now sixty-five years old, had hidden himself in his own episcopal residency of Killala with his chaplain, Father Thomas Kelly. The house had been given to Walter de Burgo, a sympathiser, who made a secret room in the house which 'contained two beds, for himself and chaplain. The apartment was feebly lighted by a window and was large enough to hold a chest. The room was infested by mice, which kept continually running over the heads of the sleepers and frequently made away with their candle'. Some years later, in exile in St. Malo, Kirwan told his story to his nephew John Lynch, who published an account in 1669 under the title *The Portrait of a Pious Bishop or The Life and Death of the Most Rev. Francis Kirwan, Bishop of Killala.*

Kirwan and his chaplain spent over eight months in the room and once Kirwan had to disguise himself in a sheet and pretend he was just a feeble old man when soldiers caught him in a surprise raid. Informers were at work in the district and Kirwan and Kelly set off for safer lodgings. On the journey he was given a meal at the house of a sympathiser.

... after he had tarried some time with his most generous host, and was on the point of taking his departure, cavalry from a neighbouring garrison unexpectedly made their appearance, and dismounted, alighting at the hall door, refusing, however, to enter the house in the absence of the father of the family; they then commanded the mistress to have supper prepared for them in the adjoining houses. Some of those troopers slept, however, in the house that night, and the Bishop spent it in sleepless vigil, giving his soul to prayer, though racked with great anxiety. His apprehensions were not for his personal safety but he dreaded that the hospitality he had received that night might prove prejudicial to the interests of his most excellent host and furnish the soldiers with a pretext for spoliation; he never doubted for a moment that the latter had seen him for he was on the threshold when they made their appearance, and it caused him to turn back. After this sleepless night had passed, one of the soldiers was heard to exhort his fellows to seize the Bishop's effects: whereas another strove to dissuade them alleging that their commander would take it exceedingly ill if any injury were done the bishop's host, who was on the most intimate terms of friendship with the aforesaid officer. Everyone subsequently attributed the Bishop's preservation and indemnity of his most kind host, to the prayers of our prelate.

After this Kirwan returned to Galway city. His life was in constant danger from informers who wished to claim the financial rewards offered for the capture of priests. On more than one occasion

...he was obliged to get out on the roof and while his pursuers were gaining on him, to descend into a neighbouring house by the dormer window. For, as most of the houses in Galway are connected, a person can safely walk on the roofs, and thus pass from one house to another and, as the interior walls support the roof, parapets raise on the outside walls, under cover of which it is easy to find shelter.

For a man of sixty-five years the life was too strenuous and he finally fell ill. He decided to give himself up to Colonel Stubber. There was a large number of priests in Galway, either in prison or on parole, among them John Patrick de Burgo, the Archbishop of Tuam. In June Stubber decided to round up all the priests and march them into prison 'all of them treated as though they were criminals, marched in bodies, surrounded by soldiers, drums beating and bugles sounding'.

Lynch says his uncle and the others were in prison fourteen months before they were 'carried off to a ship and on their way surrounded by a strong escort of spear men and musketeers'. According to Lynch 'nor had they any previous notice of the decree of banishment lest their friends might succour them with any viaticum'. Memory had played Kirwan tricks or else Lynch had taken down the matter wrongly for on December 14 the governor of Galway gave the Archbishop of Tuam and Bishop Kirwan freedom of liberty for two months on condition, at the end of the period, that they took ship for France and did not re-enter Ireland afterwards.

Kirwan arrived in Nantes, Brittany, in August 1655. He chose to live amongst his brother Celts, the Bretons, except for a brief pilgrimage to Caen and a journey to see his nephew, John Lynch, at the Augustinian Convent in St. Malo. The illness he had contracted while on the run in Ireland, and which his nephew described as 'grievous maladies', grew worse and he died on August 27, 1661, and was buried by Jesuits in Rennes.

In Ulster the Scottish Presbyterian ministers were once again meeting openly and, according to Adair, 'this poor church had a new sunshine of liberty of all ordinances and much of the blessing and countenance of God conniving therewith in those congregations where ministers had been planted'. The Anabaptist governor of Down, Colonel Barrow, was still trying to suppress all Presbyterian meetings. But the Presbyterians found help in the return to Ireland of the Presbyterian leader Sir John Clotworthy, who had raised a regiment to fight the native Irish for the King and advanced large sums of money in speculation for Irish land. He had now returned to claim his portion of the confiscated estates. The Presbyterian ministers approached him for advice on the situation through his mother, who was an ardent supporter of the Presbyterian cause. Clotworthy suggested that two ministers go with him to talk to Fleetwood. From twenty-four ministers in the latter part of 1653 there were close on eighty ministers now in Ulster. Clotworthy felt that they should claim some sort of maintenance from the state. The Presbyterians elected Adair, Andrew Stewart, Captain James Moor and a Captain Longford (who eventually did not go) to journey to Dublin with Clotworthy. Fleetwood's Commisioners apparently welcomed Clotworthy's suggestion that the Presbyterian ministers be brought under the dependency of the state. They proposed to give ministers, whom they judged worthy of a salary, allowances out of the state treasury. The suggestion was accepted by the Presbyterians 'though they saw it', says Adair, 'inconvenient to pass from their legal way of maintenance to have dependence on an usurping power, yet considered it necessary that ministers be maintained'.

On April 1 Fleetwood sent a letter to Carrickfergus.

Understanding that there is a want of godly and well affected ministers in parts of Ulster whereby good people there inhabiting become destitute of those spiritual comforts they might otherwise enjoy ... we recommend into your faithful inquiry such persons of the Scots Nation, and living in your respective precincts, as you may have reason to believe godly, of peaceable not of turbulent disposition, but qualified for that service, the which being certified we shall (through the blessing of God) make so seasonable a return as will afford them due encouragement and suit your desires.

The religious policies of Fleetwood's administration did cause some converts among the Catholics. In January the Irish converted to Protestantism in Wexford were asking that the Anglican minister Humphrey Good preach to them, while Richard Fitzgerald was preaching in Irish to a newly converted flock in Dungarvan. The attempts to convert the Irish through the medium of their own language showed the need to employ mainly Scottish colonists from Ulster who were generally at home in both Irish and English. In fact, a great many Ulster Scots were native Gaelic speakers who had come from such areas of Scotland as Galloway or Fife, which were still Scottish-Gaelic speaking in the following century. The difference between Ulster Irish and their Scottish Gaelic was merely dialectical.

Conversions of the Irish to Protestantism were not always greeted without scepticism. In July John Murcot and certain laymen were asked to examine the conversion of Irish Catholics around Athy, since they had been allowed dispensation from transplantation because of their conversion. Murcot was to see 'whether they have, upon any conscientious grounds, deserted Popery or for any feigned consideration or by-ends pretended the embracing of Protestantism'. A similar request was made to the Mayor of Dublin with regard to the Irish converts in the city.

The Army were still concerned to prevent soldiers, or even ex-soldiers, from marrying Irish women, a practice which still continued in spite of the 'non fraternisation' orders made by Henry Ireton. Intermarriage between these and Irish Catholic women usually meant that, instead of the wife adopting Protestantism, the husband adopted Catholicism and any children usually became, in the words of the poet Edmund Spenser, 'mere Irish'. On May 1, 1651, Ireton had ordered: 'Whereas divers officers and soldiers of the Army do daily intermarry with the women of this nation who are Papists . . . I say that any officer who marries such shall hereby be held incapable of command or trust in this Army . . .' Soldiers were to be dismissed and flogged. *The Moderate Cavalier* recorded, with more idealism than accuracy, that the English soldiers

> . . . rather than turn
> From English principles, would sooner burn
> And rather marry an Irish wife
> Would bachelors remain for term of life.

The truth was somewhat different; in January, 1654, the Commissioners of Revenue at Galway started to examine the number of civil and military officers who had married Irish Catholics 'and to certify their names and employment respectively forthwith to the Commissioners of the Commonwealth'. The authorities certainly did not condone the practice and on March 17, 1653, Colonel Solomon Richards had reported to Dublin Castle that a Captain William Williamson was now a prisoner in Co. Tipperary awaiting trial for having had an affair with an Irish woman while stationed in Clonmel. On June 15, 1655, Hugh Powell of Colonel Hewson's regiment was flogged after being convicted of 'fornication'.

Many Irish Catholic intellectuals and theologians, who had fled to Europe, were to die without seeing Ireland again, men like Dominican Father Pádraigín Háicead from Mor, near Cashel, who was acclaimed as one of Ireland's leading poets. Born in 1600, he had studied in the Dominican convent at Limerick and then at Morlaix, in Brittany, before returning to Ireland in 1633. He had, according to his love poem *Cuirim séad suirghe*—I put a love token—spent 'seven dead winters abroad'. Politically he stood firmly for Eoin Ruadh O'Neill and Nuncio Rinuccini's plea for Irish independence. In *Séadnadh Mór*—a political poem flaming with passion—he hailed O'Neill's army as the *Fianna Fáil*, the soldiers of destiny. By mid 1651 he had been forced to flee abroad again and settle at the Irish College of Louvain. Anguished, heart broken, vexed by the bitter feuds which he felt had led to Ireland's downfall, he died there aged fifty-four. Háicead was best remembered by a *deibhidhe*, an epigram, written in a former exile.

> While awake I am in France
>   In Ireland when I'm sleeping
> Little love have I then to wake
> To stay asleep is my endeavour

The *Mercurius Politicus* reported on August 24, 1654:

The working of transplanting is at a stand. The Tories fly out and increase. It is the nature of this people to be rebellious and they have been so much the more disposed to it, having been highly exasperated by the transplanting work. This makes many turn Tories who give no quarter, none being given to them.

The problem of the Tory raids had increased as many

landowners, with their tenants, rather than transplant to Connaught, took to the mountains and forests and engaged in a desperate warfare with the settlers. On February 6, the governor of Dublin, Colonel Hewson, paid Lieutenant Jacques £20 for the head of John Byrne, who had won notoriety as a Tory leader in Co. Wicklow. On June 14 £10 was given to a Major Henry Jones to distribute among his troops after they had killed several Tories and took others prisoner in Co. Kildare. The most active areas for Tory raids were Cos. Waterford, Wexford, Kildare, Carlow and Cork. In July a band of Tories led by the almost legendary 'Blind Donogh' O'Derrick, who controlled the area, assassinated an Irishman who served the English as a constable at Timolin. All the Irish in the area were ordered to transplant immediately to Connaught, their cabins were burnt and their possessions were taken and sold, ostensibly to provide relief for the widow of the dead man.

The method employed by Fleetwood to remove suspect Tories was wholesale transportation. In January, three Waterford merchants had been given a number of Irish prisoners to sell in the colonies. Cromwell wrote to Fleetwood early in the year to tell him that some Bristol merchants had petitioned him to transport 400 Irish 'as may be thought fittest to be spared out of Ireland for planting the Caribbee Islands'. He asked Fleetwood to see to the matter. The transporting of Tories out of Ireland was not without its hazards, as Captain Armiger Warner wrote in a petition to the Lord Protector, on June 26, 1654.

Last July my ship and men were pressed at Limerick by the Commissioners in Ireland to carry 600 Tories into Spain by which I, my wife and six children are undone, for those wicked Tories abused my men, ran my ship on a rock, which split her to pieces, robbed her of all her goods, even the seamen's clothes and went ashore and sold them. My loss is about £1,600 and I was bound in £1,000 that my ship should carry servants to Virginia for merchants of that city who threaten to sue me on my bond. I beg reference to a committee, having ever served faithfully.

The Lord Protector passed the petition to the Council of State with instructions to indemnify Warner, but only if he were sued for non-performance of his agreement with the Virginian merchants.

Some Irish soldiers sought other ways of leaving the country. Fleetwood issued orders on October 20 having heard that several Irish soldiers had been transported to Scotland 'to the prejudice of the Commonwealth'.

We do hereby strictly charge and command all masters and owners of ships or other vessels whatsoever ... not to permit or suffer any persons whatsoever of the Irish nation and Popish religion to pass in any of their said vessels into Scotland.

The transportation of Irish to the American colonies was not merely confined to fighting men; women had already been transported and children as well. Father Anthony Mac-Brody (Broudin) wrote a report entitled *Descriptio Regni Hiberniae* which remained unpublished in the Vatican archives. He commented:

The heretics at length despairing of being ever able to alienate the Irish from the ancient faith, transport their children in shipful, for sale, to the Indian Islands, that thus, forsooth, no remnant of the Irish race may survive and none escape from the utter extermination of the nation.

God alone knows the severe lot that awaits the Irish children in that slavery. We may form some idea of it from what happened to some others of our nation there last year, that is to say in 1653. The heretics, seeing that matters were prospering the Irish in the Isle of St. Christopher and being excited partly by envy and partly by hatred of the Catholic religion, seized in one night and bound with chains, three hundred of the principal Irish that were there, and carried them off to a desert island, which was wholly destitute of all necessaries of life, that there they might inevitably perish from cold and starvation. This was, alas, too sadly realised in all, excepting two, who through despair cast themselves into the sea, resolving to risk their lives rather on the waves than on the barren rocks. One of these soon perished, and the other reached the mainland, bearing the sad intelligence of the dreadful fate of his companions.

Fleetwood had other ideas about reducing the Irish and Anglicising them. On December 13 he

... proposd unto His Highness the conviency and good that probably may tend unto the nation by the yearly transportation of some fit number of Irish children into England, to be bred in the English customs and from their superstition by being distributed into such parishes in England and Wales as may be thought meet.

In spite of the harassment caused by the Tories no one

feared that the guerilla bands would unite their armed strength and menace the military administration of the Protectorate.

By the end of the year there was little activity from the Tories. One cause of aggravation had, at last, stopped. The last trials and executions of those accused of killing colonists during the war were held in Dublin in June. There were other details to be cleared up concerning the war. Brian Maguire 'notwithstanding a Papist' claimed he had revealed the plans for the insurrection beforehand to Sir William Cole. On April 5 he received a reward of £50. In March Colonel Anthony Hungerford was petitioning the Lord Protector that he was lame, in ill health and suffering from wounds he had received in Ireland. He had a wife and two children to keep. He pointed out that he had commanded a regiment which had landed in Ireland on April 30, 1647, consisting of 912 men which had been disbanded by Cromwell in August, 1649. Hungerford was given £2,000 and a pension of 20s a week. On June 27 Sir John Borlase also petitioned the Protector. He too had commanded a regiment against the Irish which had received so many casualties that Cromwell had disbanded the survivors. Officers who had died on active service had to be replaced. To aid the administration a special Commission of Public Revenue was set up under the Auditor-General, Edmund Roberts, 'a man of fawning, flattering disposition' according to Ludlow.

But above all else, the energies of the Commonwealth administrators had to be turned to the scheme to transplant the Irish into the province of Connaught and Co. Clare.

'The transplanting is now far advanced'

On July 12, 1654, *Mercurius Politicus* reported:

The transplanting work moves on but slowly: not above six score from all provinces are yet removed into Connaught. The flood gates being shut from transporting (to Spain) and one vent stopped for sending away the soldiery, part of them Irish, they begin to break out into Torying, and the waters begin to rise again upon us.

Applications from landowners seeking exemption from transplanting had almost swamped the Standing Committee on Transplantation. There was also a multiplicity of requests for extension of time. On May 17 commissions were set up for each of the fifteen precincts for the specific purpose of hearing such petitions. They continued to flow in. Margaret Barnewell had long been troubled with a shaking palsy and Mrs. Robinson, aged ninety, was blind and swore she had never been in arms against the English Parliament as alleged —despite her plea her eighteen ploughlands were given to the soldiers. Mary Archer said her aged father would die if he was forced from his land. The petitions poured in; many, such as Robert Plunkett, claimed they had given evidence against prisoners convicted of murdering the colonists during the High Court trials, and would therefore be unsafe in Connaught 'surrounded by enemies'.

Although it was supposed to be death for most Irish caught inside walled towns such as Dublin, certain dispensations were given to those whose trades or qualifications were needed. On June 5 Colonel Hewson allowed certain Irish to reside in the city and on July 8 the governor of Clonmel gave dispensation to forty-five Irishmen 'being artificers and workmen' to reside in the town.

The entire population of Cashel was given permission to stay an extra year, until May 1, 1655. They had thrown themselves on Cromwell's mercy at Fethard in February, 1650, without a fight, and he had promised the town its liberty and property. The authorities felt obliged to make some gesture of honouring the promise. The *Mercurius Politicus* reported on May 31:

And many are dispensed with: as particularly one whole town, Cashel, towards which we had no great obligation upon us. But the Lord, who is a jealous God, and more knowing of, as well as jealous against their iniquity than we are, by a fire on the 23rd instant hath burnt down the whole town in little more than quarter of an hour, except some few houses that a few English lived in which were wonderfully preserved, being in the midst of the town, and the houses round each burnt to the ground, yet they preserved.

The persons that got their dispensations from transplantation died the day before the fire, of the plague, and none else long before or since dead of the disease there.

In preparation for the transplantation, Major Myles Symner was employed in the reserved area of Connaught and Co. Clare, demolishing all the castles that could threaten the English garrisons and, at the same time, supervising the ringing of the area with forts . . . these were to be placed at intervals along the Shannon and across the nub of land sealing the Irish off from the rest of the country. On February 7 he was paid £100 for help in the work of demolition, plus £20 on account to purchase pickaxes and shovels. On May 10 Symner, with Charles Coote, Colonel Stubber and Colonel Brayfield formed a committee to superintend the demolition of garrisons and castles in the area.

It was soon obvious that the people would not transplant before the appointed day, May 1, 1654. This greatly annoyed the army officers and some petitions were drawn up asking that they be given immediate grants of land to meet their pay arrears. Colonel Robert Venables was asked by the army to represent them. Venables had a reputation among the troops as an honest, straightforward soldier. He recalled: 'After I continued in Ireland almost five years and never seen home, the Irish War being ended, the Rt. Hon. Lord Broghill and myself were, at a General Council of Officers, voted to attend His Highness with some Address from the Army in order to the settling and planting of Ireland. Which business being almost perfected it was His Highness pleasure to acquaint me that he had intended some other employment for me . . .' The other employment was the command of an expedition, with Admiral William Penn, to conquer Jamaica. Venables, who had been virtually commander-in-chief in Ulster, had to be replaced. His Lieutenant Colonel John Duckenfield was passed over for command and the post was given to Colonel Thomas Cooper, a man of moderate Anabaptist principles who was transferred from Scotland.

The popular idea at the time, which was shared even by Lieutenant General Ludlow, was that the entire Irish nation was to be transplanted to the reserved area. Ludlow recalls in his *Memoirs* that the purpose of the transplantation was the eviction of the whole Irish population so as to enable the new settlers to colonise Ireland 'without disturbance, or danger or being corrupted by intermixing with the natives in marriages or otherwise, which by the experience of former times, the English had found to be, rather than to have bettered the Irish either in religion or good manners'.

The scheme of colonisation pleased the royalists. On May 29 Sir Edward Hyde wrote a letter from Paris to Monsieur Betius.

Cromwell no doubt is very busy. Nathaniel Fiennes is made Chancellor of Ireland, and they doubt not to plant that kingdom without opposition. And truly, if we can get it again, we shall find difficulties removed which a virtuous Prince and more quiet times could never have compassed.

The penalty for not transplanting before May 1 had been death, but the vast numbers of those who had not transplanted made it impossible to impose the sentence on everyone who qualified. Nevertheless, example had to be made to prove to the population that the authorities meant what they said. On July 14 a strict search was made for those who had failed to transplant and on July 31 Peter Bath was one of several who were accordingly sentenced to death. In Peter Bath's case the sentence was commuted to transportation to Barbados.

The Lord Protector tried to ease the situation by issuing on June 22, 1654, *An Ordinance for the Further Encouragement of the Adventurers for Lands in Ireland and of the Soldiers and other Planters there on June 22*. This was followed by *An Ordinance for Indemnity to the English Protestants of the Province of Munster in Ireland* on June 27. On August 1 he issued another ordinance appointing a committee of financiers for lands in Ireland to determine differences among themselves. The committee was to comprise eleven or more leading financiers who were to decide how to settle matters if estates fell by lot in the same barony.

On September 2 Cromwell issued another *Ordinance for Admitting Protestants in Ireland to Compound*. Protestants 'having been delinquents' and fought in either the Irish or royalist armies, could now pay fines and 'upon payment of Sequestration, confiscation and forfeiture shall be discharged'.

On August 27, 1654, the Lord Protector appointed Fleetwood as Lord Deputy of Ireland and the Commission was abolished. In its place a Council was set up with Fleetwood at its head, on which councillors were to serve three years. Ludlow and John Jones naturally were dropped. Jones returned to England but Ludlow retired to his house in Monkstown, still refusing to resign his military commission. The new Council consisted of the former Member of Parliament for Sudbury, Richard Pepys, a serjeant-at-law and Baron of the Exchequer; Robert Goodwin, a former Member of Parliament for East Grinstead and a considerable speculator for confiscated Irish land; Matthew Tomlinson, who had declined to act as a judge at Charles I's trial; Miles Corbet, the only original Commissioner to sit; William Steele, a serjeant-at-law who did not arrive in Ireland until September, 1656, having been appointed Lord Chancellor in August that year, and lastly Colonel Robert Hammond, a personal friend of the Lord Protector, who died of a fever a few months after arriving to take up office on October 9. He was not replaced until December 25 when the Lord Protector, bowing to the recommendation of his Council of State, appointed his son Henry to the Council and also 'Lt. General of the States' forces in Ireland'. In case Fleetwood was angered by the appointment the Lord Protector also raised him to his Council of State.

The first major problem which the Lord Deputy and his Council had to face was the organisation of the attendance of thirty representatives from Ireland to the Lord Protector's first Parliament, which was due to meet on September 3 in London. Among those returned were Lord Broghill, Colonel Hewson, Sir Hardress Waller, Sir Charles Coote, and Colonels Ingoldsby, Sankey, Axtell and Venables. Major Generals Jephson and Reynolds and Major Anthony Morgan were also given seats, together with Vincent Gookin, still very much a civilian. Henry Cromwell had been returned for Cambridge University. Ludlow maintained that Fleetwood had taken care that all the Irish members in Parliament were friends of the Protector, despite the Anabaptists who were returned. Colonel Hewson, on the contrary, maintained that Fleetwood's 'sweet healing peaceable spirit' convinced the Anabaptists that ' the interests of God's people' could only be secured by Cromwell's Protectorate. Nevertheless, Cromwell's first Protectorate Parliament did have a considerable number of opponents to the Lord Protector, such as the republicans Bradshawe, Scot and Haselrig; even the Levellers were represented by John Wildman.

In opening Parliament the Lord Protector asked that it ratify his powers by the Instrument of Government. 'Gentlemen,' he began, 'you are met here on the greatest occasion, I believe, England ever saw, having upon your shoulders the interests of these great nations.' He said his business was 'healing and settling' the kingdoms. He went on to attack the Levellers, asking what the constitution of England had been for 300 years. 'A nobleman, a gentleman, a yeoman: the destruction of these, that is a good interest of the nation and a great one. The natural magistracy of the nation was it not almost trampled under foot under despite and contempt by men of levelling principles?' He then attacked the Fifth Monarchists and their 'pretensions of liberty of conscience'. His aim, he said, was 'to put a stop to that heady way of every man making himself a minister and preacher' and the calling of a free parliament. The Instrument of Government endorsing Cromwell's Protectorate was immediately attacked by republicans, including Levellers and Fifth Monarchists, in an attempt to destroy it. On September 22 members found themselves locked out of the House. Cromwell told them: 'I said you were a free Parliament, and truly so you are, *while you own the Government and authority that called you hither.*' He now demanded they take an oath of loyalty to the Protector and the Commonwealth. At this 100 members of republican ideology, led by Bradshawe, Haselrig and Wildman, withdrew from Parliament. The Parliament was to continue sitting for five months as prescribed by the Instrument of Government, but Cromwell decided to make their sitting five lunar months and not calendar months. The Parliament was dissolved on January 22, 1655.

The important consideration in Ireland was getting the transplantation scheme underway in a proper manner. After the increase in Tory activity earlier in the year, the climate was now quieter. According to *Several Proceedings* of October 5–12:

A man may travel and think more securely in most places in Ireland than in England, all the words of our differences here have not broken out to any breach, here is much love among officers and the country people and one with another and though there may be sometimes words about the business of re-baptising by some which is (also) less in esteem than it was, yet they all agree very well upon the main, especially as to the owning of the present power in England, and those that traffique with us find it a good trade and many that come to inhabit here find it a good climate.

There were some who were not quite sure of the wisdom of the transplantation policy. Among them was Vincent Gookin of Kinsale, the son of a colonist, Sir Vincent, who had been a constant opponent of Lord Strafford when he was Charles I's Lord Lieutenant. Gookin, as a Member of Parliament, had become a confidant of the Lord Protector. He felt that the Irish chiefs and the Irish social system should be smashed but he felt that the transplantation policy decreed the ruin of the whole Irish population and merely replaced Irish chiefs with English officers. He became a special adversary to the militant Anabaptist pressures for colonisation and resolved to spend the autumn of 1654 preparing a treatise on the subject. The Physician-General, William Petty, was a friend of Gookin, and agreed with his views: in fact, he collaborated with him on his treatise. Petty pointed out, however: 'It was for the security of the English and the English interest to divide the Irish one from the other, especially the commonality from the chiefs.'

Secretary Thurloe had written to Fleetwood on September 6, 1654, asking him to stop the survey of confiscated lands and the distribution under it. Henry Cromwell's report that the Surveyor-General, Benjamin Worsley's survey was ill conducted had caused the Protector to take action. William Petty was now summoned before Fleetwood and the Council to explain his objections to the survey and was asked if he could do a better job.

Petty said that he could survey the forfeited lands starting with civil and natural divisions, adding county, barony and townland boundaries as necessary for constructing a map of forfeiture, and he undertook the responsibility for the ultimate sub-division of land among claimants. The whole task he promised to complete within thirteen months from an appointed day 'if the Lord give me seasonable weather and due provision be made against Tories and that my instruments be not found to stand still for want of bonders'. As for payment, he would accept £6 per 1,000 acres or a gross sum of £30,000, out of which he would pay all expenses. 'Upon the fieldwork, it being a matter of great drudgery to wade through bogs and water, climbing rocks etc.' he would instruct foot soldiers to whom such hardships were familiar.

The Lord Deputy and the Council were impressed. Worsley had insisted that his survey would take thirteen years. A preliminary agreement was drawn up on October 27 in spite of the objections of the infuriated Worsley. To mollify him, he was allowed to retain the office of Surveyor-General and Petty's contract was made responsible to him, although the Council supervised the matter closely. On December 11 'after a solemn seeking of God performed by Colonel Tomlinson, for a blessing on the conclusion of so great a business' the final contract for the survey was signed. It was further ratified on Christmas Day.

The very same day, December 11, Petty started work on a pilot scheme, spurred on by the eagerness of the army officers to get their land. In spite of winter hardships, he chose the 'most troublesome and almost endless' counties of Dublin and Meath to survey. It tested his organisation severely for the land was flooded 'the mears not to be seen, the quality of the land not to be discerned, the measurers, mearers, chainmen and spadesmen discouraged, going up to their knees and middle in bog and water, the rain spoiling the instruments'.

A few days later Petty ran into his first difficulty. Four surveyors arrived in Dublin to find a new surveyor and themselves out of a job. They complained to Fleetwood's Council:

> some of us, upon our repair to town, tendered our assistance to the Dr. profering to do the same thing for lesser rates than are allowed unto him but he, minding nothing but to make himself extraordinary gains by other men's labours, will not hearken to any proposals of ours ...

The men rejected Petty's claim that he was undertaking a new method of surveying and said 'we find him informing the private soldiers, whose labour he may have at an easy rate, in the ordinary and common method'. They said they could do the same job at less cost in the same time as they were experienced surveyors and 'shall be better able to perform the same than such who are raw and unexperienced'.

He was called to the Council to answer these criticisms. Petty, in fact, looked upon the soldiers 'only as handy men and fitter than most others for the difficulties'. Soldiers were less likely to return work injurious to the state and, as no soldier knew where his allotment of land would fall, he would be fair in his survey lest it was his own land he were surveying. The Surveyor-General, angered that the Council still favoured Petty, accused Petty of employing Irish Catholics to conduct the survey. To this Petty answered: 'there was no more danger to have the measurer a Papist than the mearsman ... the only scandal in this point was employing Irish Papists when English Protestants might be had.'

Petty was now allowed to continue the survey, taking the whole of the province of Munster, except Co. Clare, the whole of Leinster, except Co. Louth, all Ulster except Cos. Fermanagh, Monaghan, and Cavan and excluding the whole of Connaught. The survey soon became known as the 'Down Survey' because of Petty's continued reference to it as 'by survey laid down' or 'laid down by admeasurement'. All Petty's surveyors were also required to take an oath.

You shall, in the presence of fear of the Lord, swear that you will faithfully and truly according to your best skill and knowledge, perform the duty and trust of a surveyor in all such surveys as you shall be employed in, according unto the instructions you either have or shall receive from the Surveyor General, or such others as are or shall thereunto, authorise, and shall make true returns thereof, and shall neither for fear, nor favour, malice or reward, or hope of reward, violate the trust reposed in you.

On November 30 the order publishing the Act of Settling Ireland and the subsequent ordinances and acts restating the transplantation policy were ordered to be republished. All transplantable people were again ordered to cross the Shannon, this time by March 1, 1665, Fleetwood, explaining the failure of the previous deadline, wrote: 'We are on the gradual transplantation though the hopes the people have from England of a dispensation makes them keep off, and not transplant so readily as otherwise. They would, if their thoughts were free from expectation out of England.'

By the end of the year there was little chance of a change of policy from the Lord Protector.

'A very strange and scandalous book'

The Hon. Robert Boyle wrote to his friend John Malet, in Somerset, on January 22, 1655, 'We inhabit but a desert scarce peopled with anything but four legg'd or two legg'd wolves'. Taxes, he declared, were 'unsupportable'. The native Irish were removing to Connaught 'except for the inoffensive ploughman' yet, he adds with pride, 'amongst all this ruin and these distractions' his brother, Lord Broghill, had found time to print the first four parts of his epic romance *Parthensia*.

Now realising that the Protectorate administration was in earnest about the transplantation, the Irish landowners were obeying the summons to move across the Shannon. The *Mercurius Politicus* was delighted and reported on January 4–11:

> The transplantation is now full advanced, the men being gone before to prepare their new habitations in Connaught. Their wives and children and dependents have been and are packing away after them apace and all are to be gone by the 1st of March next.

Fleetwood and his Council were proceeding with a determined ruthlessness. On January 24 they had issued an order that no quarter was to be given to any Irishman, woman or child, found in possession of arms. On January 9 Major David Shorne received £20 for the heads of Tories he had brought into Athlone and on May 14 Nicholas Power of Knockmore received £2 for the head of one Daniel Mulcahy 'a notorious and known Tory' which he delivered to the governor of Dungarven. On May 23 orders were issued to commanders in Wicklow and Waterford that 'the inhabitants of Carnew, Coolattin and Clohamon, or so many of them as appear liable to relieve the Tories, be forthwith transplanted and the rest brought into some more secure place . . .' On May 7 the city of Dublin was to be cleared of Irish Catholics 'and superfluous Irish cabins and other noisome places be demolished'. The Irish who had built cabins and creaghts near Athlone, to house them while waiting to hear from the Athlone Commissioners where they should transplant to, were ordered to remove them on March 31. In spite of the fact that the High Courts of Justice had ceased to function the judges had resumed their normal circuits through the country, and in February, for the first time since the outbreak of the insurrection, trials for 'massacres' occasionally occurred.

Threats of the overthrow of the Protectorate rule were a constant worry. In England the dissolution of Parliament on January 22 had been followed by several riots while Anabaptists, Fifth Monarchists, Republicans and Levellers sought ways to topple the Lord Protector. Most serious was a Royalist revolt in Wiltshire under John Penruddock. The governor of Athlone, Major General John Reynolds, was despatched to England with a brigade of 2,600 infantry and 600 cavalry. The foot was commanded by the governor of Wexford, Colonel Thomas Sadler, and the horse by Major Daniel Redman. For his services, the Lord Protector conferred a knighthood on Reynolds on June 11, 1655. To strengthen his power Cromwell divided England into districts, each under the control of a Major-General, who were to see to the execution of the Protector's ordinances, to keep a register of inhabitants and their movements, to break up public meetings not in the interest of the state and likewise search dwellings and close ale-houses. When Reynolds' 'Irish' brigade returned to Ireland Colonel Sadler was appointed governor of Galway, replacing Colonel Peter Stubber, who now retired having bought a great deal of land in the vicinity of the city from the transplanted Irish and having also acquired an estate in Co. Tipperary.

Cromwell was bitter over the dissension his rule was causing and wrote to Fleetwood that summer: 'The wretched jealousies that are amongst us and the spirit of calumny turn all into gall and worm-wood.' Fleetwood meanwhile was keeping a worried eye on his own extremists, such as Ludlow. On January 26 he ordered the arrest of Colonel William Eyre who had arrived in Dublin from England and was known to be a friend and supporter of the republican general. Eyre was arrested 'on suspicion of promoting a disturbance of the public peace' and was thrown into Marshalsea jail where he stayed until June. He was allowed to return to London on June 12 but was re-arrested and imprisoned there.

With increasing tensions and problems, Fleetwood and his Council were faced with an attack from an unexpected quarter. An anonymous pamphlet was published on January 3, and distributed to every Member of Parliament before the dissolution. It was entitled: *The Great Case of Transplantation in Ireland Discussed or certain considerations wherein the many great inconveniences in the transplanting the Natives of Ireland generally out of the three provinces of Leinster, Ulster and Munster into the Province of Connaught are shown. Humbly tendered to every individual member of Parliament by a well wisher to the good of the Commonwealth of England. 1655.*

It was an attack on the whole policy of the transplantation which, although published anonymously, was the work of Vincent Gookin of Kinsale. His friend Petty later claimed that he, too, aided in the preparation of the work. Introducing his criticisms, Gookin presents a sorry picture of the problems facing the ordinary Irish.

...touching the Irish, for the bloody persons (known) are all dead by Sword, Famine; Pestilence, the hand of civil justice or remain still liable to it, or are fled beyond the sea from it; the priests and soldiers (the kindlers of war in the beginning and formentors of it since) are for the first universally departed the land, and for the second, to a vast number, and are most dangerous and the remaining are weary of war having long since submitted, and those that are out sue for nothing but mercy, for the poor Commons, the Sun never shined (or rather not shines) upon a nation so completely miserable. There are not one hundred of them in 10,000 who are not by the first and fourth articles of the Act of Settlement under the penalty of losing life and estate. The tax sweeps away whole subsistences, necessity making them turn thief and Tories and then they are prosecuted with fire and sword for being so. If they discover not Tories the English hang them, if they do, the Irish kill them, 'gainst whom they have nothing to defend themselves, nor any other that can, nay, if any person melted with the bowels of man, or moved by the Rules of Common Esq., labour to bring home to them that little mercy which the state allows, there are some ready to asperse them as favourers of Tories, coverers of blood guiltiness and briefly, in a probable computation, five parts of six of the whole nation are destroyed, and after so sharp an execution is it not time a length to find a retreat? Must we still cry justice! Justice? wherefore is justice invoked against them, was it not for cruelty? God has avenged it, let others take heed now they become guilty, especially they that avenge it.

Gookin argued that the transplantation would lead to an almost continuous guerilla warfare with the Irish and increase the numbers of Tories roaming the countryside. He stated that the English settlers should not fear the Irish any more, since so many of the nobility had fled to Spain, and all the priests had been transported. He added:

... the remaining part of the whole nation are scarce the sixth part of what were at the beginning of the war, so great a devastation has God and Man brought on the land, and so far as they from those formidable numbers they are (by those that are strangers to Ireland) conceived to be, and that handful of natives left, are poor labourers, useful, simple creatures, whose design is only to live, and their families, the manner of which is so low, that it is a design rather to be pitied than by anybody feared, envied or hindered.

It was a ridiculous policy to put the Irish people into Connaught where they would be 'under the power of the chiefs, who have engaged them in so much blood in the late Rebellion'.

They are seated in a country furthest distant from England, and for the sea shore most remote from the course of the English fleet, where therefor they may receive arms from any foreign prince with most security, modelise themselves into arms and be furnished irresistably for a new war, by means of these advantages, the English in the last rebellion first lost Connaught, and last regain'd it ...

To those who argued that the Irish could be contained in the reserved area and that the colonists would be free from any attack, Gookin wrote:

... they exceedingly mistake who imagine that the passage out of Connaught into the other three provinces is difficult, or may be easily defended against the Irish, if they should thus be armed and fitted for a new war.

Whereas it is evidently for the security of the English and English interest to divide the Irish one from another, especially the commonalty from the chief, and both from the advantages of receiving probable assistance from foreigners.

He criticised the cruelty of the soldiers and concluded that 'transplanting is an impossible work'. He added:

The unsettling of a nation is an easy work, the settling is not, it has cost much blood and treasure there, and now prudence and mercy may accomplish the work ...

Fleetwood was angry at the publication of the pamphlet and on February 7 he wrote to Thurloe that 'there is a very strange and scandalous book entitled *Arguments against Transplantation* that is now come forth, which doth very falsely and unworthily asperse those that did and now do serve in state here'. He claimed 'it will be a great discouragement to the state servants if such may be allowed their liberty to traduce them' adding, in justification 'the Irish are abominable, false, cunning and perfidious people . . .'

The Lord Protector, influenced not only by Gookin's arguments but by his friendship with Gookin, was becoming increasingly worried about the transplantation. He suggested to Fleetwood that, if he felt it to be in the public interest, the survey of lands could be stopped and the orders for the transplantation modified. Fleetwood considered the public interest best served by the rigid enforcement of the policy and had set up a Committee of Officers in Dublin to consider the best ways to allot lands going to the military. Petty, if he did, as he claimed, have a hand in Gookin's book, now resigned himself to the task in hand, writing: 'As for the bloodshed in this contest, God best knows who did occasion it, but upon the playing of the game or match, the English won, and had amongst other pretences a gamester's right at least to their estates.' He had now been joined by his cousin, John Petty, a talented map maker and surveyor. With John, Thomas Taylor and William Shaen, as Commissioners for the civil survey, Petty organised a staff of 1,000 persons, including forty clerks at headquarters and an army of surveyors who worked on site in each district. These men were prey not only to natural working hazards but to merciless attacks by Tories. It was not until April 12 that the disgruntled

Worsley handed over to Petty his records of the previous survey, by which time the survey of most of the baronies had been completed.

The Lord Protector was still far from happy about the situation, and after discussions with Lord Broghill the latter appeared before the Council of State in February with some propositions on the problem. Broghill was not to return to Ireland for nearly a year for, in March, Cromwell appointed him President of the Council in Scotland with a salary of £1,000 a year. The Council of State elected to give him £3,000 worth of land in Ireland in payment of his services. In August, 1656, he left Scotland to sit for both Edinburgh and Cork in the second Protectorate Parliament. In the meantime the Council of State announced a grant to Henry Cromwell to cover his expenses on becoming a Major-General and commander of the armed forces in Ireland. He had already been made a member of the Irish Council on December 25. The appointment caused another spate of rumours and speculation, one such rumour being that the Lord Protector was about to be crowned King and his son Richard appointed High Admiral, with Henry as Lord Deputy in Ireland, while Fleetwood, his son-in-law, was to return to be Lord Treasurer.

'Their courage is exhausted'

In March, 1655, the new governor of Wexford, Colonel Richard Lawrence, who was serving on the committee of officers supervising the transplantation, published a reply to Gookin's attack on the policy. It was entitled *The Interest of England in the Irish Transplantation Stated—being chiefly intended as an answer to a scandalous, seditious pamphlet entitled 'The Great Case & etc. by a faithful servant of the Commonwealth'. Richard Lawrence. 1655.* Whereas Gookin claimed that the intention was to transplant the entire Irish nation west of the Shannon, Lawrence reiterated that only proprietors and those who had fought against the English

Parliamentary forces would qualify. To justify the transplantation, Lawrence repeats many of the Irish atrocity stories, and mentions the undesirability of Papist infiltration, were the two nations to mix.

A few months later Vincent Gookin replied to Colonel Lawrence's criticism, this time naming himself as the author of the previous work, dedicating his second volume, perhaps with a sense of irony, to Fleetwood, who had called his first work 'scandalous'. He entitled this second pamphlet *The Author and Case of Transplanting the Irish into Connaught Vindicated from the Unjust Aspersions of Col. Richard Lawrence by Vincent Gookin Esquire. Printed by A. M. for Simon Miller at the Sign of the Star in St. Pauls Churchyard, 1655.*

Gookin replied to Lawrence's criticisms point by point. Firstly, Lawrence had complained that Gookin had written that they were grinding the Irish with heavy pressures to the destruction of more families under Commonwealth rule than out of it. 'To which I answer—That this was a narrative of what has happened to them not a complaint that it has befallen them nor an accusation of those instruments by whom it has befallen...' Secondly, Lawrence had criticised Gookin for mentioning the divisions among the Protestant sects in Ireland. 'Surely if my not speaking of those things (which I so much bewail) would have contributed to their not being, my tongue should first cleave to the roof of my mouth ere I would publish the divisions...' He adds: 'I seek to tax the neglect of sending ministers to convert the Irish.' Lawrence had also criticised him for saying the Irish were under a miserable condition, tied to impossible laws and reforms 'and revered only for slaughter, and those frowned upon that dispense any equity to them'. He had been particularly vehement against Gookin's talk of the oppression of the ordinary people by the soldiers. Gookin, claimed Lawrence, was also accusing the officers of the army of similar conduct by saying that the Irish had just cause to fear to complain if they were ill treated by soldiers. Gookin replied:

I do believe the Army in Ireland is the best disciplin'd Army in the world, except that in England whereof it is a part: Yet I believe likewise that there never was an Army (except of Angels, where the

Lord of Hosts was Captain) that had not some that swerv'd from the integrity of the rest. I said no more (but some) and I believe themselves will say no less. I do not accuse all, neither will they excuse all, and for these things going unpublished, for their just fear to complain, it touches not the most subordinate, much less the Supreme officer; for the officers not knowing it, keep him just— and yet the private soldiers' power over the peasant may make his fear just too: for though it be in the Irishman's power to complain of a first injury, yet it has in the poorest soldiers' power to do him another, that shall put him (it may be) past complaining, or put such a specious colour on it, as may give it the face of Justice, and then who will not believe an English soldier rather than an Irish Teige (Tadhg), if the matter should come to dispute: So then, though the cause be unjust in the soldier, yet it may be just in the labourer who may fear justly to complain of injury lest he be injured more by complaining.

Gookin reiterated that he thought the Irish were now too weak to fight.

Their courage is exhausted, their numbers decayed, their soldiers (most of them) sent beyond the sea, their priests banished, the remainder be at your feet. Therefore do not transplant them (though heretofore you thought on that course) since now there is not the same necessity which made it then fit, but many expedients which made it now unfit.

He believed the 1641 insurrection need never have occurred had three things been done by the English colonists in Ireland.

1. Care taken for spreading the Protestant religion, the neglect of which left them to their own, and the strongest incentive to rebellion, and tie unanimity in it, and this would do well to be heeded in times to come, which would work a change in their minds, for changing of place will never make them honest. 2. Educating the gentry in civility and religion, for which the Court of Wards was errected, and doubtless was then convenient therefore the nation. 3. suppressing their language, manners, laws, septs etc.

These were the very things he now advocated and, he reminded his readers, the Romans had been successful in their colonisation policies because they had intermarried with the natives in their colonies and had gradually absorbed them. They had not segregated themselves.

But Gookin's arguments were ignored by Fleetwood and his Council. The deadline of March 1 came and went. A correspondent from Athy writing on March 4 to *Mercurius Politicus* said:

I have only to acquaint you that the time prescribed for the transplantation of the Irish proprietors and those that have been in arms and abettors of the rebellion being near at hand, the officers are resolved to fill the jails and to seize them; by which this bloody people will know that they are not degenerate from English principles: though I presume we shall be very tender of hanging any except leading men: yet we shall make no scruple of sending them to the West Indies, where they will serve for planters and help to plant the plantations that General Venables it is hoped hath reduced.

On March 9 Fleetwood ordered all the passes over the Shannon between Jamestown and Sligo to be closed, so that the area of Connaught and Co. Clare was blocked off. Ten days later a general search was made for all people who had not transplanted and courts martial were set up to try them. The jails were soon overcrowded;—some of those caught, such as Edward Spring of Killeagh, Co. Kerry, were allowed to go free when they agreed to renounce Catholicism. Others were not so fortunate. At the end of March a court martial sitting in St. Patrick's Cathedral, Dublin, sentenced Edward Hetherington of Kilnemanagh to death. Hetherington appealed and on April 2 the findings of the court martial were studied by the Council. At this stage depositions from two Englishmen were brought forward claiming that Hetherington was a Tory leader who, in 1643, had taken them prisoner near Naas, boasting that he had killed seven Englishmen. However, Hetherington was duly hanged on April 3 with placards on his breast and back bearing the legend 'For Not Transplanting'.

To give further encouragement to the rest Fleetwood decided that produce owned by transplantees should be seized, sold, and the money used to aid those who had already transplanted. The *Mercurius Politicus* reported on April 12:

The Lord Deputy and Council in Ireland have published a Declaration for making sale of the corn of such Irish proprietors and others that did not transplant themselves into Connaught, according to the Declaration of 30th November last, for buying stores to relieve those that do transplant themselves according to the said declaration.

There were few people now exempted from the order. Even the Ulster Protestant minister, Jeremiah O'Quinn, who had worked for the new administration by converting the Irish to Protestantism in the medium of the Irish language, was now ordered to transplant. His transplantation had been deferred a year while he had been on a missionary tour of Connaught and Clare. It was no wonder that Fleetwood now reported that O'Quinn had become 'somewhat bitter against the interest of England'.

Some moderate men were now swinging to Gookin's views on transplanting. Then came news from Europe which killed all feelings of sympathy for the Irish Catholics. The Waldenses or Vaudois, who lived in the Alpine valleys west of Turin, had been a Protestant people since the Reformation. The Duke of Savoy, a Catholic, had claimed that the Waldenses had broken their treaty with him, under which they were to inhabit only the mountain valleys. In the spring of 1655, under the pretext that the Waldenses were encroaching on his territory, he began to drive them back into the mountains, with great brutality being shown by his troops. These troops, it was reported, included a brigade of Irish exiles. Religious feeling in Protestant Europe was aroused as stories of massacres of men, women and children were told. Political pressures on Savoy led to the pacification of Pigneral in October but in the meantime Protestant horror against tales of Catholic atrocities led to the establishment of a public fund to relieve the suffering of the Waldenses. Cromwell himself led the list of subscribers with a gift of £2,000. The poet John Milton, who was a member of Thurloe's staff, wrote, in his famous sonnet:

> Avenge O Lord thy slaughtered saints whose bones
> lie scattered on the Alpine mountains cold . . .

In Ireland, on July 9, Fleetwood held a meeting of army officers in Dublin Castle which resolved to subscribe to the fund for the relief of the Waldenses. Officers were asked to send two weeks' pay and private soldiers were to subscribe one week. Several officers subscribed as much as a month's pay while others subscribed three weeks'. It was decided that no one should be compelled to give money to the fund 'but that such of the officers and soldiers as would be free therein should contribute but otherwise nothing be expected from them'.

Now, as the rumours grew that Irish troops had been involved, there was no stopping the Council's resolve to strictly obey the settlement scheme. At the very same meeting the army officers drew up a petition asking that wounded and maimed soldiers, widows and orphans be quickly put in possession of the land allocated them.

Lorenzo Paulucci, the Venetian secretary in London, wrote to Giovanni Sagredo, his ambassador in France on June 5, 1655, saying that the army officers were over-reacting to the news of the Waldenses. 'This government has one sole and devout object, to root out the Catholic faith from Ireland and introduce Protestantism in every corner of it.' The moderation of Gookin was now completely forgotten.

As the long, straggling lines of Irish poured across the Shannon with their few meagre belongings more problems began to present themselves. The indigenous people of Connaught and Co. Clare were angry at the arrival of strangers from other parts of the country who were taking over what little land they had left. On June 18 the Commissioners for Revenue at Athlone had to make an order enabling them:

...forthwith to transplant such Irish proprietors or others from their present habitations into some remote part of Connaught that shall no menace and assault etc. there to live.

At the beginning of the transplantation Co. Clare had been deserted of inhabitants. Out of nine baronies containing 1,300 ploughlands only forty ploughlands in Bunratty were inhabited by June, 1653. A few people lived in the safety of garrisons, castles or mansions. But in 1654 Major Myles Symner had commenced demolishing these garrisons and major buildings as a threat to the line of English forts being established along the Shannon up to Sligo. On January 1, Edmund Doherty, a mason, received £32 10s for demolishing thirteen castles in the country. Some of the earliest transplantees assigned to Clare commented bitterly that there was not enough wood to hang a man, water with which to drown him, or earth enough to bury him. The area was depressing and made many transplantees take to the woods with the Tories rather than live there.

Seán Ó Conaill, of Iveragh, poured out his feelings in a lengthy poem he entitled *Tuireamh na hÉirinn* (The Dirge of Ireland). Seán's father, Muiris of Caherbarnagh, who had been active in 1641, was ordered to transplant to Co. Clare. He died on the long, agonising journey. Seán wrote bitterly:

> *Ca nGead Geabham feasda? No cad do dheanam?*
>
> Whither shall we go in future? Or what shall we do?
> No shelter for us, hills, woods, mountains,
> there is not our remedy with a physician in Ireland
> but God to pray to, and the saints together.

But could the Irish still believe in aid from God? Even Ó Conaill's faith was wearing thin. Of God he demands:

> Are you deaf, or whither are you looking?
> Was it not you who overthrew the monsters with thy nod?
> What little to you the time that you are patient?
> Our faith is gone . . . there is not living but a spark of it.

No cries to God for aid, nor pleas for moderation were to deter Fleetwood now. On July 27 *Mercurius Politicus* reported:

> The business of transplanting is not yet finished. The Irish choose death rather than remove from their wanted habitations. But the State is resolved to see it done.

'No restraint on the soldiery'

In spite of Father Peter Talbot's efforts to reorganise the Catholic priesthood, the church had been badly hit by executions, imprisonments and transportations. Arrests were continuing at an alarming rate, about £5 being the reward for each priest captured. The elderly priests were still allowed to go to the continent. On June 16 thirty priests who were imprisoned in Galway were ordered 'to be shipped away for Spain, Portugal or Flanders'. Younger priests still went to the colonies, such as Father Thomas FitzNicholas, who was shipped to Barbados on November 15 and, on the same day, a lay friar named John Stafford was ordered to be transported 'into the plantation islands in America to work for his living'. Many more arrests were made towards the end of the year.

Inroads into the frail structure of the priesthood had become almost irreparable. The conditions under which the priests worked were described by an anonymous Jesuit father on a mission to Ireland during that year in a report to the head of his order.

The heretical enemy having overcome every obstacle, and obtained possession of the whole kingdom, raged with such fury against all ecclesiastics and everything dedicated to religion, that the Turks or the very demons from hell could not display greater impiety or ferocity.

There was no restraint on the soldiery when pursuing the Catholics, the persecutors were at the same time accusers, witnesses and judges; by day and night they burst into the houses of Catholics; they broke open rooms and desks and private drawers under the pretence of searching for ecclesiastics, and even when no resistance was offered them, they invented whatever suited their designs. It was a capital crime for any ecclesiastic to enter a city, or town or garrison, to offer the Holy Sacrifice, or to administer the sacraments: and for doing so many suffered death: the same penalty was incurred by whosoever received a priest into his dwelling. No individual could sleep in any of these places without signing his name and receiving express permission from the governor; those who came were minutely examined, as to who they were, whence they came, what their business & etc.

On January 7, 1655, Pope Innocent X (Gian Battista Pemphila) had died four months before his eighty-first birthday. He had become Pope in 1644 and during the eleven years of his pontificate the Papal prestige had fallen into a serious decline for he had been dominated by his sister-in-law, Olimpia Maldalchini, who advised him on all matters of foreign policy. While her advice was aimed at keeping the Papacy aloof from international entanglements, her greed for money led her to adopt devices which destroyed the very prestige upon which the success of such a policy depended. On April 7, fifty-six year-old Cardinal Fabio Chigo was elected as Pope Alexander VII. He had been Nuncio at

Cologne between 1639 and 1651 before becoming Secretary of State to Innocent X and a cardinal in 1652. He had been an excellent Nuncio but he was inclined to indolence and, under his pontificate, he left an increasing amount of the administration in the hands of the congregations.

As soon as Alexander VII was elected, the Lord Protector, who personally favoured religious liberty for those English Catholics who did not act against his regime, decided to send a secret mission to the Vatican. Talks were opened by an English delegation led by William Mettam and Thomas Bayly. The aim was to secure an 'engagement' with the new Pope by which English Catholics would be allowed to worship in private and the penal laws respecting them removed if the Pope, in return, would no longer preach rebellion against the Protector's administration. To give a cover for these talks the laws against Jesuits were renewed in April that year. Alexander VII resented the renewal of the penal laws and this, with the surly conduct of the negotiator Bayly, led to a breakdown of the discussions. Edward Hyde wrote soon afterwards: 'It would be very strange if after so much hypocrisy and juggling, Cromwell should gain credit at Rome and be looked upon as a person who would perform any civil office to the Catholics, when it is notoriously known that his interest and power is only in those persons who are irreconcilable to them.' But few English Catholics could curse Cromwell's attitude to them. Antoine de Bordeaux, the French Ambassador, and Eamonn O'Reilly, after his election as Irish Primate, observed that English Catholics fared better under Cromwell than at any time since the reign of Mary Tudor. Cromwell's domestic policy towards Catholics was almost the opposite of that adopted towards Irish Catholics. Having, in Ireland, the extreme Puritan wing of his army to satisfy and revenue to raise from a wasted country, his policy was based on a typical English ignorance of Irish history and a blind resentment of the Irish who had, in the insurrection, nearly overthrown English power in Ireland.

For the Catholic Church the reconstruction of the Irish Province was a pressing matter. The Franciscans in particular had been badly decimated and on May 12, 1654, the

Minister-General of the order, Father Peter Manero, had, while in Madrid, appointed Father Bonaventure Mellaghlin from North Leinster, as Vicar-Provincial. Mellaghlin was slow to establish his authority and it was not until November 21, 1655, that he appointed Father Francis O'Farrell as Minister-Provincial. In the meantime the Irish Franciscans, not aware of these developments, appealed to the Pope to appoint leaders for them. On July 3, 1656, Alexander appointed his own Minister-Provincial. For a while, therefore, the Franciscans had two hierarchies issuing differing orders.

Since the Archbishop of Tuam and Bishop Kirwan of Killala had left Ireland, the only remaining bishop was the aged and bedridden Eugene Sweeney, the Bishop of Kilmore. It was precisely because of these conditions that Fleetwood did not force the old man to transplant or transport. The Irish priesthood therefore pressed that Cardinal Albezzi, of the Sacred Congregation, who was in charge of appointing the Irish Hierarchy, make such appointments immediately. Not only was a Hierarchy needed, as much to boost the morale of the remaining priests as to administer the church organisation, but batches of trained priests were also urgently required. The Sacred Congregation seemed in no hurry to consider the matter though they encouraged the various orders to smuggle young priests into the country on missions, priests such as Father Ignatius Brown, a twenty-five-year-old native of Wexford, who had trained as a Jesuit at Compostella.

Irish scholarship, always a vital force, still continued on the continent. Indeed, Irish scholarship had flourished in Europe for many centuries from the time Irishmen took the lead in reconverting Europe to Christianity during the Dark Ages. They had established churches and monasteries in France, Belgium, Germany, Austria and Italy, which still housed libraries of Irish scholarship and literature. It was to the Irish Colleges, such as those at Louvain, Rome and Cologne, that scholars had fled after the Cromwellian conquest to continue their work in peace. In 1655 the renowned Irish doctor of medicine, Neil O'Glacan from Co. Donegal, published his classic thirteen volume study *Cursus Medicus* in Bologna. O'Glacan had been physician to Louis XIII of

France in 1629 and Louis had been so impressed with the young Irishman that he had made him a Privy Councillor. The plague had suddenly broken out in Paris and O'Glacan had thrown aside honours and comparative safety under Louis' patronage to establish a hospital for plague victims in the poorest quarter of the city where he devoted all his waking hours to combating the plague. He survived and wrote a medical study on the disease called *Tracta de Peste*. He had then gone to Bologna and devoted himself to the writing of *Cursus Medicus*.

Another important work of Irish scholarship was published that year in Antwerp by another Donegal man, Father Seán Mac Colgan of Priests' Town, then called Muff, near Carndonagh. His study was on the great ninth-century Irish philosopher, John Scotus or Eriugena (not to be confused with John Duns Scotus of the thirteenth century), entitled *Tractus de Ionnis Scoti, Doctoris Subitis theologorumque principis, vita, . . . authore RPF Ioanne Colgano*. Mac Colgan was ordained in 1618, and entered the Franciscan Order of St. Anthony's College at Louvain. He was appointed commissary of the three Irish Franciscan colleges of Louvain, Prague and Vielum. His ambition was to show the world that, in spite of English propaganda, Irishmen were citizens of no mean country, a country with a rich and superb native literature and with philosophers the equal of those of most other countries. In 1649 an Englishman, Father Angelus Mason, had published a work on Eriugena in which he maintained he was an Englishman for obviously, the Irish being an inferior breed, could never have produced such a philosopher. Mac Colgan, with assistance from Philip O'Reilly of East Brefni, the new Provincial of the Irish Franciscans, produced a 200 page rebuttal. 'Scotus' to ninth-century Europeans simply meant 'Irish' while Eriugena is simply 'Irish born'. Eriugena was perhaps the most considerable philosopher in the western world between Augustine and Aquinas —an idealist, poet and mystic who takes his place in a long line of thinkers from Heracleitus and Plato. Although he was not wholly an original thinker, he had an extraordinary power of synthesis. Father Mason, in claiming him for England, was merely exercising the English prejudice of the day, namely, that no Irishman could make any original contribution to 'civilisation'.

Yet another Irish work to appear in 1655 was published in Lisbon by one Craesbeck. This was a history of Ireland entitled *The Rise, Increase and Exit of the Family of Geraldines*, the Fitzgeralds being Earls of Desmond. The author of this work was Dominic de Rosario O'Daly. O'Daly was born in Co. Kerry in 1596. When Portugal, which had been incorporated into the Spanish kingdom in 1580, regained her independence under the new Braganza dynasty in 1640, O'Daly became Confessor to the Queen. He was soon appointed Censor of the Supreme Court of the Inquisition, Vicar-General in the kingdom of Portugal and Vicar-General and Founder of the Irish Convent of the Dominican Order in Portugal. At the time of the publication of his history, John IV sent him as Portuguese ambassador to the court of Louis XIV of France. O'Daly displayed a simple piety and refused to have any ambassadorial residence other than that of the Dominican Convent in the Rue St. Honoré. He became well liked by the French but returned to Portugal in 1656 after the death of John IV.

From the English point of view the 'barbarous Irish' were still a source of worry. To the Lord Protector Ireland was always a problem, whether it was approving a Great Seal for the Irish Council on March 6 or dealing with innumerable petitions for compensation due to the Irish war. The Lord Protector passed petitions, such as that of Lieutenant Richard Palmer, to his Council of State. Palmer had written:

I commanded a foot company under General Monck in Ireland and lost both my eyes so that I cannot see, therefore the Irish Committee settled on me £100 a year from Guildhall which is £75 in arrears. Parliament made this into 40s. a week to be paid from crown revenue. This being stopped your Highness gave me an order for regular payment and arrears. Consider my wife and four small children and order me the £84 due, the 40s weekly and the £75 from Goldsmith's Hall.

The same month, February, the Lord Protector sent another plea, this time from an ex-naval captain named William Hamilton, to the Admiralty Commission. Hamilton had written sorrowfully:

I have pawned my clothes for attendance, my money is gone, and I have now no surgeon and my solicitor has not dealt honestly with me. I have been faithful to the State in England, Scotland and Ireland, and received a shot from an Irishman which will cause my death unless I have a speedy release from this woeful prison which I beg may be without fees or chamber rent.

Cromwell now urged his son Henry to take up his appointment as commander of the army in Ireland and as a member of the Irish Council as soon as possible. The Lord Protector was eager not to give offence to his son-in-law Fleetwood and to ease the change-over of the administration in Ireland without trouble. The problem was how to recall Fleetwood and leave Henry Cromwell in full control of Ireland. On June 15 Henry, his wife Elizabeth and his first born child, left London en route for Ireland. Henry was never to see his father again.

CHAPTER 3

HENRY CROMWELL

'you would find him very troublesom'

After a stormy crossing of the Irish Sea, and a night spent mostly in his cabin suffering from the effects of sea sickness, Henry Cromwell arrived in Dublin at mid-day on Monday, July 9, 1655. The Council of Ireland, and the army officers, had spent most of that morning discussing the plight of the Waldenses. The entire company then retired to Ringsend, at the mouth of the River Liffey, to await Henry's arrival. According to Ludlow:

> ... upon his arrival in the Bay of Dublin, the men of war that accompanied him and other ships in the harbour rung such a peal with their cannon, as if some great good news had been coming to us, and tho' the usual landing place for those who come in ships of war was near my house, yet he and his company went up in boats to the Ring's End where they went ashore and were met there by most officers civil and military of the town.

The journal *Perfect Proceedings* reported:

> On Monday morning the Lord Henry Cromwell arrived at the Bay of Dublin, and was met on the sands by the Lord Deputy and Council, most of the officers and gentry of Ireland, nigh 500 horses, with ten coaches of six and four horses apiece, and a very magnificent entertainment, more than could be expected from so poor and ruined country.

Lord Deputy Fleetwood gave no outward displays of animosity towards his brother-in-law but he must have realised that his rule in Ireland was now coming to an end. So far he had ignored the Lord Protector's diplomatic overtures to return to England where, Cromwell hinted, he would be more usefully employed. Fleetwood was determined to remain supreme ruler in Ireland for as long as he could. But with Henry's arrival he was placed in a difficult position. Firstly, Henry, as a Major-General, now outranked him as military commander and, secondly, pressure from the Lord Protector to return home was increasing. Cromwell, however, was acting carefully with Fleetwood because of Fleetwood's backing from the Anabaptists.

It was with some resentment that Fleetwood watched his brother-in-law's reception in Dublin and his inauguration as Lord Chancellor of Trinity College, during the course of which the Dean, Dr. Dudley Loftus, unfortunately referred to Henry as the future ruler of Ireland. It probably made Fleetwood increasingly bitter that Trinity College had bestowed the honour on Henry while it had been Fleetwood's administration which had resurrected the college. Trinity College had been built in 1591 as 'a college for learning, whereby knowledge and civility might be increased by the instruction of our people there, whereof many have usually heretofore used to travel into France, Italy and Spain to get learning in such foreign Universities, whereby they have been infected with Popery and other ill qualities'. Catholics were received into the college and many sons of prominent Irish chiefs took their education there. In about 1650 the Chancellor of the College, Anthony, Bishop of Meath, died, and for a while its fate was uncertain. Fleetwood decided to restore it but to exclude any Catholics and maintain it as a rigid Puritan establishment. Major Myles Symner, a graduate of Trinity who had recently been employed preparing Connaught for the Irish transplantees by demolishing castles there, was appointed professor of mathematics. He also taught young men in the art of land surveying and, as a concession to Petty, he allowed soldiers to attend his lectures as well. The new Provost, Samuel Winter, had a love for good horses. He had shipped thoroughbreds from England and caused a furore when one of them was stolen while he was on a trip to Ulster. He liked indulgent living and acquired estates in King's County (Offaly), Westmeath, and a house in Dublin and another in Drogheda. He hated Anabaptists and most of his sermons were directed against them. Therefore he was pleased at the arrival of Henry for he felt that Fleetwood was merely a puppet of the Anabaptists.

Under Fleetwood, however, the College had been revitalised and twelve Bachelor of Arts degrees were granted in May, 1654, as well as Master's degrees. Winter made a sound knowledge of Hebrew necessary for the Master of Arts degree. Fleetwood allowed John Kerdiff, a senior fellow at Trinity, to tour the country to identify college estates so as to make them exempt from confiscation. The former tenants, if not killed or outlawed, were ordered to pay rent and arrears to the College, which came to a quite considerable sum. Fleetwood saw the appointment of Henry as Lord Chancellor as a deliberate affront.

Five days after Henry's arrival Fleetwood reasserted his position as Lord Deputy by issuing two declarations which showed that he intended to carry on the policy of transplantation according to the Act and ordinances. Replying to the authorities at Limerick, Fleetwood defined those liable to transplantation for bearing arms against the English Parliamentary forces as those who had attended a rendezvous and kept watch for the Irish insurgents, even if they had been forced or pressed into doing it. Secondly, he issued orders to the army, although Henry was now commander of it, pointing out that some officers and men had not only neglected to search for people condemned to transplantation but were actually keeping such persons as tenants or servants on their lands. If this state of affairs was not altered they, the officers and soldiers, would be dealt with under the Articles of War. There were also a number of people living in Dublin itself who had been condemned to transplantation, and ordered to give up their property to the colonists, who had not done so. On July 18 Fleetwood ordered that the Commissioners of Revenue appoint bailiffs to evict these people and to make sure that the new tenants were safely installed. However, on July 29, he ordered that Irish people attending the Court of Qualifications at Loughrea to show why they should be exempt from transplantation, 'be not arrested till 20th September next, nor molested in any way'.

The Lord Protector now decided it was time to order Fleetwood to return to England in plain language. On August 7 Fleetwood wrote to Secretary Thurloe: 'I have now received His Highness' positive command to return to England and now undertake my journey with my comfort, trusting the Lord hath given me a call thereunto . . .' Henry appeared to be worried by Fleetwood's departure. 'What we shall do in the absence of my brother Fleetwood, I do not well know,' he wrote to Thurloe on August 22. 'I shall have little comfort to stay behind further than to answer duty, in the doing of which I shall trust the Lord will assist me with His presence.' Whether Henry was genuinely worried by the enormity of the task that now lay on his shoulders alone or whether he was merely play-acting is not certain. One thing is sure, he knew well enough before reaching Ireland that he was going there to replace his brother-in-law. His appointment had even been welcomed in some quarters earlier that year as a sign of a new positive policy in Ireland. One writer voiced the opinion that he would be a more efficient administrator than Fleetwood. 'The Irish are unwilling to transplant or prove their qualifications but they will be forc'd to go and make way for the English planters.'

There were certainly many tough problems facing Henry. The Tories had recently increased their activities. The Irish Council had received reports that ships from France and Spain, as well as landing Catholic priests in Ireland, were also supplying the Tory bands with arms and ammunition. On August 16 the Council issued an order aimed at preventing shelter being given to the guerillas.

... it is hereby ordered and declared that the governors within the respective precincts in Ireland do take special care that all such Irish, as are not comprehended in the Rule for transplantation into the Province of Connaught and the County of Clare, and that live scatteringly in the several counties of Ireland (and thereby can make no resistance against Tories but rather are a relief to them and hold correspondency with such bloody persons and others) do at or before 20th August next draw themselves into villages and townships and cohabit together in families, and that every such village or township shall consist of at least thirty families, and shall not stand or be placed within half a mile of any fastness, whether it be wood, bog or mountain, that may be adjudged a shelter for Tories or other enemies of the Commonwealth. And it is further ordered and declared that in each of the said villages or townships there must be appointed a headman, constable or tithing man, who is from time to time to take care that the cattle belonging to that village be brought together every night and that there be a watch set in convenient places and cause at least thirty men to be at every watch, to end such mischiefs as is above mentioned, for the future may be prevented and the thieves, Tories, and other loose persons the better discovered and apprehended.

Fleetwood had previously issued orders 'for the prevention of the many rapines, thefts, burnings and spoils done and committed on the poor inhabitants of this nation by Tories, Irish rebels and other desperate persons, their confederates and accomplices'. If a murder was done and the murderer not found, four Irish living in the area were to be seized and jailed as hostages. If the people responsible were not delivered to the authorities within twenty-four days, the four Irish would be shipped off to Barbados, and every other Irish person in the district would be immediately transplanted to Connaught or Co. Clare. At the same time as issuing this order, Fleetwood had ordered all the Irish who had not manifested constant good affection to remove two miles outside of Dublin's city walls. Henry saw no reason to alter these orders.

The next problem facing Henry was the initiation of the second disbandment of the army. Some 10,000 soldiers had been disbanded in 1653 and now a further 5,000 were to be disbanded by September 1. Two horse regiments were to go (those commanded by Sir Charles Coote and Lieutenant-General Ludlow) together with the remainder of Ingoldsby's regiment of dragoons, three foot regiments and several unattached companies.

Henry wrote to Thurloe on August 29: 'Never so great a work was performed with so much quiet. I believe we reduced near 5,000 men and as good soldiers as are in three nations. I am afraid few of them will betake themselves to planting, if you could find some employment for them abroad, it would be of good service to the public.'

New pay scales were drawn up for the army commanders. Oliver Cromwell, as commander in chief, received £10 a day while Henry, as Major General, received £3 a day. The next job was to see that the disbanded soldiers who wished to remain in Ireland as colonists were allocated their land and on September 8 Sir Charles Coote and Thomas Herbert wrote to Petty asking him to organise the allotment.

... observe carefully in the first place this general rule: not to admit any person to satisfaction that produceth not his original debenture: and where any of the said single persons, whose arrears

are left doubtful in the said list, shall produce their original debenture to you, yet you are to suspend his satisfaction if it appear to
you he was formerly a disbanded person and that he hath been since
taken in again.

Petty was told to cross out each man's name in the margin
of the debenture list when he had collected the man's
debenture.

Henry was finding that the Chancellorship of Trinity imposed various obligations. His father, Oliver, had been particularly keen to extend education facilities in Ireland and
had decided to found a second college in Dublin, endorsed
by an Act of March 8, 1650. Henry approached Dr. John
Owen, a leading member of Trinity's trustees, to discuss the
project. A site was selected between College Park and St.
Stephen's Green and Baggot Street 'and the Cork House with
its gallery leading towards Cork Bridge were transformed for
the purposes of a library'. But the organisation of the project
was to take some time, and Henry was full of the problems
of his office. Nevertheless, he was to entertain the royalist
Lord Cork, Lord Broghill's brother, at his new residence at
Phoenix House. He assured Lord Cork that his brother Broghill had especially recommended him to his care and that
Cork would find him 'a real friend'.

On September 6 Fleetwood left for England. Henry Cromwell saw him and his sister, Bridget, as far as Lieutenant
General Ludlow's house at Monkstown, where Fleetwood's
frigate was waiting for him. Fleetwood wanted a confidential
talk with Ludlow before leaving Ireland. He had tried to
persuade him to give up his military commission or, if not,
at least not to participate in the distribution of anti-
Protectorate literature. Ludlow had steadfastly maintained
his opposition, refusing to give an inch on any count. Knowing what was in the Lord Protector's mind, Fleetwood
warned Ludlow that he was faced with a choice of returning
to England of his own free will or returning as a prisoner.
He suggested that Ludlow might try to delay any return to
England until Fleetwood had seen the Lord Protector in
case he dealt harshly with him. Ludlow agreed to follow
Fleetwood after a month or so and, in the meantime, Fleetwood could assure Cromwell that Ludlow would not engage

in any activity against him before seeing him personally and explaining his position. What Fleetwood and Ludlow did not know was that Cromwell, following Henry's advice, had decided that the best thing would be to let Ludlow vegetate in his house in Ireland where he would be out of harm's way.

With Fleetwood's departure, Henry Cromwell became president of the Council of Ireland as well as commander of the army, but Fleetwood still retained the title Lord Deputy.

Having left Fleetwood at Monkstown, Henry set out for Kilkenny. Here he received a number of petitions relating to army matters. Optimistically the *Mercurius Politicus* correspondent stated: 'The disbanded forces are all satisfied. His lordship intends to see them in actual possession and to take a view of the plantation wherein they sit down before his departure to Dublin.' But the common soldiers were far from happy with the grants of land in lieu of their backpay. They recalled that they had never wanted to come to Ireland in the first place, they remembered the mutinies and how they were crushed into submission. It was the officers who had promoted the idea of land in lieu of pay. In a great many cases those officers had cheated the soldiers out of the lands due to them. Some officers, however, sided with their men and while Henry was in Kilkenny, Lieutenant Colonel Scott had to be arrested for agitating disbanded companies of soldiers against the administration. On September 26 Henry left Kilkenny for Waterford: 'It was of the opinion of some,' wrote the *Mercurius Politicus* correspondent, 'that the disbanded soldiers would not be content but the discreet carriage and wise behaviour of the lord Henry Cromwell, hath given them such comfort that they are all very well satisfied.'

Henry arrived back in Dublin at the beginning of October to a 'great Flood such as have not been seen in Ireland for many years'.

Ludlow was once again the cause of consternation. Henry found that he had left Ireland in his absence in spite of explicit orders not to do so. He had reached Beaumaris where the governor had placed him under arrest until orders came from the Lord Protector. On October 14 Henry also had Ludlow's brother-in-law, Colonel Nicholas Kempston arrested 'on suspicion of being privy to the departure of Lieutenant General Ludlow'.

Ludlow was a prisoner for six weeks in Beaumaris Castle before being allowed to journey to London where he was interviewed first by the Council of State and then by the Lord Protector in his bedchamber in Whitehall.

'What can you desire more than you have?' asked an exasperated Cromwell when Ludlow refused to recognise his Protectorship.

'That which we fought for,' replied Ludlow, 'that the nation might be governed by its own consent.'

Cromwell said he was as much for government by consent as any man 'but where shall we find that consent. Amongst the Prelatical, Presbyterians, Independent, Anabaptists, or Levelling parties?'

'Amongst those of all sorts who have acted with fidelity and affection to the public,' replied a determined Ludlow. He went on to deplore the bloodshed which had taken place in order to suppress the disturbances and demonstrations against the Protector. There was a difference between a sword in the hands of Parliament to restore the people to their ancient rights and one in the hands of a tyrant to rob and despoil them of the same. Ludlow told Cromwell that the Lord Protector could not longer appreciate the difference.

Ludlow was forced into retirement and Cromwell put a stop to his attempt to be elected for his native Wiltshire in the second Protectorate Parliament in 1656. But Ludlow was not to be away from Ireland for very long.

'others they transported . . .'

Henry had not thought the 5,000 soldiers disbanded at the beginning of September would settle down in Ireland and had asked Thurloe to find them 'some employment abroad'. The subject of colonising the New World and especially the West Indies had been a problem. Some of the soldiers could certainly be sent there as planters but how could women be encouraged to go to the new dominions to ensure the colonies flourished? For years, since Cromwell had started the practice after Drogheda, the Cromwellian administration had been shipping off its Irish enemies, vagrants and other 'loose, idle persons' to the West Indies. It was Lord Broghill who suggested to Thurloe that a supply of women and young girls could be seized from the Irish and transported to the colonies. Thurloe had immediately written to Henry suggesting that 1,500 soldiers be sent to Barbados as colonists with 1,000 'Irish wenches'.

Henry agreed with the plan and quickly justified the moral issue. He wrote back to Thurloe:

Concerning the young women, although we must use force in taking them up, yet it being so much for their own good and likely to be of so great advantage to the public it is not in the least doubted that you may have such a number of them as you shall think fit to make use upon this account.

Henry also added that 1,500 to 2,000 young Irish boys of twelve years to fourteen years of age could also be sent. 'We could well spare them and they might be of use to you: and who knows but it might be a means to make them Englishmen . . .' There seemed nothing abhorrent to Henry in the idea of his soldiers descending on an Irish village and seizing women, young girls and boys—wives, mothers, daughters and sons—carrying them off for transportation to a strange country, never to see their families or friends again. It was, after all, 'for their own good'. He did, however, display concern about the arrangements to transport them. Writing to Thurloe on September 11, he pointed out:

Care must be taken for ships and provisions for their transportation. It's thought at present that Galway or Kinsale are the finest places to send your ships to receive them, but we shall inform ourselves more fully and give you a particular account by next (frigate).

Barbados, the island where the majority of the Irish were transported, had been claimed for England in 1625. By 1629 there were between 1,600—1,800 settlers on the island. On May 3, 1650, the colonists there declared for Charles Stuart but, on January 11, 1652, they surrendered to Parliamentary forces under Sir George Ayscue. The island had grown from a small band of struggling English colonists to a flourishing community. The colonists ran their settlements with the aid of white servants whom they treated far worse than their African slaves of which, at this time, there were only a small minority. The white servants were mainly political prisoners. After the Parliamentary victories during the English Civil War batches of prisoners were sold to London merchants to be transported to the colonies. A large number of Scots were sold in this way, after Preston and Dunbar, and the Irish were similarly treated after the Cromwellian victories there. On March 11, 1655, Thomas Carlyle wrote: 'A terrible Protector this... he dislikes shedding blood but is very apt to Barbados an unruly man... he has sent and sends us by hundreds to Barbados so that we have made an active verb of it "barbados you"!'

The white servants were called *engagés*. When they arrived in the colony they were forced to indenture themselves to a plantation owner for five or seven years in return for a free passage to the colony (the owner would pay the merchant of the ship who had brought the unfortunate to the colony), for maintenance and, at the end of the contract, a strip of land. On paper the contract sounded reasonable but during the indentured period the servant was treated as a mere chattel at the absolute disposal of the master. Cases of extreme cruelty occurred all too often. The Irish servant was treated as inferior to the African slave, for the slave was a permanent possession for which good money had been given. It was therefore to the advantage of the master to preserve the slave as long as possible by good treatment. Servants were cheaper and treated accordingly.

In 1657 a former servant, having managed to escape his servitude, published *A True and Exact Account of the Barbados*, in London. The man, Ligon, describing the life the servants led, said that at 6 a.m. a bell was rung summoning the servants to work in the open fields, in grinding mills and boiling rooms. At 11 a.m. when the tropical heat became too intense for the work, the servants were given a meal of loblolly, a mixture of crushed Indian corn worked up into a paste with water. At 1 p.m. work recommenced but at 6 p.m. it was broken when they returned to their huts for another meal of loblolly or of potatoes in water. Ligon adds:

To this no bread nor drink but water. Their lodging at night, a board, with nothing under, nor anything on top of them ... If they be not strong men, this ill lodging will put them into a sickness. If they complain they are beaten by an Overseer, if they resist their time is doubled. I have seen an Overseer beat a servant with a cane about the head till the blood has flowed for an offence that is not worth speaking of.

Another such servant, named Esquemeling, who worked in the French colonies in the West Indies, described conditions there in 1664. He claimed the planters of the Caribbean islands were extremely cruel to their servants and one planter was known to have 'killed a hundred with stripes and blows'. Of conditions on the English settlements, of which he claimed to have some experience, he said 'the cruelty they (the English) exercised towards their servants was, that when they had served six years of their time (the usual term of their contract being seven) they used them so ill as forced them to beg their masters to sell them to others, though it were to begin another servitude of seven years'. Esquemeling had known many who had thus served for fifteen or twenty years. 'The toil imposed on them being much harder than what they enjoined the Negroes, their slaves, for these they endeavour to preserve, being their perpetual bondmen, but these white servants they care not whether they live or die, seeing they are to serve them no longer than seven years.'

Not all the Irish transplantees received such treatment. Some of them fell in with kind masters such as the plantation owner who remembered his servants in his will of May 1, 1657.

I give all my Christian servants, Dermot O'Doyle and Hannah, six months a piece off their time, provided they do continue dutiful servants to my wife: but, if they be anyways disobedient or refractory then this bequest to be void and of none effect. And unto Dermot O'Doyle I give my best suite of clothes and my best hat.

Another plantation owner, Cornelius Kelly, whose will was dated May 8, 1659, stipulated that his servant Dermot Daniel, who had been engaged for nine years, be freed in seven, and that another servant, Kathleen Wilson, who was to serve seven be freed after five years.

Other Irish servants lived in fear. One Patrick Miller complained on December 7, 1656, that his master, James Cornelius, had 'inhumanely beaten and bruised (him) insomuch that he is incapable of doing him any service for the present'; Tadhg Donoghue and Walter Wester, servants of Edward Hollingshead, received thirty-one lashes each because they had 'rebelliously and mutinously behaved towards him and their said mistress whereby they have been in fear of their lives'. There was also the case of Cornelius Bryan who was flogged in January, 1656, because he 'did say as he was eating meat in a tray that if there was so much English blood in the tray as there was meat he would eat it'. He was given 120 strokes of the whip on his back before the jail at Indian Bridges Town by the common hangman. Bryan, who was described as an Irish piper, was under 'great suspicion of raising a mutiny'. He survived the flogging and was ordered to be banished from the colony.

The Irish in Barbados found fellow sufferers in the African slaves who were now a growing section on the island. In December, 1656, Colonel William Brayne had written to the Lord Protector urging that he increase the number of Africans in Barbados 'because the planters would have to pay for them, they would have an interest in preserving their lives, which was wanting in the case of bond servants, members of whom were killed by overwork and evil treatment.' In 1649 the African slaves made an attempt to throw off their bondage but the plot was betrayed by a slave of Judge Hothersall and eighteen of the leaders were executed. In November 1656 the Irish and Africans joined forces against the English, but the rebellion was brutally crushed.

Many Irish managed to escape from the plantations to which they were allocated. On September 2, 1657, the island's governor, Daniel Searle, issued a proclamation.

Whereas it hath been noticed that several of the Irish Nation free men and women who have no certain place of residence, and other of them, do wander up and down from Plantation to Plantation as vagabonds, refusing to labour, or to put themselves into any service but continuing in a dissolute, lewd and slothful life, put themselves on evil practices, as pilfering, thefts, robberies and other felonious acts for their subsistency . . .

They were to be arrested, flogged and put into some service on the plantations. No Irishman or woman was to be allowed to keep any arms. All were to be given some means of identification. On September 22 Colonel Lewis Morris was ordered to make sure all arms were in safe keeping.

The Irish were a continued problem to the administration of the island. On June 11, 1660, while the news of the Restoration had not reached Barbados, contingency plans were drawn up in case of a royalist invasion. Daniel Searle asked all field officers in the island to draw up a list of all the Irish living in their precincts; no Irish person was allowed to be in charge of or own any type of ship or boat; if the enemy approached the island, ten troopers and an officer from each troop were to arrest all the Irish in their precincts. Likewise church wardens were also asked to make an 'exact list of all the Irish that live or be in their parishes and such amongst them as are of turbulent, seditious, troublesom or dangerous spirits . . .'

In other American colonies treatment given to Irish servants was slightly better. In 1655 the colony of Virginia passed an act declaring all Irish servants from 'the first of September, 1655, (who) have been (brought) into this colony without indenture shall serve as follows viz. all above 16 years old to serve six years and all under to serve till they be 24 years old.' After that the servants would be freed.

Cromwell's administration kept strict control of the numbers of Irish being shipped to the colonies. The numbers transported by explicit orders ran into many thousands—on September 3, 1655, several hundred Irish prisoners in Plymouth 'not thought fit to be tried for their lives' were sent to Barbados. Some 10,000 Irish were probably transported 'officially' while many unscrupulous merchants were known to have seized Irish people indiscriminately and shipped them off for profit. In a pamphlet published in 1660 entitled *A Collection of Some of the Massacres Committed on the Irish,* the author accuses Colonel Peter Stubber of this practice when governor of Galway.

It was a usual practise with Colonel Stubber, the governor of Galway, and other commanders in the said county, to take people out of their beds at night and sell them for slaves to the Indies, and by computation sold out of the said county about a thousand souls.

Lord Broghill and Sir John Clotworthy were also rumoured to be behind this Irish 'slave traffic'.

Henry tried to enforce the law against 'unofficial' transportation and on May 7, 1656, Robert Bonker and Edward Smyth were arrested for seizing men and women and taking them aboard a ship bound for Barbados without a warrant from the Justice of the Peace. Fleetwood, too, had kept a careful watch on such traffic. Three days before Henry's arrival he had ordered a ship in Dublin Bay to be searched on suspicion that people were being forcibly taken on board to be sold to the Barbados.

The exact number of Irish who were 'Barbadosed' or sent to the other English colonies in the New World will never be known. It was probably in the region of 50,000. Indeed, the common language on the isle of Montserrat in the Leeward Islands until the late eighteenth century was reported to be Irish dating from the Cromwellian period.

'they will never change their bloody nature'

As soon as Henry began his administration he came up against opposition from the dissident officers who supported Fleetwood and Ludlow. Henry's supporters, the Commissary-General Sir John Reynolds, Sir Hardress Waller and Theophilus Jones, had written to the Lord Protector suggesting that Henry be given the title of Lord Deputy. But a group led by Colonel John Hewson, the governor of Dublin, Colonel Henry Pretty and Colonel Richard Lawrence, demanded that Fleetwood be sent back to Ireland. They argued that Henry would be too lenient with the Irish and that people would 'abuse his lordship's good nature on the one hand and weaken the godly interest on the other, to the promoting their private interest thereby to prepare this people for some other dangerous designs'.

The strongest opposition group, of course, were the Anabaptists. Dr. Thomas Harrison, writing to Thurloe on October 17, 1655, said he knew of at least twelve governors of towns, ten colonels, three or four lieutenant colonels, ten majors, nineteen or twenty captains and two salaried preachers who were Anabaptists. One of the two preachers was Thomas Patient, one of the ablest ministers of the day. There were also ten Anabaptist churches.

The main activists against Henry were Quartermaster-General John Vernon, Adjutant General William Allen and Advocate-General Philip Carteret. Henry knew Colonel Richard Lawrence was an Anabaptist but believed him 'quiet though not contented'. Adjutant-General Allen had only just returned to his post in Ireland, having been arrested earlier in the year in Devon for 'multiplying disaffection'. He supported Ludlow in opposing the Protectorate. Now he began to lead the Anabaptist opposition against Henry.

Henry pressed on with trying to make the transplantation policy work. Some soldiers who had settled in Co. Wexford had applied to the Council of Ireland for permission 'to retain a number of Irish husbandmen and servants, of whose faithful demeanour towards the Commonwealth a good account may be given' until such time as the planters could get sufficient English labour to enable them to dispense with the Irishmen. There seemed no doubt that most people were beginning to accept that the transplantation policy applied to all Irish people. On October 3 Henry deferred the matter until a full Council meeting could discuss the problem. More and more colonists were applying for exemptions on behalf of the native Irish in order that the Irish could work on their estates, yet under the Acts the labouring Irish were already exempt unless they had borne arms. The Council had, in fact, made October 20 the deadline for the removal of the native Irish living in Dublin, south of the River Liffey, and in Cos. Wicklow, Wexford and Kildare, and in Co. Carlow, north of the River Barrow, to Connaught or Co. Clare. Because of the large number of appeals from the colonists for servants and workmen the Council, on October 19, 'thought fit to allow some time for the stay of such tenants and servants as belong to the petitioners until further order, and as shall be conceived fit and constant with the public good'.

On October 3 Henry also raised the £2 reward for the capture of a Tory, dead or alive, to £5. He ordered that sums ranging from £30 to £5 'be offered for the heads of certain Tories that hold out in the fastness of Wicklow and Wexford'. £30 was offered for the capture of 'Blind Donagh' O'Derrick, whose guerillas had captured eight of William Petty's men, engaged in mapping confiscated lands at Timolin, Co. Kildare, in March of that year. O'Derrick had taken the captives to a nearby wood, given them a drumhead court martial and executed them. A reward of £20 was offered for O'Derrick's lieutenant, Dermot Ryan.

Worried by the problems and obvious flaws in the transplantation scheme, Henry decided to set up a committee on October 9 to consider ways and means to encourage the colonisation 'and likewise how the Irish may be brought to conform to the English nation in their apparel, speech, names etc. as also how the Irish may be persuaded and won to hear the preaching of the Word and brought to embrace the truth of the Gospel and abhor the error of Popery'.

Henry expanded plans to instruct the Irish in the principles of Protestantism through the medium of their own language. In the Civil List of 1655 Alderman Hooke, Dr. Henry Jones, Robert Chambers and John Price, or any two of them, were ordered to oversee a lecture delivered in Irish to be given in Dublin. A converted Catholic priest, Seamus Corcy, was appointed in March, 1656, to preach in Irish at Bride's parish every Sunday. He was also ordered to go to Drogheda and Athy to minister to the Irish speaking flocks there. His ministry did not prove successful for, in August, he was complaining that his congregations preferred to spend the hours for service at the local ale houses or indulging in 'unwarrantable exercises'. Henry had taken steps to bring over a number of ministers to convert the Irish. One of the best known of these was Dr. Thomas Harrison from the American colony of New England, who preached at St. John's on July 23, 1655, before being settled at Christ Church for £300 a year. The cry for ministers to preach in Ireland made in the spring and summer of 1655 brought from America Samuel Mather, who became the minister of St. Nicholas Church, Dublin, and Increase Mather, his brother, who followed him to Ireland in 1657. Increase Mather took up his ministry at Magherafelt but the climate did not suit him and he soon returned to New England where he became a notorious witch-hunter.

Strangely enough, there was only one case of a witchcraft trial during the Cromwellian administration. In September, 1655, Marion Fisher was condemned to death at Carrick-fergus for bewitching one Alexander Gilbert. She was never executed for, in a subsequent examination by Sir James Barry it was established that Gilbert had died from natural causes and that Fisher was 'often distracted'. A pardon was given to her in February, 1657. There were no other cases of witchcraft trials in spite of the fact that the Ulster Scottish colonists, both clergy and laity, had come from Scotland at a time when an hysterical anti-witch epidemic was raging.

The Scots Presbyterians had seen hope for their future with the arrival of Henry. Adair commented: 'Fleetwood was too much an Anabaptist to carry on Cromwell's designs . . .'

Henry, in fact, had arrived in Dublin with a Presbyterian chaplain named Francis Roberts and 'acted more the governor and politician than Fleetwood had done, not only in civil and military office but in reference to the Presbytery in the North . . .' He increased the number of Presbyterian ministers on state salaries from fifteen to forty-five.

He tried to get all religious factions talking with one another and when he was in Kilkenny in September he had asked Dr. Harrison to seek out Christopher Blackwood, the 'oracle of the Anabaptists in Ireland'. Harrison proposed that the religious factions get together. Blackwood told him that the Anabaptists would join in a day of prayer and lectures provided they could always speak last so that if anything was said against their orthodoxy they might be enabled to correct it and so vindicate the truth. The meeting did not take place and not long afterwards Dublin Anabaptists excommunicated a member of their sect 'and delivered him over to Satan' for attending the Anglican church. Blackwood went to Dublin where he remained until 1659 writing his books, the most famous being *Exposition and Sermons upon the first ten chapters of Matthew*, dedicated to Fleetwood, and published in London in 1658. The Anabaptists declared that Henry was under the dominance of Independents, mainly because some Independents were in the habit of going to his home in Dublin in the evening, where the Cromwells liked to entertain.

One religious group actively disliked by Henry was the Society of Friends, popularly known as the Quakers. They were the extreme left wing of the Puritan movement. The threefold emphasis of Quakerism was the immediacy of Christ's teachings and guidance, therefore the consequent irrelevance of special buildings or ordained ministers, and the application of Christian teaching to life as a whole. Sporadic local persecution led to clashes and Cromwell issued a proclamation in February, 1655, directing magistrates to prosecute 'unless they (Quakers) forbear henceforth all such irregular disorderly practises'. William Edmunds, an Englishman discharged from the army, became a trader and went to live in Dublin. He finally set up a business in Co. Antrim. On a visit to England in 1653 he met George Fox and James Naylor, the Quaker leaders, who converted him to their belief. He returned to Ireland and organised the first Quaker meeting at Lurgan, travelling and preaching first in Ireland, then in England, America and the West Indies. His first convert in Ireland was an Anabaptist preacher named William Parker and a man called William Norris 'an elder of the Baptists, captain of a company, justice of peace, commissioner of revenue, chief treasurer in that quarter (Belturbet) and chief governor of three garrisons' who, as a consequence, was discharged from his command. The administration disliked Quakers intensely because of their refusal to pay tithes or contribute towards the repair of meeting places or churches, 'steeple houses' as they contemptuously called them. The fact that they would not take oaths not unnaturally brought them into conflict with civil and military powers, and their peculiar mode of addressing people, their refusal to do 'hat honour', their extravagant methods of preaching in the streets and interrupting at meetings all aroused the ire of ministers and the anger of the mobs. Henry wrote to Thurloe:

I think their principles and practices are not very consistant with civil government, much less with the discipline of the army. Some think them to have no design but I am not of that opinion. Their counterfeited simplicity renders them to me the more dangerous.

Early in 1655 Elizabeth Fletcher and Elizabeth Smith, two Quaker preachers, as women were equal with men in Quaker eyes, visited Dublin and spoke at an Anabaptist meeting and at St. Audoen's church. They were committed to jail but after their release went to Cork to start preaching. Two more Quakers, Humphrey Norton and Willie Shaw, held a meeting at Samuel Newton's house in Galway. Sir Charles Coote's soldiers turned out, 'the meeting was broken up and (they were) turned out of the town and not suffered to go in to fetch their horses'. On December 17 Henry ordered that all Quakers, 'blasphemers and anarchists', were to be arrested and held pending their transportation the following month.

His general order was designed to apprehend the ring leaders of the sect in Ireland but it had no effect on converts. They were especially strong in Cork. At Kinsale, at the close of the Sunday service, a Quaker rose to his feet to start speaking, the congregation made to leave but a sergeant and soldiers with muskets and lighted matches prevented them. One soldier actually flashed his pan, whereupon, it is rather incredulously reported, the congregation disarmed the soldiers and handed them over to the civil authorities without hurting them. Major Holden, governor of Kinsale, who seems to have been a convert himself or at least extremely tolerant of them, was blamed for the affair.

On October 23 Dublin celebrated the 'anniversary commemoration of that great deliverance which the Lord wrought in the preservation of this place when the blood thirsty rebels first rose up against it . . .' Dr. Thomas Harrison conducted a service at Christ Church before a congregation which included the Council of Ireland. Later the city was given over to celebrations and 'the night was entertained with bells and bonfires that the whole city seemed as enflamed with joy'. But all was not entirely at peace in Dublin and two days later, Henry, for the greater safety of the Council, ordered that no Irishman or woman should be allowed within Dublin Castle after sunset. He was still involved with the problem of clearing the city of the Irish condemned to transplantation. On November 17 the Judge-Advocate, Philip Carteret, was ordered to start proceedings against those people in Dublin who had not transplanted.

Towards the end of October Henry turned his attention to Galway. The town was a seaport of great strategic value which could provide a suitable landing place for any projected invasion from the Continent. Henry wrote to Sir Charles Coote, Lord President of Connaught, on October 30:

> ... it is held advisable that the said town of Galway be forthwith cleared of all the Irish and other Popish inhabitants that do inhabit therein; and in order thereunto your lordship's speedy and effectual care is desired for the speedy removing of all the said Irish and other Papists out of the said town, that better accomodation may be made for such English Protestants, whose integrity to the state is well known, and may be conceived fit to be trusted in a place of such concernment.

Sir Charles was to give Catholic proprietors of houses in the town liberty to sell their lands 'to any Protestant that had not been in arms against the Commonwealth' but, if by a certain date they had not been able to sell the property, he was to seize it and dispose of it himself. By this means Henry thought to make Galway secure against any potential enemy. Coote reported that he had 'dispensed only with a few persons who, through extreme age and sickness, and unseasonableness of the weather were unable to remove, but the security of that place was well provided for'. Later, on November 14, Henry confidently wrote to Thurloe: 'We have cleared the town of Galway of the Irish, and shall have a special care of that place.' Five days later he wrote to Coote giving him permission to keep in Galway twenty masons, labourers, and other handicraftsmen 'of the Irish nation' until May 20, 1656. But he was to ensure that priests over the age of forty were shipped to the continent, and those under forty to Barbados or other American plantations.

In spite of the steps taken against the Tories, the guerillas continued their activity throughout the autumn. The *Publick Intelligencer* reported that two people who had been active against the Irish had been 'lately murdered by Tories in

Kildare' but 'Colonel Hewson is sent down to the town where they were murdered and will secure them all to be sent to the West Indies: they will never change their bloody nature. Our disbanded forces are taking possession apace'. The area where the raid had taken place was that in which the notorious 'Blind Donagh' O'Derrick operated and Hewson was eager to claim the £30 reward on the guerilla chief's head. However, the Tories had disappeared and Hewson contented himself with rounding up all the Irish in the vicinity, hanging four as warning and delivering the remaining thirty-seven, including three priests and twenty-one women, to Captain Colman on November 27 for transportation to Barbados. Among those seized happened to be the wife of 'Blind Donagh' O'Derrick, together with the entire family of Henry Fitzgerald of Lackagh Castle. Fitzgerald and his wife Margery were over eighty years old. On November 27 Thomas Herbert and Charles Coote ordered Philip Peake, the Marshal of the Four Courts, to escort the priests and 'others such as are committed for murder' as well as those arrested by Hewson 'together with the reputed wife of Donagh O'Derrick alias Blind Donagh' to Captain Robert Colman, commander of the Wexford frigate. Colman was to transport them to Wexford where they were to be handed over to the merchant John Norris for transportation to Barbados. The actual transplantation was carried out by Nicholas Norton, a Bristol merchant and sugar planter. There was some delay and the order was repeated on December 4. On December 10 Father Richard Shelton was put on board the Wexford frigate together with Father James Tuit, Father Robert Kegan and Father Redmond More. They arrived in the Barbados on May 21, 1656, but were given fifteen days to leave the island. Governor Searle felt the island was becoming over-populated with Irish priests. In merely banishing them, however, Searle disobeyed a directive from Colonel Thomas Herbert, clerk of the Council of Ireland, who wrote to him at the beginning of December stating:

It is desired by the Council that care may be taken in especial concerning those three priests, that they may be so employed as they may not be at liberty to return again into this nation where that sort of people are able to do much mischief by having so great an influence over the Popish Irish here, and of alienating their affections from the Government.

'Blind Donagh' O'Derrick's anguish at the transportation of his wife made him fight with an intense fury, but his anger caused him to be careless. Within a few weeks he had been caught at Timolin, Co. Kildare, 'in the house whence he and his party took the eight English surveyors, who were thence carried to the woods and most barbarously murdered'. On December 25 Colonel Henry Pretty, the governor of Carlow, was given £100 with which to pay his men for the capture of 'Blind Donagh' and several of his followers. O'Derrick was summarily tried and executed. The most famous of the Tory leaders had been eliminated but his lieutenant, Dermot Ryan, escaped to hold out against the English for two more years.

'Blind Donagh's' execution in no way deterred the Tories from continuing their attacks. On December 3 the governor of Cork, Colonel Robert Phayre, wrote to advise the Council that a band of Tories from Waterford had raided the county and taken many English settlers prisoner. Phayre suspected that many of the Irish living in Co. Cork were harbouring the guerillas and he had rounded up some suspects, sentenced two to be hanged, six to be transported to the West Indies and five entire villages to be transplanted to Connaught immediately. He wished to know if he had the support of the Council. They did not oppose his action.

In spite of the problems, as the year 1655 drew to a close, the Cromwellian administration seemed well pleased with developments in Ireland. According to the *Publick Intelligencer*:

As touching news, Ireland affords little, save that we are now very much blessed in our governor, the Lord Henry Cromwell, who gains very much every day upon the affections and hearts of all sober men and especially in his giving countenance to the said orthodox ministry and his lordship's consistant attendance on public ordinance gives general satisfaction and I may truly say Ireland hath been and is as happy in their governor of late as any place.

'Oh God! What an age you have made us spectators of!'

For the Catholic priesthood there was no improvement in their conditions under Henry's rule. The Jesuit Father Quinn, writing in 1656, described the conditions under which the priests existed:

We live, for the most part, in the mountains and forests and often, too, in the midst of bogs to escape the cavalry of the heretics. Catholics flock to us, who we refresh by the Word of God and consolation of the Sacraments; here, in those wild mountain tracts, we preach to them constancy in faith, and the mysteries of the Cross of Our Lord: here we find true worshippers of God, and champions of Christ. In spite of all the precautions used to exercise our evangelical ministry in secret, the Cromwellians often discover it; and then the wild beast was never hunted with more fury, nor tracked with more pertinacity, through mountains, woods and bogs, than the priest! At present it is a common saying among the misbelievers 'I am going to hunt the priests.'

He added:

One priest, advanced in years, Father John Carolan, was so diligently sought for, and so closely watched, being surrounded on all sides, and yet not discovered, that at length he died of starvation.

As if such conditions were not bad enough, Father Quinn continued:

To crown our other miseries the plague is raging in all quarters: but the more frightful its ravages, the more prompt and zealous is the vigilance of the missionaries. We lately ordered prayers to be offered up in all the province to appease the anger of heaven, and every Catholic in the whole kingdom fasted three days on bread and water —even the children, babes of three years old, fasted as well as others, and all not disqualified by years received with great devotion the sacrament of the Eucharist and Penance.

In spite of the persecution of the priesthood and the severe penalties incurred for sheltering priests, the majority of Irish Catholics clung doggedly to their faith. On February 2 a number of Irish people were arrested for going to Marshalsea Jail, in Dublin, to hear Mass celebrated from a cell window by a priest being held there 'in high contempt of Authority and scandal of the Government'. Charles Coote and Thomas Herbert issued orders to the Mayor of Dublin to examine the prisoners, take a list of their names, addresses, families and what property they held 'and to take care that they be secured in such place as shall be held fit'. But not all Irish Catholics remained steadfast to the faith, many being converted while others proved quick to accept rewards for the betrayal of priests.

Some priests paid the supreme penalty, although executions of priests were now a rare occurrence. On March 26 Father Patrick Archer was found guilty of high treason at Carlow Assizes by Judge Gerard Lowther and sentenced to be hanged, drawn and quartered. On April 1 Henry intervened to remit the quartering part of the sentence. Such an act against a priest, he felt, would only stir up unrest. John Hay, the High Sheriff of Kildare and Carlow, was asked to see the sentence carried out. Thomas Benny, who had captured Father Archer, was duly paid his £5 reward. Thomas Wadding wrote to the former Nuncio to Ireland, Rinuccini, from Nantes on October 21:

> There is no corner of Ireland but is now filled with heresies and atheism, and iniquity of every sort, never was the Catholic name so persecuted; malice is triumphant, all vices flourish, justice has decayed, true faith and mercy, and modesty, and sincerity are banished, violence and audacity everywhere prevail, no one had any property but what he has acquired by fraud and violence, the good are exposed to prosecution and mockery, the bad alone are prosperous, and abound in wealth ... so that we are tempted to cry out Oh God! What an age you have made us spectators of!

The Sacred Congregation now realised it to be imperative that the Irish Province be reorganised. Since mid 1655 they had increased the numbers of Irish priests being sent back into the country on missions. The priests were not only ministering to the needs of the Catholic faithful but encouraging any resistance to Cromwellian rule they could find. Many, in fact, lived with the prowling Tory bands and were agents for their supplies of arms and ammunition. Henry had noted on January 24:

> ... Irish Papists, who had been licensed to depart this nation, and of late years have been transplanted to Spain, Flanders and other

foreign parts, have nevertheless, secretly returned into Ireland with arms, occasioning the increase of Tories and other lawless persons.

Father Thomas Talbot, the brother of Peter, had written to Charles Stuart on May 5, via a Father Plunkett, with the proposal for recruiting 3,000 men in Ireland and placing them in the hands of a Galway merchant named Bodkin. His idea was to prepare 'all the Irish to rise in arms when the King thinks fit'. Father Peter Talbot had, however, written to the Earl of Ormonde on July 31 saying that his brother told him so many lies he could never believe him. Sir Edward Hyde wrote to Father Peter Talbot telling him 'the King is very angry' that Talbot's brother 'should meddle in matters relating to him without his privity or consent and will complain to his Superior or write to the General (of his Order) if he will not be quiet till he be called upon'.

The priesthood, as in the days of the Irish Confederacy, were deeply split as to their political aims. Many still believed in the policies advocated by Nuncio Rinuccini and Eoin Ruadh for Irish independence. Others, such as Peter Talbot, of old English colonial stock, firmly believed in the English right to rule Ireland. The two sides were constantly warring with each other and, in August, Peter Talbot discovered that an Augustinian brother had been sent to see a Dr. Creagh, one of the Pope's chaplains, to plead for the cause of Irish independence. Writing to Edward Hyde from Ghent on August 13 he said:

... it is necessary that such seditions and suspected persons of the Irish clergy as have any title or authority in Ireland, be disposed of, that honest and learned men, who know the duty of subjects according to the tenets of Catholics may be put in their places, that the simple people of Ireland be not again seduced by factious and ignorant clergy; the Internuncio will have this done if the King's pleasure be signified.

On February 3 a Congregatio Generalis had met in Rome to begin the reorganisation of the shattered Irish church. They decided that Cardinal Albezzi should continue to be responsible for the appointment of bishops to the Irish Sees and for the selection of a new Irish Primate, which office had been vacant since the death of the former Primate, Bishop Hugh O'Reilly, some years before. There were, in fact, eleven surviving bishops of whom only one was still in Ireland. Eugene Sweeny, Bishop of Kilmore, who was the only bishop to remain in Ireland from 1654 to 1659, had been allowed to do so because he was bedridden and not an active apostolic. Of the other ten surviving bishops, all but one were now elderly men, most of them broken by the terrifying experiences they had undergone. Cardinal Albezzi realised the futility of trying to send them back into Ireland. Only Anthony MacGeoghegan, Bishop of Clonmacnoise, now studying in Rome, had the mental and physical strength to return.

Albezzi decided to nominate Eamonn O'Reilly, the Vicar-General of Dublin, who had recently made his way to Europe after his trial and imprisonment in Dublin, as the new Primate, the Archbishop of Armagh. MacGeoghegan would be removed from Clonmacnoise to become Bishop of Meath. As the other bishops, although inactive, were still alive, Albezzi thought it best to appoint Vicars-Apostolic to the dioceses of Dublin, Cashel, Emly, Clogher, Down, Connor, Killaloe, Ross, Ossory, Limerick, Clonfert (Ferns) and Waterford. Pope Alexander did not give final approval for the new Hierarchy until April 16, 1657.

There was, of course, the ordinary priesthood to be strengthened. The Sacred Congregation considered a report assessing the Irish Province from the General Chapter of the Dominican Order, meeting in Rome at the same time.

Of the 43 convents that our Order possessed in that island, there is not one now remaining; all, through the heretical fury, having been consumed by fire, razed to the ground, or devoted to profane uses. In the year 1646 we numbered 600 friars there now not a fourth part remains, and even they are exiles from their native shores the others being all either crowned with martyrdom or condemned to a lengthened death in the island of Barbados.

The Society of Jesus had fared little better. The Jesuits had been eighty in number before 1649 with six colleges, eight residences and several oratories and schools. Only seventeen Jesuit Fathers now remained in Ireland. Moves were set afoot for recruiting and training replacements to fill the depleted Orders and by September 23 Henry Cromwell was writing in alarm of the great number of priests

Roger Boyle, Lord Broghill, fifth and youngest son of 'The Great Earl of Cork'. He was one of the leading members of the Cromwellian administration, although his sympathies were always Royalist, and is reputed to have originated Cromwell's 'Hell or Connaught!' policy. He was created 1st Earl of Orrery at the Restoration.

Photograph: Charles White

Sir William Petty, who came to Ireland in 1652 as Physician General to the Army. He devised and carried out the plan of surveying and allocating the confiscated lands of the Irish and, by so doing, became one of the biggest landowners in the country.

Erasmus Smith, a London merchant who made money by supplying the English troops in Ireland. He invested in the confiscated estates and by the end of the Cromwellian period had become the largest landowner in the country. Faced with the prospect of having some of his land seized at the Restoration, he 'generously' donated it for the purpose of building schools and achieved fame as a benefactor to education in Ireland.

Sir John Clotworthy, a Presbyterian colonist whose family settled in Ulster. A staunch Parliamentarian, he speculated in confiscated estates and increased his property holdings. He was created 1st Viscount Massereene in 1660.

Ballinakill, Co. Galway, in the province of Connaught, where the Irish were forced to resettle on pain of death.

The island of Inishbofin, off Co. Galway, where Henry Cromwell had a special camp set up for captured Catholic priests. The prisoners were to remain on this desolate, rocky island until the Restoration.

arriving in the country, particularly from Spain, whom he thought were preparing plans for a Stuart uprising. He had, in fact, issued orders on August 20, for a special search to be made for returned Catholic priests.

A new method of combating the priesthood had been evolving in Henry's mind throughout 1656. While shipping priests under forty years of age to the American colonies could usefully serve as a deterrent, merely sending those over forty years of age back to the Continent in no way decreased the ardour of the missionaries. Henry was toying with the idea of using some of the remoter western islands as internment camps where all priests would be incarcerated without hope of reprieve. By April the prisons were crowded with captured priests and on May 3 Henry wrote to the governors of the fifteen precincts to send all priests under guard to Carrickfergus, where they were to be put on board such ships as would transport them to Barbados. One priest, Father Paul Cushin, who was very elderly, had been arrested and sent on to Philipstown where he fell sick and was in danger of dying. On August 27 he pleaded that he be allowed to wait in Philipstown until he was better. The Council allowed him 6d per day during his illness until he could be sent to Carrickfergus.

At Carrickfergus, Colonel Cooper, the governor, noted that the horror of approaching exile shook many of the younger priests so much that a number of them said they would renounce Catholicism and become Protestants.

It was on September 23 that Henry decided to implement his 'internment camp' idea. He wrote to Colonel Cooper telling him to cancel the transportation of the priests until he had approval for the new plan to build a prison camp for them on the Aran Isles.

The Catholic priesthood were not the only religious sect against which Henry felt obliged to use tough measures during that year. Following the big round up of members of the Society of Friends, the Quakers, a large number were held in jails in Dublin and Waterford. In January Henry ordered that they be banished. Those in Dublin were to be put on a ship to Chester and those in Waterford were to be transported to Bristol. In spite of this the Quakers continued their activities. Edward Burrough and Francis Howgil visited Limerick and towns in Co. Cork. In Bandon they converted Cornet Edward Cook of the Lord Protector's own regiment of horse. Cook was several times roughly handled by his fellow soldiers when he sought to convert them. Burrough and Howgil's meetings became popular and were attended by prominent army officers, such as Colonel Robert Phayre, the governor of Cork. Phayre's interest, though, was strictly academic for he was a convinced Muggletonian. This sect was formed by Ludowick Muggleton, a Bishopsgate (London) tailor who, in 1651, claimed he had received revelations from God. He proclaimed that his cousin John Reeves and himself were the two witnesses mentioned in Revelations xi, 3-6: 'And I will give power unto my two witnesses and they shall prophesy a thousand two hundred and three score days, clothed in sackcloth...' In 1652 they published *A Transcendent Spiritual Treatise* and in 1656 an exposition of their doctrines entitled *A Divine Looking Glass*. They believed the three persons in the Trinity were merely nominal. God had a real human body. To disbelieve the prophets, Muggleton and Reeves, was an unforgivable sin. 'And if any man will hurt them, fire proceedeth out of their mouths and devoureth their enemies, and if any man will hurt them he must in his manner be killed.' Muggleton had already been imprisoned in 1653 for blasphemy.

Phayre himself was the son of Emanuel Phayre, the Anglican vicar of Kilshanning, Co. Cork. He had become a lieutenant colonel in Colonel Richard Townshend's regiment, raised in September, 1649, which had served under Fairfax in England. He had been commander of the halberdiers at Charles I's trial and was one of the three officers to whom the warrant of execution was actually addressed. Returning to Ireland in November, 1649, with a foot regiment, he had become governor of Cork where he displayed his administrative talents. Phayre did not become a convert to Quakerism but he did attend many of the Quaker meetings. Other army men did become converts. At Kinsale Burrough and Howgil had considerable success. Major Holden, the governor, encouraged them to preach to his troops. They converted Susaneh, wife of Dr. Edward Worth. Major Holden even wrote a letter to Henry in their favour. Henry was not impressed and, on his instructions, the High Sheriff of Cork arrested them and transferred them to Dublin under guard where Henry, with members of his council, questioned them before they were banished from the country.

In March, 1656, Barbara Blagdon, from the English West Country, arrived in Dublin and had a meeting with Henry. This prominent Quaker preacher warned Henry that he should follow the advice of Gamaliel as in Acts v, 34–42. 'Refrain from these men, and let them alone; for if this counsel or this work be of men, it will come to nought: but if it be of God, ye cannot overthrow it; lest haply ye be found even to fight against God.' She reported that Henry had given her a fair hearing and was not as hostile as he was reputed to be but that he was stirred up to persecution by others. She went on to Limerick only to be arrested by Colonel Ingoldsby, imprisoned for a time and banished.

In Limerick Quakerism grew, especially among army circles. Meetings were held regularly in the house of a Captain Robert Wilkinson, 'a man that had received some illuminations but too much a stranger to that silent and humble waiting in the divine light, which would mortify the carnal will', commented a fellow Quaker. Other meetings were held in the house of a Captain Holmes. The Quakers in Limerick became so powerful that in November, that year, the Council deemed it necessary to write to Ingoldsby directing him to turn all Quakers out of the town or to arrest any of the inhabitants who professed to adhere to Quaker principles. Several complaints were addressed by John Perrott to Henry about the severe way Ingoldsby clamped down on them. Ingoldsby wrote defending himself against these 'vipers . . . in our bosom'. He cashiered several officers and used corporal punishment freely on the soldiers. He had a sergeant flogged for writing him an abusive letter and suspended a Lieutenant Waller who had resisted arrest while attending a Quaker meeting at Captain Holmes' house.

Waterford, Cashel and Kilkenny became centres of Quakerism and in that year of 1656 they rented a farm in Co. Cavan in order to put into practice their doctrine of non-payment of tithes. However, after some years, there was a disagreement with the owner, Colonel Kempston, and the colony removed itself to Mountmellick in Queen's County (Leix) in 1659. After 1656 Henry's persecution of the Quakers died down and only nine were imprisoned between 1657–59.

The year 1656 did not start well for Henry. The attacks from the Anabaptists continued. Colonel Thomas Cooper had just arrived in Ireland to take command of Colonel Venables' regiment in Ulster. Henry believed that Cooper, whom he called a 'moderate Anabaptist', would have a stabilising effect on the Anabaptist opposition. He decided on a bold policy and in the first few weeks of January he called together the dissident officers 'that they might all of them of that judgement expect equal liberty both in their spiritual and civil concernment with any others'. He gave them the opportunity to express any grievance against him 'either as a public person or a private Christian'. While his officers did not say anything openly to Henry they had, within a few days, on January 16, written a letter to the Lord Protector asking that Fleetwood be sent back to Ireland as Lord Lieutenant while Henry, so as not to give offence to the Protector, could be given the title of Lord Deputy.

Henry was infuriated by the continued opposition to his command. The Quartermaster-General, Vernon, was now openly preaching against him saying it was a great judgment for 'the people of God' (Anabaptists) to be under a young or wicked governor, such being apt to be lifted up and to believe lying reports about 'poor saints'. Henry, he declaimed, was too 'priest ridden' to be moderate against beliefs not his own and he compared him with Absalom, the son of David, who led a revolution against his father. Henry, went on Vernon, was endeavouring to grasp unlawful power at the expense of his father, and to steal away the hearts of the people. The Lord Protector wrote to 'my son, Harry Cromwell' on April 21.

I am glad to hear what I have heard of your carriage; sturdy still be innocent, and to answer every occasion, roll yourself upon God—which to do needs much Grace.
I think the Anabaptists are to blame in not being pleased with you. That's their fault ... Take care of making it a business to be

hard for the men who contest with you. Being over concerned may
train you into a snare. I have to do with these men, and am not
without exercise. I know they are weak because they are so peremp-
tory in judging others.

Henry, however, was extremely sensitive to the Anabaptist criticisms and felt he should resign his office. On July
8 Thurloe wrote to give him some advice.

If opposition, reproach, hard thoughts and speeches of all sorts,
would have made His Highness to have quitted his relations to the
public, he had surely done it long since. And I persuaded myself
your lordship is not ignorant how he hath been exercised in this
kind. Everybody can keep his place when all men applaud him, and
speak well of him; but not to faint in the days of adversity is the
matter. He that looks for more than his own integrity and sincerity
in public work at this time of day for his reward will be mistaken;
and truly he hath that can look difficulties in the face.

Henry continued to be vexed by the Anabaptists even
when his first son, Oliver, was born on April 19, 'a lusty,
hopeful són'. His wife Elizabeth was reported to have had a
comfortable labour and bonfires and banquets were held in
Dublin. But when Henry had the child publicly christened,
the Anabaptists, with their creed of adult baptism, took it as
a deliberate insult. A more diplomatic person would have
avoided the incident. The Lord Protector felt that men who
would back Henry should be sent to Ireland to offset the
opposition. There was still a vacant seat on the Council
caused by the death of Robert Hammond. Thurloe wrote to
Henry, saying that everything was being done to find a suitable and trustworthy person to assist him.

Strangely enough, Colonel John Jones, Ludlow's friend
and former supporter on the Fleetwood administration, was
suggested. Henry's reaction was immediate. 'I know no old
Protestant in Ireland can be more dangerous and prejudicial
to the public upon that account than this gentleman.' He
said that Jones would use the factions in Ireland to make
use of power for his own republican ends. Thurloe pointed
out that Jones was a suitor to Mrs. Catherine Whitstone, the
Lord Protector's sister and widow of Roger Whitstone. Jones
was therefore almost one of the Cromwell family. Grudgingly
Henry wrote on April 2:

When I wrote you about Colonel Jones I did not know that he was likely to be my uncle. Perhaps that may serve to oblige him to faithfulness to His Highness and Government. I wish it hath as good an influence upon him as to other things, but you have silenced me as to him . . .

The final choice made on August 4 fell on William Bury and William Steele was eventually persuaded to go to Ireland to take his seat on the Council. He became a supporter of Henry although he, too, was an Anabaptist.

By April, 1656, the greater part of Petty's survey was finished and its total completion took place in the autumn. Worsley had to approve the end result but maintained it to have many defects and omissions. Petty pointed out the difficulties under which he and his men had worked, the confusion of the country and lack of money. Henry's Council paid scant attention to Worsley's grousings and decided the survey had been adequately carried out. Worsley, according to Petty, 'rackt himself and his brain to invent racks for the examination of my work . . .' but the survey was accepted. Henry, now weary of opposition to the scheme of transplantation and the policies he was following, decided there should be no further delays and the land should be distributed to the army according to the survey. On May 20 he set up a committee of six officers to supervise the allotment of land to the army.

The financiers were now moving into Ireland to claim their allotments. In February John Pitts of Devon arrived to take up an estate he had been allocated at Iffa and Offa near Clonmel. The fine rich lands of Co. Tipperary induced Pitts to give up his English property and settle in Ireland. Pitts returned to England to escort his family to their new home but when they arrived on June 12 they found themselves kept off the estate by 'the insolency of the Irish rebel' . . . the dispossessed owner Philip O'Neill. Mr. Pitts called in Robert LeHunt, the High Sheriff of the county, who immediately had O'Neill and his wife and daughters arrested and forcibly removed to Connaught. Mr. Pitts and his family moved into their new estate.

Another financier, Gregory Clements, had been allotted 7,000 acres of Coughlan land in Barrycastle, Banagher,

King's County (Offaly). On May 7 he was complaining that
Mary Coughlan of Kilcolgan was still in residence there and
had kept him off the property for two years. The land was
once the property of Terence Coughlan who had been Commissary of Stores to Ormonde's Army, during the campaign
of 1649–50. He was related by marriage to Lord Clanricarde.
Terence died in exile but his son Francis served Charles
Stuart as a captain in a foot regiment in Flanders. Gregory
Clements was one of those who suffered death as a regicide
after the Restoration and Francis was restored to the Barrycastle estate.

Some settlers who had gone to the American colonies were
attracted back to take advantage of the colonisation of Ireland. On May 5 John Stone and his family from New England
petitioned to become a tenant at Garristown and, on July
30, John Barker, arriving from New England, made a
similar application. Some of the old landowners, however,
managed to keep the new colonists at bay. Viscountess
Thurles, mother of the Earl of Ormonde, and daughter of
Sir John Poynting of Gloucestershire, owned the castle and
town of Thurles in Co. Tipperary. Her estate was of 4,000
acres. During the long years of the Confederate war she
naturally gave her powerful protection to the English and
supplied the royalist armies with large sums of money to
help them suppress the insurgents. When a Major Peisley was
forced to surrender the neighbouring garrison of Archers-
town to the Irish, she gave him her protection. In spite of
the fact that her son Ormonde was a Protestant, Viscountess
Thurles was a Catholic. Her son had been made a ward of
the King and brought up in England with the family of Dr.
Abbott, Archbishop of Canterbury. John Gunn, the agent for
the financiers, described her as 'a Papist recusant and transplantable'. She was, indeed, ordered to transplant to Connaught but because of her powerful connections the order
was dispensed with from time to time until her son Ormonde
returned to Ireland with increased power and honours.

The Lord Protector himself sometimes intervened to prevent transplantation of certain people. Pierce Butler, Viscount Ikerrin of Lismalin, had been ordered to transplant.

Because of 'a distemper' he was allowed to go to England for six months in search of a cure, his wife and servants meanwhile being allowed two months' extra time to transplant. Having received his cure, Lord Ikerrin return to Ireland on November 26, 1654, and started to consider ways and means of avoiding transplantation. He made himself useful in hunting down Tories in his area, many of them former neighbours who had sought shelter in the woods rather than transplant. On February 27, 1657, the Lord Protector took up his case and, writing to his son Henry, pointed out:

> ... the lord Viscount Ikerrin hath been of late time serviceable to suppress the Tories and we being very sensible of the extreme poor and miserable condition of his lordship even to the want of necessaries to support his life, we could not but commiserate his said distress and condition by helping him to a little relief, without which he could neither subsist here nor return back to Ireland, and therefore earnestly desire you to take him into speedy consideration by allowing him some reasonable portion of his estate without transplanting him...

The estate and castle of Lord Dunsany in Skreem, Co. Meath, was also confiscated, in spite of the fact that he had written, on March 11, 1642, that he had resolved 'rather to be hanged with the imagination that I died a loyal subject and lover of the prosperity of England, than to live in the quiet posession of all the north of Ireland'. He had died not many years after and his widow now lived at Dunsany Castle. On July 13, 1655, Hans Graham, a Bristol merchant, sent his agent to claim the estate. Lady Dunsany announced that the castle would have to be carried forcibly before she would quit. The agent was quite prepared to hire some men to storm the castle but the local sheriff, perhaps on friendly terms with Lady Dunsany, advised a delay. However, on July 4, 1656, Hans Graham came over himself and Major Thomas Stanley, the governor of Clonmel, forcibly removed Lady Dunsany and her children.

The Royalists, while they admired the Cromwellian scheme of colonisation, began to wonder whether things might lead to a reaction which would overwhelm the colonists. Colonel John Brampfield wrote from Paris on April 18 to his friend Sir John Hobart:

If they (the Irish) massacred such vast numbers of English in Ireland unprovoked at the beginning of the war, what will they do in revenge of what they have justly suffered since?

Many landowners still held out against transplantation and not all had the power or influence of Lady Thurles. In the summer of 1656 some petty landowners at Mallow refused to transplant despite orders given them at a sitting of the Court of Qualifications at Mallow on Saturday, August 29. The landowners simply refused to go to Connaught.

The court threatened and cajoled. The landowners were adamant. One was heard to say he would rather go to Barbados than into Connaught amongst the rebels. A letter was sent to the Council of Ireland asking what should be done. The resistance of the landowners of Mallow was a victory for them for, by a special ordinance, they were exempted from transplantation provided they went to live in the baronies of Barrymore and Muskerry.

The work of the confiscations and allocation of lands was not carried out without some graft and corruption on the part of officials. When the financier Sir Nicholas Crispe subscribed £1,700 of his own money, and a further £1,500 with some partners, to get an estate, he found himself a victim of a fraud. His allotted estate at Limerick was in the middle of a bog. But when corruption was discovered it was punished by Henry. On November 7 Robert Mason, a clerk at Loughrea, confessed to receiving £60 in bribes from transplanting Irish to use his influence to get them well appointed tracts of land in Connaught 'contrary to the trust reposed in him'. He was immediately dismissed from his post.

With the transplantation properly under way, financiers, at a meeting in the Grocers' Hall, London, decided to ask Worsley and Petty to survey their land. On September 3, Charles Coote and Thomas Herbert signed an order to that effect. Petty was becoming one of the richest men in Ireland. By 1656 his cash resources had increased to £13,000 from the meagre £480 he had arrived with in 1652. He was making the money mostly by buying land debentures from soldiers and conducting highly suspect deals at considerable profit.

'the desire to be rid of that race'

For some people in Ireland life continued with semblance of what could be described as normality. On April 17, 1656, marriage articles were drawn up for Dáibhí Ó Dubhda of Castleconner, Co. Sligo, and Derbhla, daughter of Tadhg Rua Ó Dubhda of Castletown. The prospective groom, Dáibhí Ó Dubhda, was without any estate, everything had been confiscated by the English. However, as he pointed out to his prospective father-in-law, he had strong expectation of an appeal made to the Commissioners at Loughrea. Tadhg Rua apparently thought these expectations were enough for he agreed to the wedding and gave more than generous terms in the matter of a dowry.

> Tadhg, in consideration of the said marriage, gives to Dáibhí as a marriage portion to and with the said Dáibhí, the number of cows, sheep, cattle following: viz. forty great cows, to be milch cows next summer, 15 heifers to two years, 15 yearling heifers, 100 sheep, one horse and a plough.

Dáibhí's expectations were well founded for a few months later, in August, the Commissioners allotted him a small estate in the parish of Kilgarven, in Gallen, Co. Mayo, among the ancient clan lands of the Ó Dubhda's. The grant was made on August 4. Dáibhí settled there with Derbhla and had five sons, three of whom were to die in the Williamite wars of the next generation. His marriage articles had been drawn up at the Castle of Lecan, Kilglass, Co. Sligo and witnessed by the famous Irish scholar Duald Mac Firbisigh. Duald, or Dubhaltach, was Ruairí Ó Flaithearta's teacher. Among his great works was *The Geneaologies, Tribes and Customs of Hy-Fiachrach* which he started writing while at St. Nicholas College, Galway, in 1650. After the fall of Galway he continued working on his manuscript, enlarging and correcting it until 1664. He was murdered in Dunflin, Co. Sligo, in 1670, 'and by his death our antiquaries received an irreparable blow', commented a contemporary.

For the majority of Irish people there was little normality

to their lives, though the *Mercurius Politicus* of March 20–27 commented:

Things are in a fair way here towards a settlement. A gallant country it is far improved, and great advantages are to be made by planters and good encouragement is given them by the authority. The Irish retain still their old native (sic) but their sting is taken out.

It was true, the journal admitted, that the Tories were as active as ever but 'they will hardly design anything without a discovery'. It would seem there were many 'designs' by the Tories, aided by the exiled royalists. Writing to the Doge and Senate on April 7 the new Venetian secretary in England, Francesco Giavarina, commented:

In Ireland we hear of some rising against the government plotted by the Spaniards and just now encouraged by King Charles. The people there were working secretly but with great activity to put their plans into execution. Men in disguise travelled through the country to rouse the people and incite them to rebellion. But their plans became known here and the Protector immediately took steps to check it at its birth and not allow matters so prejudicial to his authority and seat to get a start. Instructions have accordingly been issued for the arrest of some of the most mutinous and for a strict and thorough surveillance of everything.

Colonel Richard Lawrence had pointed out that the areas in which the Tories were most active were the counties of Wexford, Kildare and Carlow, where the local guerilla leaders seemed to have undertaken a policy of assassination of the colonists.

Of which number one gentleman living in a strong castle and sitting by the fire with his wife and family in the evening, heard some person, whose voice he knew, call him by name to come to his gate to speak with him: the poor gentleman, supposing no danger in a country where no enemy was heard of, presently went to the door and was murdered, where he was taken up dead off the place. Another of them, walking in his grounds in the day time, about his business, was there found murdered, and to this day it could never be learned who committed either of them. And when these horrid murders are done, the poor English that do escape know not what means to use. As for his Irish neighbours, it's like he may not have one near him that can speak English, and if he have a hue and cry (or hullaloo, as they call it) to be set up, they will be sure to send it the wrong way, or at least defer it until the offender be far enough out of reach, and not unlikely but the persons that seem busiest in the pursuit may be them that did the mischief.

The administration made an agreement early in 1656 with the former Royalist Major Charles Kavanagh of Co. Carlow. In return for dispensing with his order to transplant he agreed to combat the Tories in Cos. Carlow, Wicklow, Wexford and Kilkenny. He selected thirteen fellow Irishmen for the job and made his headquarters in the old castle of Aghadagh which lay in boglands in the barony of Idrone. The lease for the castle was made out to Major Boulton, of Colonel Pretty's regiment, who was to be Kavanagh's commanding officer and also provide communication between Henry's Council and Kavanagh. The castle lay four miles due east of Leighlin Bridge on the River Barrow, which was a well known spot used by the Tories for ambushing convoys from Kilkenny to Carlow. Major Kavanagh's force was used in a counter-insurgency rôle, fighting the Tories on their own terms and showing no mercy. The capture, execution or transportation of Tories in no way deterred their activity. Many of them were still sent to the West Indies. On March 26 Martin Noell, Thurloe's brother-in-law, contracted to transport 1,200 men from Knockfergus, Ireland, and Portpatrick, Scotland, to Jamaica at £5 10s. a head.

The transplantation policy continued to act as a means of recruiting for the Tories. It was observed that many people were slipping back into the country with arms and Irish privateers had also become active against Commonwealth shipping around the Irish coast. On April 7 Captain Henry Hatsell reported to Colonel John Clark that his ship The Friendship, out of Plymouth, had been bound for Ireland with salt and deal timber, when it had been attacked and 'taken off Scilly by Nicholas Hayes, an Irishman, holding a commission from James, Duke of York, who put his quartermaster, Harry Wade, and six other men, four being desperate Irishmen, into her, with an order to carry her to St. Sebastian for condemnation'. Wade appears to have been either tired of the royalists or of serving his captain for he sent two of the four Irishmen under his command off to the nearest island in a boat on some errand and when they were gone he seized the other two Irishmen and had them bound. When the first two returned he similarly bound them and put all four into a boat. He then freed Captain Hatsell and his crew.

In Dublin, Henry had settled down into the routine of administration. On April 6 the city celebrated its deliverance from the clans of the O'Byrnes and O'Tooles of Wicklow, who had been defeated two miles from the city. 2,000 armed men in fifteen companies led by the Mayor of Dublin marched 'with colours flying and drums beating' to the scene of the colonists' victory. Henry and his Council were in attendance. Dublin had cause to celebrate again thirteen days later when Henry's first son Oliver was born.

But apart from ceremonies there were countless problems to be considered. Major Daniel Redman, at Kilkenny, was worried about instructions for deploying his troops 'for the winter approaching'. On June 11 Captain William Webb, the surveyor of the fortifications, was sent a further £300 to help him build Fort Cromwell at Ballahy Pass, Co. Sligo. Some £600 had already been spent on it. It was one of several forts which were designed to cut off the Irish in Connaught and Co. Clare, forming a line with the River Shannon.

On May 1 Colonel William Moore had to be given £200 to help him leave Ireland to take command of a foot regiment in the American colonies. On May 12 the Venetian secretary Giavarina reported that M. de Bardeos had been granted permission to raise 6,000 soldiers in Ireland from the natives to serve in Flanders.

The Protector agreed to this solely from the desire to be rid of that race as the most prone to sedition, the most opposed to the present government and professing the Catholic religion, so detested and persecuted by this state. Accordingly the ambassador has already begun to grant patents to colonels to enrol them.

Not the least among Henry's problems was that of coping with the wolves. By March, 1655, some £243 5s 4d had been paid out in rewards for wolves. On July 1 Henry published new rates of rewards: £6 for a bitch, £5 for a dog, 40s for a cub and 10s for a suckling cub. There was also the problem of eliminating base coinage and introducing some credible form of currency into the country. In April Henry had considered ways to set up a mint in Ireland for Irish coinage and had passed on his proposals to the Council of State in

London. In July the Council considered a proposal from a French coiner, Monsieur Pierre Blondeau, who offered his services as a coiner for the English mint.

Blondeau was given a London house for a trial period while he prepared designs, with Cromwell's head on one side and his coat-of-arms on the other, for the new Irish coinage.

A postal service was also in preparation. Evan Vaughan had organised the stages of a post for the delivery of public letters, much to the relief of the cavalry regiments of the army 'who were formerly the only post to convoy the public letters'.

Throughout the summer there were rumours of invasion by the Royalists in conjunction with Spain, with whom the Commonwealth was in open conflict since the English attack on Hispaniola and the taking of Jamaica. Ambassador Alonso de Cardenas had quit the country and English troops were now fighting the Spaniards in Flanders. Trouble did break out in Ireland in September and on the second of the month Lieutenant Colonel John Nelson was ordered into Co. Kerry 'by reason of malignants raising their heads'. He was authorised to arrest heads of clans, septs 'or otherwise considerable and leading men formerly in arms'. The Venetian secretary, Giavarina wrote to his government on September 15:

In Ireland, which is the part most opposed to the present rule and the easiest place in which to start trouble and revolt, they have recently discovered a plot to be exploded at the time parliament meets, supposed to be most favourable to the designs of those who do not like this government. They soon put everything right by imprisoning some, by putting others on their trial, and by punishing the guilty, much to the chagrin of the House of Stuart who have been planning this for a long time in the hope it might do some good for their cause.

He added, on September 22:

Besides the conspiracy discovered in Ireland they have found another being planned in England to be kindled at the time of Parliament.

Pressing financial needs, mainly caused by the war with Spain, forced the Lord Protector to call his second Protectorate Parliament on September 17. The main purpose of the

Parliament was to raise money. The credit of the government was now treated with suspicion as two city merchants, Vassell and Avery, once men of great wealth and formerly Members of Parliament, were languishing in debtors' prisons because the government had not returned money the merchants had lent them. This in no way encouraged other merchants to loan sums to the government.

But financial affairs had to wait while moves were made to alter the Instrument of Government which had made Cromwell Lord Protector. William Jephson, the former Major General, who had been returned to Parliament for Co. Cork, proposed on October 28 that the Protectorship should be made hereditary in Cromwell's favour and not elective. Lord Broghill, who had now risen into the élite circle who counted as Cromwell's closest advisers, was strongly in favour. The Protector declined the idea. The discussion of finance was again postponed when Parliament decided to try a case of blasphemy. It was fortuitous that Captain Richard Stayner had, in September, captured a Spanish treasure fleet. The gold was sorely needed although the poet Edmund Waller suggested the gold should be melted down to make a crown for the Lord Protector.

> With ermine clad and purple, let him hold
> A royal sceptre, made of Spanish gold ...

The case of blasphemy concerned the Quaker leader James Naylor, whose followers, mainly women, had staged a humble imitation of Christ's entry into Jerusalem when they welcomed Naylor into Bristol. Naylor said the women saluted him on account of that part of Christ which is in all men and that he made no claim to be Christ. Although eighty-two members voted for the death sentence, by a sixteen vote majority he was allowed to live ... but sentenced to three whippings and pillories to be followed by close imprisonment. The Lord Protector intervened to ask by which laws the Parliament had taken the case out of the civil courts, and a year later, was still busying himself over the fate of Naylor.

With the attempted uprising in Ireland having been suppressed by Nelson, Henry set out on what was to become an annual tour of inspection. From Kilkenny on September 16 he wrote a long and practical letter to Thurloe, now serving as a Member of Parliament for Ely, as well as Secretary of State, commenting on the disposition of the army. Henry suggested that an extra militia be organised 'in the several counties of this nation for the defence and security thereof'. On September 29 he was at Cashel and then went on to Limerick and Galway 'which as things now stand is most especially to be looked after and secured'. Especially, because General Monck had reported to Henry that some fifteen or sixteen enemy ships had been lying off the coast for three weeks and he thought that they intended to fall on the next convoy bound for Jamaica. Henry had been asked to provide escorts for the convoy, which was due to go through St. George's Channel, in late October. Some seamen were recruited and gathered at Carrickfergus where they were shipped to rendezvous at Cork or Kinsale.

On October 14 Henry was at Athlone, writing that Galway 'is as considerable both for Western trade and of as great strength as any town I know in these nations, and would if fully planted with English have a very good influence for awing (sic) the Irish in that province'. Nathaniel Brewster, who accompanied Henry, wrote to Thurloe on October 22 pointing out

... that the principal seaports and land towns of this county are sadly decayed and unpeopled being likely to continue so till better encouragements be offered to planters, especially merchants.

The Lord Protector did not greet Henry's suggestion for a militia with enthusiasm. He 'judged it to be a thing of very tender consideration as to the hands where in it is to be placed'. Henry, always sensitive to criticism, was hurt by his father's lack of response to the idea. In early November he sent Colonel Cooper to London with a letter for the Lord Protector and another one for Thurloe. His commission was to report on the situation in Ireland. At the same time Vincent Gookin was also supporting Henry in his counsels to the Protector.

In the first few days of November news of a disaster reached Henry. The two ships he had sent as additional protection for the West Indies convoy had met with tragedy. The *Two*

Brothers, out of Kinsale, had been wrecked in the Bay of Timoleague. Of 250 soldiers commanded by Lieutenant Colonel Brampstone on board only forty managed to get ashore while sixteen out of twenty-nine seamen were saved. Reverend Edward Worth, the vicar of Ringrone, thanked God the wreck had been swept ashore in the barony of Couries 'for the greater part inhabited by English and such Irish as were never in rebellion: divers of the English and many more of the Irish attended all that evening on the coast, not to get plunder, but to preserve the men whom it should please God to bring ashore'. The *Two Brothers* had made the West Indies run several times, but the ship was old and hardly seaworthy. A second ship *Sapphire*, out of Carrickfergus, started to founder and was driven back to Cork harbour in a near sinking state with 260 men commanded by Colonel Moore. According to the official report the ship 'sprang a leak and was forced back to Cork, the vessel being so old and crazy that she was not able to abide the seas'. Colonel Moore and his men finally embarked for the West Indies in March, 1657, in a ship called *Plain Dealing*.

Henry was angry that the two ships, which were so obviously in a bad state of repair, could have been allowed to go to sea. He wrote: 'I think that those who were employed to contract for those ships are deeply guilty of the loss of those poor men.' Later in the month another ship from Barbados put into Kinsale and reported she had 'met a fleet bound for Jamaica in the trade wind safe and well which we hope may be Lt. General Braine and the rest of the fleet that went hence'.

In November Henry himself had a narrow escape from severe injury or even death. On November 15 the Earl of Cork wrote in his diary that he had gone hunting with Henry on his estate 'and at my return did dine with him and spent most part of the afternoon with him. That day his horse fell upon him and he was saved from being dragged, his foot hanging in the stirrup, by my catching hold of the bridle'.

Henry was back in Dublin again towards the end of the month where a new crisis awaited him. For some months now the Anabaptist opposition had remained remarkably quiet. In October, in fact, the Anabaptist preacher, Thomas Patient, had even called upon Henry and expressed satisfaction with his administration. Now four prominent Anabaptist officers had announced their intention of resigning in protest at Henry's rule. They were Quartermaster-General Vernon, Adjutant-General Allen, Colonel Daniel Axtell and Colonel Robert Barrow. In a discussion with Henry they announced they were resigning because 'the Godly were discouraged and wicked men countenanced', according to Vernon. Axtell said Henry had interfered with his command and Allen simply said he was dissatisfied with the change of government.

The officers clearly thought their threatened resignation would cause Henry and his Council some consternation and that he would either refuse to accept the resignations or make martyrs of them by imprisoning them for disaffection. Instead Henry merely accepted the resignations which left them powerless. Henry wrote to Thurloe on December 3:

The Anabaptists, whose ways and principles were inconsisted with settlement and our interest, do find themselves disabled from doing much harm. My inclination now is, having brought them to good terms, not to crush them quite, lest through despair they attempt things dangerous; and withal lest others take the occasion to become insolent and violent, and so put us to new trouble. Besides it is against my conscience to bear hard upon any merely upon account of a different judgement, or to do anything that might make them think so.

On December 16 Thurloe, who approved of Henry's action, wrote to tell him that his father was considering who to send in place of the officers. He added: 'His Highness meets with his trials here at home of all sorts, being daily under exercise from one hand or other, and I wish he may not have occasion to say, my familiar friends in whom I trusted have lifted up the heel against me'. Just before Christmas Henry wrote that he did not want his father 'burdened by any miscarriage' of his. He had been under the doctor's care that morning and his little daughter who had been ill for some time was now 'well recovered'.

One piece of news did cheer Henry. On December 27 the lawyer, Bulstrode Whitelock, has proposed to Parliament that the 4,000 acre estate of Portumna, its manor, park and lands, which had formerly belonged to Lord Clanricarde, should be awarded to Henry. Vincent Gookin also suggested that a further 2,000 acres in Connaught be added to this estate. Parliament enthusiastically approved the proposal.

CHAPTER 4

THE LORD DEPUTY

'droves of fluffy Saxons'

In 1657 the Cork poet Dáibhí Ó Bruadair of Cnoc Rátha wrote of Ireland as *A Bheith na Lubh*—O Lady of the plaited tresses. He addressed Ireland as the faithless wife of ancient heroes, asking why she had forsaken her true lovers who used to guard her honour. Why had she left them to gaze at her ringleted tresses while she delivered herself up to the English?

> It pains my breast to see her fertile sloping mantle
> trodden, trampled down by droves of fluffy Saxons.
> Those lands which proudly swelled with dewdrops dazzling
> while strains of music sounded in the cloudy mansion
> her grass meadows fair, adorned with branching thickets,
> without defect or flaw beside the river harbours,
> therefore is my fear construed to flow, o stately darling,
> calm and condescending, yet so false and fickle.

Things were not going well for 'the droves of fluffy Saxons'. In January, 1657, there were three separate attempts to assassinate the Lord Protector under the general direction of the Leveller colonel Edward Sexby. Arrests were made including that of another Leveller, Miles Sindercombe, who escaped execution by committing suicide. Thurloe revealed the plots to a horrified Parliament on January 19 and a service of thanksgiving was ordered for January 23. In an address congratulating the Lord Protector on his escape John Ashe, a member for Somerset, moved a rider 'that His Highness would be pleased to take upon himself the government according to the ancient constitution so that the hopes of our enemies in plots would be at an end'. The interpretation was clear; Oliver Cromwell was offered the Crown.

On Monday, February 23, a document entitled *The Humble Address and Remonstrance*, later adapted into the *Hum-*

ble Petition and Advice, asked the Lord Protector to revise
the constitution so as to permit the assumption by himself
of the 'name, style, title and dignity of King'. The address
was moved by the former Lord Mayor of London, Sir Christopher Packe. Lawyers like Thurloe, Bulstrode Whitelock and
Sir John Glyn supported the idea together with Broghill and
the majority of representatives from Ireland. Of the military,
however, only Skippon favoured it. The scheme was presented
to the Lord Protector on March 31. Europe as well as the
Commonwealth waited, firmly believing that Cromwell
would accept. On April 3 the Protector called the petitioners
into the Banqueting Hall in Whitehall. He prevaricated on
a definite answer and deferred the matter. It was on Friday,
May 8, at 11 a.m. that the Lord Protector met representatives
of Parliament in the Painted Chamber to deliver his answer.

> You do necessitate my answer to be categorical; and you have left
> me without a liberty of choice to save as to all ... I am not able
> for such a trust and charge ... I have not been able to find it my
> duty to God and you to undertake this charge under that title.

He added:

> ... I say, I am persuaded to return this answer to you, that I
> cannot undertake this government with that title King, and that's
> my answer to this great weighty business.

Henry's personal feelings had been entirely against the
assumption of kingship. Kingship, he had written to Thurloe, was merely 'a gaudy feather in the hat of authority'.
There were, however, more immediate problems to be con-
tended with. Henry had clashed with the Ulster Presbyterians when they had refused to celebrate the Lord Protector's escape from Sexby's assassination plots. He wrote to
his father that the Presbyterians had kept a day of religious
humiliation instead. Nevertheless, he ordered Colonel Arthur
Hill to draw up a list of all Presbyterians whose names appeared on the civil list who had not celebrated the day accordingly. The Presbyterian ministers sent two of their
number to see Henry in Dublin, John Hort and John Greg,
and these further enraged him by saying that the matter was
not a worldly consideration but a question of conscience.

Rumours of insurrection and invasion were still rife. On

February 24 General Monck wrote to Henry 'that Charles Stuart intends this summer (if monies do not fail him) to give us some trouble both in Ireland and Scotland and I hear the Earl of Ormonde is come over to Ireland and also Inchiquin'. Monck adds: 'I have a great ambition to be a planter under your Excellency if I could get but liberty to be loose from my command here which I hope in a short time I shall have.'

Two months later a message in cipher was sent to Lord Muskerry and Sir George Hamilton, who were living in Spain, requesting them to ask the King of Spain for aid with men, arms and ammunition to be transported to Ireland. This was the same month that Major-General John Reynolds was withdrawn from Ireland to command 6,000 foot against the Spanish in Flanders. Reynolds was soon to marry the sister of Henry's wife. When the Lord Protector had tried to send Reynolds on the Jamaican expedition the previous year Henry had written: 'If you take him from hence you deprive me of my right hand.' But now Henry was more sure of his position. On January 20 the royalist agent, Sir Alan Broderick, wrote to Sir Edward Hyde: 'Will Pate (Henry Cromwell) has rendered himself almost master of Little Lewes (Ireland).'

But to be 'almost' master of Ireland was not good enough in Cromwellian eyes. The problem was a threefold one and was summed up by Major Anthony Morgan, elected Member of Parliament for Wicklow, when addressing Parliament on June 10, that year.

We have three beasts to destroy that lay heavy burdens on us. The first is the wolf, on whom we lay five pounds a head if a dog, and ten pounds if a bitch. The second beast is a priest, on whose head we lay ten pounds—if he be eminent, more. The third beast is a Tory on whose head, if he be a public Tory, we lay twenty pounds and forty shillings on a private Tory. Your army cannot catch them. The Irish bring them in: brothers and cousins cut one another's throats.

In the early months of 1657 the Tories had been fairly quiet. In April Lt.. Francis Rowlestone was paid £6 13s. 4d. for his good services in killing two Tories. One was Henry Archer, a former officer in the Irish army and now a guerilla leader of some repute, and the other was William Shaaffe, a brogue maker, who was under Archer's command. Rowlestone delivered the severed heads of the Tories to Major Redmond at Kilkenny. On May 12 Captain Adam Loftus was paid £20 for seizing Daniel Kennedy, another Tory leader. Kennedy was executed and his head was spiked on the walls of the castle at Carlow to serve as a warning.

To the English colonists the Irish were all scathingly known as Teigs, derived from the common Irish Christian name of Tadhg. To the Irish, all the English colonists were similarly known by the name of Ráif, from the then common English Christian name of Ralph.

But while the Tory activity was not so noticeable in the early months of 1657, there was increased activity from the Catholic priesthood which was meeting with increased repression from the administration. In spite of Henry's new policy of imprisoning all priests in Ireland some 'irreconcilables', like Father Rowland Comyn, were still shipped for Barbados. The majority, in accordance with Henry's plan, were exiled to the Aran Islands, lying thirty miles out in the Atlantic opposite the entrance to the bay of Galway. Later, it was the stormbeaten isle of Inishbofin off the northwest Connemara coast which became the prison for the remaining priests. On March 5 it was agreed that the sum of 6d a day be set aside for the maintenance of the priests and the order was transmitted to Lieutenant Colonel Hunt, the governor of the island.

In spite of the repression the priesthood worked on. Father Agapitus of the Holy Ghost, who was running the affairs of the Carmelite Order, was in Dublin in 1657. He reported that there were two Carmelites in Dublin at the time plus a few Jesuits, several Dominicans, three Franciscans, a secular priest—one Father Patrick Reilly—who ministered to their flocks in disguise within the city boundaries. Father Agapitus had several narrow escapes from arrest and once, in the company of Father Charles Nolan, Vicar-General of the Diocese of Leighlin, he just managed to escape from pursuing troopers by running into a wood and hiding. After staying in Dublin for a time, Father Agapitus spent two years in Wexford and was the only priest in the city until the arrival of two secular priests, two Franciscans and a Teresian friar. He then went to Kildare and Meath, where he became friendly with Bishop MacGeogeghan before leaving Ireland in 1660.

In 1657 another Carmelite, Father Lawrence of St. Teresa, who had been born in Drogheda in 1625, arrived in Meath to minister to the Catholics there. Father Lawrence had studied in Aquitaine, France, and in Rome. He was later to acquire a reputation as a leading Teresian theologian, being made professor of theology at the College of Bologna and also lecturing at Cremona. He finally became Prior of the Missionary College of St. Pancratius in Rome. In Meath he began to try to organise the shattered diocese. Informers soon reported his presence to the local garrison but Father Lawrence managed to avoid arrest until September 11, when he was seized and imprisoned. He remained in Drogheda jail for three years. At the same time Father Keirnan, another Carmelite, was arrested and imprisoned for six years before finally being transported. Yet another Carmelite, Father Patrick, managed to escape execution as a rope was being placed round his neck. He made his way to Italy where he gained a reputation for his missionary work.

In June, that year, the Protector's Parliament decided to make an Oath of Abjuration statutory for all suspected Catholics.

I ... abhor and abjure the authority of the Pope as well in regard of the Church in general, as in regard of myself in particular. I condemn and anathematize the tenet that any reward is due to good works. I firmly believe and avow that no reverence is due to the Virgin Mary, or to any other saint in heaven, and that no petition of adoration can be addressed to them without idolatry. I assert that no worship or reverence is due to the sacrament of the Lord's Supper or to the elements of bread and wine after consecration, by whomsoever that consecration may be made. I believe there is no purgatory but that it is a Popish invention, so is also the tenet that only the Pope can grant indulgences. I also firmly believe that neither the Pope nor any other priest can remit sins, as the Papists rave. And all this I swear.

Cromwell, with his usual leaning towards liberty of religious conscience, told the French Ambassador, Antoine de Bordeaux, that the oath would only be mildly enforced. Any

Catholic refusing to submit to the oath would have to forfeit two-thirds of his property. Nevertheless, however mildly
enforced the oath was in England, it was rigidly applied in
Ireland. The Irish Catholics immediately resisted. A report
to the Sacred Congregation of Propaganda reported that the
inhabitants of Cork refused to take the oath. A young man,
who had listened to the authorities read the oath in the
cathedral, had then requested them to read it in Irish so
that the people could understand it. He then refused to take
the oath and was applauded by the people, who followed his
example.

A former friar, John Coffey, who took the oath, reported
that he had been threatened with physical violence by out-
raged Catholics. But many people did take the oath as the
poet Seán Ó Conaill recalled in his poem, written that year,
Tuireadh na hEirinn (Dirge of Ireland).

> After all they sent across the Shannon in slavery...
> others took oathes, framed for their oppression.
> They are without wealth but with much lies.

Henry realised the dangers involved in enforcing the oath
too strictly. He wrote to Thurloe on September 23.

> The oath of abjuration begets much disturbance here, for the Irish,
> upon apprehension thereof, sell off their cattle to buy horses to put
> themselves into a shifting condition either for force or flight... I
> wish His Highness were made sensible hereof in time.

Dr. Henry Jones added that the oath 'was the great engine
by which the Popish clergy stir up the people, and whereby
they move foreign states to their assistance'.

But the over-riding problem for Henry was still the
colonisation scheme. In April William Wallace, an agent
for financiers settling in the barony of Duliek, Co. Meath,
adjoining Drogheda, complained that many Catholic proprietors were still on their estates. Henry was being pres-
surised to take stronger action. Rumour had it that Henry's
liberalism would again be replaced by Fleetwood's harder
policies if the colonisation did not proceed satisfactorily.
Cormac MacCarthy, the son of Lord Muskerry, wrote to Sir
Edward Nicholas on July 6, reporting as fact that Henry
was returning to England to be replaced by Fleetwood. But
there was little danger of this for the Lord Protector seldom

interfered in Henry's administration except to send notes of recommendation or fatherly advice.

Despite the slowness of the colonisation policy it was, at least, proceeding. Early in the year Cromwell had personally intervened again to point out a case worthy of investigation to Henry. William Spenser had had his land confiscated as an 'Irish Papist'. William was the grandson of Edmund Spenser (1552–99), the English poet famous for the moral allegory *The Faërie Queene*. Spenser had been a colonist in Munster under Elizabeth's administration, having settled at Kilcolman beside the River Blackwater. He had a great hatred for the native Irish and deplored those of his fellow English colonists who were learning their language and adopting their ways, becoming, as he put it, 'mere Irish'. Now, ironically, his grandson was being ordered to transplant as an 'Irish Papist'. Spenser wrote to Cromwell pleading for exemption from transplantation. He was renouncing Catholicism, he said, and added that at the start of the 1641 insurrection he and his mother had gone to Cork city and lived in the English quarter there and had never engaged in any activity against the English. Cromwell wrote on March 27, 1657, to Henry: 'If upon enquiry you shall find his case to be such, we judge it just and reasonable and do therefore desire and authorise you, that he be forthwith restored to his estate and that reprisal land be given to the soldiers elsewhere.'

In the early summer of the year one of the richest of the new landowners arrived in Ireland. He was forty-six-year-old Erasmus Smith. Smith had been apprenticed to a poultry merchant named John Saunders of London at the age of seventeen. After seven years he was made a freeman of the Grocers' Company. His father, a London merchant and alderman of the city, Sir Roger Smith, had been a supporter of Parliament. A cousin, Sir Edward, was one of the first members of the Irish Adventurers' Committee and subsequently one of the Commissioners for the Court of Claims in Dublin, which approved of the land grant to Erasmus. Sir Edward became a Chief Justice of Pleas in Dublin, was converted to Catholicism and left Ireland in 1680 .

Erasmus' father, Sir Roger, first took out bonds for Irish

land in 1642/3 worth £375. He gave them to his son 'in consideration of his natural love towards him'. Erasmus, in the meantime, had gone into business on his own and, in 1649, was supplying the Parliamentary Army in Ireland. As an army contractor over the next four years he made a tremendous profit and during 1653/4 purchased debentures from other financiers and from soldiers to the value of £2,698 to which he continued to add until in 1657 his total allotment of land was worth £13,082.

On April 28, 1657, he had been elected an Alderman for Billingsgate ward in London but resigned, gave up his London business and moved to Ireland as the country's principal landowner. He bought a house in St. Stephen's Green, Dublin, and applied himself to education problems. As a friend of many highly placed people, whom he carefully cultivated, Smith managed to retain hold of all his possessions during the Restoration and Williamite confiscations. In 1657 he had obtained 5,750 acres in Connaught, an area in which no financier was supposed to hold lands under the Cromwellian ordinance. These lands he gave away in trust in December, 1657, for education purposes in which £300 per annum was to be laid out in support of five schools 'for teaching of grammar and the original tongues, and to write, read and cast accounts'. Had Smith not given away the lands they would doubtless have been confiscated when the mistake became known. This astuteness on Smith's part won him a place in Irish history as a benefactor to Irish education.

The 'clearing of the Irish' was also proceeding slowly. On April 3 the Protestant coopers in Dublin had their Catholic counterparts removed from the city and on October 10 the Protestant shoemakers had a similar order made against their Catholic rivals in business. But the Irish were still a strong community in Dublin. In fact, that year the colonists in Dublin presented a petition to the Municipal Council.

Whereas by the laws all persons ought to speak and use the English tongue and habit—contrary whereunto and in open contempt thereof, there is Irish commonly and usually spoken and the Irish habit worn not only in the streets and by such as live in the country and come to this city, to the scandalising of the inhabitants and magistrates of this city. And whereas there is much of swearing and cursing used and practised, as in the English tongue too much, so also in the Irish tongue.

Acts 'for the assuming, confirming and settling of lands and estates in Ireland' on June 9 and an 'Act for the Attainder of Rebels in Ireland' on June 26, were passed by Parliament to help the process of transplantation.

Lord Broghill, who had been a prime mover in asking Cromwell to assume the kingship, was very active in the Parliament. He was impressed by Cromwell's spy system and tried to institute his own. By his efforts he secured the release of the Royalist Sir Robert Walsh on condition that he forwarded intelligence from the exiled court of Charles Stuart. After Cromwell refused the crown, Broghill approached him with a startling suggestion—a marriage should be arranged between Charles Stuart and Cromwell's daughter Frances. According to Broghill's chaplain, Morrice, Cromwell thought about the matter but believed Charles would never forgive him the death of his father. Cromwell's guilt 'lay so heavy upon him' that to Broghill's regret 'that business broke off'.

On June 26 Cromwell again assumed the title of Lord Protector in a state ceremonial at Westminster. The news reached Dublin on an English packet which docked on July 4. The Council issued a proclamation that July 9 would be a day of celebration in honour of the event. On that day the Council met at 8 a.m. in the Council Chamber at Cork House and proceeded to Christ Church to listen to Dr. Harrison preaching 'a most judicious and religious sermon'. There was a large parade afterwards and the proclamation of the Protectorship was published at Castle Gate, Bridge Gate, the Corn Market and Toll Gate. There were 'bonfires, fireworks and noise of cannon which, with other expressions, concluded the day' says a chronicler, obviously not waiting till the day was over because of the departure of the packet for England that evening. *Mercurius Politicus* of July 23–30 reported 'the great concourse of people who came out of the remoter parts of that province into this city were not the least thing considerable in this day's work'.

'I am at my wit's end'

The time had now come for Henry to set out on his annual tour of inspection. This year he decided to go to the province of Ulster and then on to his estate at Portumna 'intending', wrote William Steele to Thurloe on July 22, 'I believe, to be abroad five or six weeks to see in what posture the north part is in, as to garrison and otherwise'. The tour of inspection was the only thing which brought satisfaction to Henry that autumn. Before he left on the tour Henry had discovered that another petition was being sent to his father asking that he be made Lord Deputy of Ireland. He asked Steele and Bury of the Council 'to prevent further spreading of that business' but it was too late. The petition had already been sent to London. Henry wrote to Thurloe on August 8.

If the rumour of any such things come to His Highness ear I desire you would oblige me to assure him that no part of this whole proceeding was in the least with my privitie or consent, either before or afterwards being a course which I extremely dislike.

Thurloe assured Henry that Cromwell realised it was not of his doing.

Henry was back in Dublin on September 9. He was seething against the Anabaptists who were still making difficulties for his administration. In particular he was angry with the governor of Athlone, Lieutenant Colonel Alexander Brayfield, who was also the field commander of Henry's own regiment of foot. Henry, who regarded Brayfield as one of the Anabaptists who had been intriguing against him, decided to court martial him and wrote justifying himself to Thurloe. Thurloe thought that cashiering Brayfield was too strong a measure and Broghill, who had arrived back in Ireland at the end of August, offered to mediate between Henry and Brayfield. Even the Lord Protector wrote admonishing his son on October 13. But Henry remained unforgiving and Brayfield was dismissed from the army.

Henry did not remain long in Dublin before he left for Kilkenny. Broghill came from his residence at Youghal to meet him there, and wrote to General Edward Montague on November 6:

I make, by conversing with him (Henry) and observing of him every day new discoveries of eminent things in him; such truly convinces us all he is fit to be our Chief Governor before he have a patent for it, which is both our trouble and satisfaction. He has indeed a great gift in reading men.

In spite of the offices of state, Henry had found time to occupy himself with his estate at Portumna, Co. Galway and had employed an architect to redevelop it. Daniel Thomas, senior, reported to Henry on October 6 that a new bridge would have to be erected at Portumna. Thomas had managed to get some English sawyers of timbers. 'Sawyers, especially English, both in Dublin and all the nation over are very rare and scarce to be had,' he pointed out. Thomas 'would speedily settle into the business at Portumna, that by this time twelve months I would by God His good assistance be able to give your Excellency a great and good account'. He would also bring some good English families to settle on Henry's estate. But his work was delayed by reason of the oath of abjuration for 'the Irish workmen are run away from me, for since the oath of abjuration is come amongst them, they had rather do any man's work than build places of strength what may subdue and keep them in obedience and have scattered themselves some ten, some twenty and some forty miles from me'. On October 15 he added: 'how much overjoyed the country on both sides of the Shannon is in the hopes of your lord's good intentions concerning the building of the Bridge of Portumna.'

On November 21 Colonel Walters arrived from England and 'immediately attended His Excellency and presented him with his commission'. Henry was to replace Fleetwood as Lord Deputy of Ireland. On Tuesday, November 24 'about two o'clock in the afternoon' the Council Chamber was packed while the commission was read. Dr. Harrison offered a prayer, 'then the great guns fired, the town bells rang, fireworks and bonfires were made with great testimonies of

rejoicing among the people', said the *Mercurius Politicus* of
November 26–December 3.

At the same time that Henry received the news of his new
office he heard that his sister Mary had married Lord Fauconberg, who was subsequently to become a close friend by
correspondence. General Monck was writing again, expressing his 'great ambition to be a planter under our excellency
if I could see His Highness a little better settled in his
affairs'.

It was, however, a bad month for Henry. On December
14 Henry's 'right hand', Sir John Reynolds, had perished in
a great storm when his ship was wrecked on the Goodwin
Sands. It had only been two short months since Reynolds
had married the sister of Henry's wife. Although Henry felt
the loss greatly the affairs of Ireland could permit no mourning. He was in a great quandary over the financial situation,
which was growing to crisis proportions. On December 2 he
had confessed to Fleetwood that 'the army being eight
months in arrears and no money in the treasury . . .' To his
father on the same day he asked for leave 'to come to England
and for a small time at a convenient season' to see the Lord
Protector. He asked that £180,000 be sent immediately. 'It
being no more than what will appear to be justly due as the
arrears of our allowance from England.' To Broghill Henry
confessed 'there is still some secret cause in England why we
are thus neglected here. I confess I know not what will become of us without speedy supplies. I wish I could be in
England to untie this knot which entangles our affairs'.
Broghill promised to support Henry's plea when he returned
to England on December 24 to take a seat in a new 'upper
chamber' of Parliament which Cromwell had decided to
form. In the meantime Fleetwood was unsympathetic to
Henry's complaints and wrote to tell him so in no uncertain
terms. Henry waited a week before replying on December 30.

> I take no pleasure in complaining and am sorry that those griev-
> ances, among their other ill effects, should raise any misunderstand-
> ing between us. The truth is, when I look around about upon our
> affairs, I am at my wit's end and too apt to resent things too
> deeply. . . .

On January 5, 1658, Henry despatched Major Anthony

Morgan to London to acquaint the Lord Protector with 'the state of several matters fit for your knowledge'. Morgan and Lord Broghill were to press the importance of the economic crisis. Henry also sent another agent, James Standish, the Paymaster-General, to explain the situation more fully. To Thurloe on February 24 Henry explained:

> ... besides the country, to whom the army is in score, will be all in a flame for poor people must not loose their debts, who are daily peeled so many other ways; as namely the assessments (a heavenly charge) collections for repairing the bridges, session houses, market places etc. add to all this the great misery of base coin ...

Henry already 'had a hint of some design of Londonderry but I shall eye the place with other garrisons'.

London had its own problems. Parliament, having recessed in the summer of 1657, opened a new session on January 20, 1658. As well as the House of Commons, the Lord Protector had re-constituted an Upper House, generally known as the 'Other House' which was made up from some of Cromwell's ablest supporters—men like General Lambert, Broghill and others who were made 'lords' by Cromwell. In the Lower House 100 opponents of the Protectorate, excluded from office by Cromwell's Council of State, managed to take their seats under the new constitution. Republicans led by Arthur Haselrig and Thomas Scot immediately attacked the Upper House. They were in a strong position, for Cromwell needed finance and the Commons aggressively declared that grievances must be redressed before they would vote him more funds. While the republicans were organising a petition to deny any right of House of Lords status for the 'Other House', the Royalists were also intriguing. In late January Cromwell informed Lord Broghill that 'a great friend of his was in town'. The 'great friend' was Lord Ormonde who, in disguise, was staying in the capital, firstly with a Catholic chirurgeon and then a French tailor somewhere near Blackfriars. He was being hidden by a Catholic secret society, the Sealed Knot, one of whose members, Sir Richard Wallys, was an agent for Thurloe and kept him informed of every move made by Ormonde. Cromwell did not want to order the arrest of Ormonde, which would probably lead to his trial and execution, because such action

would do more harm than allowing Ormonde to escape
quietly abroad. Broghill, taking Cromwell's hint, warned
Ormonde who immediately left for France. Thurloe reported
to Henry:

> It's certain that Ormonde was here to treat with our great men and
> some that never were before in open arms against the Parliament, but
> I believe his encouragements were not so great as he expected.

Such was the republican opposition in the Commons on
the subject of the 'Other House' that Cromwell's next action was predictable. On February 4 he dissolved Parliament. Even Fleetwood remonstrated with him over this at
which the Lord Protector cried: 'You are a milksop! By the
living God, I will dissolve the house!'

Broghill decided to retire from too close a connection
with the Protector's regime. He maintained that his gout
was troubling him, using this as an excuse to leave active
politics. But he was an astute man. The Protector had recently had two bouts of severe illness and so Broghill
reasoned, if he collapsed, with the current unrest caused by
the Royalist party, the restoration of the monarchy would
be inevitable. So Broghill thought it prudent to detach
himself from the Protector's circles. Cromwell, now entering his sixtieth year, was a much altered man, melancholy
and pensive. According to Broghill he 'seem'd afraid of
everybody'. Assassination attempts certainly made Cromwell
extremely cautious. On one occasion Broghill was riding
with him in his coach from Westminster to Whitehall when
it was halted in a narrow street. A man with a pistol opened
the door and lunged at the Protector. Broghill narrowly
averted his death by striking out at the man with the scab-
bard of his sword. Dropping the pistol, the man fled. In mid
August Broghill quietly returned to Ireland and took up
residence at Ballymaloe House, near Cork.

In the meantime the financial problem was no nearer
a solution. Paymaster-General Standish returned to Ireland
in June without any decision being made. On March 16
Thurloe wrote to Henry:

> The great want is money which puts us to the wall in all our
> business. But truly, my lord, nothing troubles us more than your

condition which I find everybody sensible of and this afternoon we are to come to a meeting with the money men to turn every stone for the supply of Ireland. What will come of it I know not.

Henry tried to forget the money problem by attending to his own estate at Portumna. Sir Charles Coote had gone to inspect it and he wrote to Henry on March 20:

...if your lordship will accept of the rents mentioned in this rent roll the tenants will submit unto the same.

Most of the tenants, 'as will appear by their names', were English and would make improvements, and for a lease of twenty-one years Coote's Lieutenant Colonel would undertake to repair the Castle of Lismore and 'bestow £200 thereon and on the lands'. Henry's lands would yield up £665 5s. annually from some 1,782 arable acres 'which lies in a waste country on the Shannon side and at present, I fear, will not yield much, yet it is good land and nobly wooded and in the future may rise to a considerable interest'.

But the worries of state were telling on Henry's health. Both he and his wife were prey to sickness. His wife had been seriously ill although, in March, she had borne his third child at Dublin Castle. The season was bad and there was generally more illness than was usual.

For the native Irish there seemed no respite from their sufferings. That year a poet named Eamonn Mac Donnchadh an Dúin from Ulster wrote a poem which opened with the lament:

> Mo la léoin go deo go n-éagad
> My day of grief forever until I die
> and go to lie alone under a stone,
> until the resurrection of Judgement Day
> that sets back the flood that has reached you, O Ireland!

His poem was no vague lament but a detailed and vivid picture of the ravages of the sword, famine and plague, the transportations and transplantations and the executions. Mac Donnchadh wrote of his anguish as he saw the slaughter and the heads of executed Irish heroes put on spikes. 'Were I to die or my limbs to be torn apart I could not colour the story of the fate of the progeny of free princes,' he wails.

While Tories hunted in the mountain, claimed Mac Donnchadh, those left inside towns and villages who had done
no wrong had to pay for everything the Tories did. If a man
had a relation with the Tories he was arrested. Some people
tried to bribe the judges. Other people took up the trade of
spying to betray the Irish to the English, some sold their
relations to the enemy, others betrayed the hiding places of
the clergy.

Mac Donnchadh cries:

> Transport! transplant! my ears are deafened by English,
> Shoot him, kill him, strip him, tear him,
> A Tory, hack him, hang him, rebel,
> a rogue, a thief, a priest, a papist . . .

Dáibhí ó Brudair of Cnoc Rátha found he could only
write *Guagán ghiega*, jingling trifle. In this short poem,
which describes things of frequent occurrence in the lives of
the ordinary people with a shrewd wit, common sense and
keen observation, the Cork poet explains:

> *An uair nach chuni cion ar cheil i nduan*
> When I see how people set no value on poetic wit
> and when to run in steps of sages brings to no one any joy
> when heroes of the Fenians stand no longer up erect
> an empty jingle is the only poetry which suits my mind.

Father Richard Shelton, now the Superior of the Jesuits
in Ireland, reported to the Sacred Congregation on April
28 that two priests of his order had been arrested. He adds:

> . . . every effort is now made to compel Catholics by exile, imprison-
> ment, confiscation of goods and other penalties, to take the sacrilegi-
> ous oath of abjuration, but all in vain, for as yet there has not been
> even one to take it, with the exception of a stranger residing in our
> island, who had acquired large possessions and being afraid of losing
> them, and at the same time being ashamed of the other Catholics,
> undertook a journey of more than 200 miles to present himself to one
> of Cromwell's Commissioners.

The Pope had sent a Brief consoling the Catholics of
Ireland and seeking to animate them to greater faith in order
to endure their persecution. Although Irish Catholics signed
a petition on April 22 asking the government to relieve their
sufferings, there were hardly any arrests of priests in the

early months of 1658. Significantly on June 9 Major Brian Smith reported that the numbers of 'desperate Irish' sheltering priests in the mountains were increasing. On February 28 William Handcock was given £50 to build cabins on Inishbofin for the priests interned there. Henry had not become lax in searching for priests, who were also, in a large number of cases, Royalist agents. In May he noticed that more messengers than usual were arriving in Dublin and had a search made of the city at midnight in order to 'have an account of every stranger and his business'. On August 23 he ordered that any horses or arms belonging to Catholics in the city were to be confiscated.

The Irish in Meath embarrassed the administration on October 27 by carrying out a daring rescue of a priest who had just been imprisoned. Towards the end of the year the arrests began again, but Father Galatius Hickey, writing from Clonmel, reported to the Sacred Congregation that the administration's attempts to suppress the clergy and convert the Catholics were not as strong as they had been before.

The Irish now had a new Primate. O'Reilly was consecrated Archbishop of Armagh on May 26 at Brussels. On July 20 he wrote a letter to Pope Alexander announcing that he was going to London for a few weeks before proceeding to Ireland. His appointment had upset the Royalist priests, such as Father Peter Talbot and Walsh. It was, in fact, Walsh who approached Cromwell's Council of State and betrayed O'Reilly's presence to them. O'Reilly, who had just reported to the secretary of the Sacred Congregation that English Catholics were enjoying more religious freedom under Cromwell than at any time since Mary's reign, was ordered to quit England on December 26.

In the meantime O'Reilly's other antagonist, Peter Talbot, had just published a book in Antwerp that year under the pseudonym of 'N.N.' The title of the study was *The Politicians Cathecisme for his instruction in divine faith and moral honesty*. In this work Talbot argued that Protestantism induced the ruler to tyranny and the people to rebellion, and that the Pope's spiritual jurisdiction was not dangerous to sovereigns but rather the ground of fidelity and obedience to them, which was utterly destroyed by denying the Pope's supremacy. Catholicism was the foundation of all justice.

Talbot maintained that Catholicism had been recognised by the English Parliament in 1649 and 1652 to the effect

... that the oath of abjuration shall not be administered to any in Ireland, but also an express article granted in a treaty to the Catholics of Ireland at Kilkenny the 12th May, 1652, in confidence whereof, and of much more to the same effect, the Irish submitted and laid down their arms, being assured that they should enjoy the freedom and liberty of their conscience, and not be molested ...

Henry was not as deeply troubled by Catholic opposition as he was by the problems of colonisation and the difficulties now arising from the occupation of the lands which had been surveyed for the army by Dr. Petty. The officers did not want to take up their estates before the financiers were allotted all the lands due to them. They felt they could obtain a better result by claiming 'dubious' lands not claimed by the financiers. Their eyes were on the rich lands in Co. Louth. Henry suggested that Petty go to England and meet with members of the Committee of Adventurers for Land in Ireland and give the army's petition on the matter to Thurloe. Henry wrote to Fleetwood on May 5: 'I shall say only this for him (Petty) that he has in all late transactions shown himself an honest man.'

While Petty was in London, Oliver Cromwell, Lord Protector of the Commonwealth of England, Scotland and Ireland, died. An era had all but ended.

'What shall become of us ...?'

Tragedy had first struck the Cromwell family that year, in 1658, when the Lord Protector's grandson, baby Oliver Claypole, youngest son of his daughter Elizabeth, had died in June. Elizabeth herself had died on August 6. Cromwell was so distracted with grief by this double tragedy that he had collapsed. By August 17 he had recovered a little from his prostration but Thurloe wrote to Henry to inform him that the Lord Protector's illness was causing 'great alarum'.

On the evening of August 17 the illness, characterised by pains in the bowels and back, returned. The Lord Protector was taken from Hampton Court to Whitehall. On August 24 Thurloe wrote to Henry that he was having what he termed as 'fits' but he had faith in Cromwell's ability to recover. He added: 'the doctors do not conceive there is any danger to his life'. It would seem that he was suffering from the 'tertian agues—a form of malaria, classified as P(plasmodium) Viviax, a usually non-fatal form of malaria which he had picked up during his campaign in Ireland. While the disease was rarely a cause of death it did weaken the sufferer by destroying haemoglobin in the red cells so as to make them susceptible to other diseases.

On Thursday, August 26, Cromwell was well enough to dine with the former commander-in-chief of the New Model Army, Sir Thomas Fairfax. The following day he was ill again. Thurloe wrote to Henry of his worry for the future. 'How we are like to be left as to outward appearances, I need not mention.' On Tuesday, August 31, Henry's brother-in-law Fauconberg wrote that Cromwell was beyond all hope of recovery. He rallied a little on Tuesday evening and learnt that the republican Ludlow had just arrived in London. He was sufficiently in command of his senses to send Fleetwood to find out what Ludlow was doing in the city. Ludlow assured Fleetwood he was merely on a visit to his mother-in-law.

On Thursday, September 2, the Council of State, realised all hope had ended, gathered round his bed to ask the semi-conscious man to nominate his successor. The name of his son Richard was put to him and he managed to make an affirmative sign. In the mid afternoon of September 3, 1658, Oliver Cromwell died.

The news did not reach Dublin until September 10. Henry had been increasingly depressed by the various reports from London. Now he raised himself momentarily from his grief to have his brother Richard proclaimed Lord Protector and then, on September 11, he wrote to Thurloe:

Let her highness, my dear mother, know that my affection is doubled when I think of her condition. Pray God comfort her. I do pray for her and I shall not cease but shall continue her obedient and affectionate son whilst I live. I shall not tell you how unexpressable my grief is.

In the meantime Richard sent to Ireland a Mr. Underwood, of the Lord Protector's staff, who had 'attended him in all his sickness'. Underwood was to give Henry full particulars of the illness as Royalist rumours were current that Cromwell had been poisoned. The news was received quietly in Ireland, as quietly as it had been in England where Thurloe reported:

God hath given His Highness, your brother, a very easy and peaceable entrance upon his government. There is not a dog that wags his tongue so great a calm are we in.

Dr. Harrison, Henry's chief chaplain and a preacher of some eloquence, preached a funeral sermon at Christ Church before Henry 'with divers of the nobility, gentry and commonality there assembled to celebrate a funeral solemnity'. This discourse was later published and dedicated to Richard Cromwell under the title *Threni Hybernici or Ireland sympathising with England and Scotland in a sad Lamentation for loss of their Josiah.*

Such a watchman of Israel was Josiah (Harrison said) such a watchman was our Josiah. It was no easy matter to surprise him. How securely did we sleep while he watched over us ... what shall become of us now that this watchman is fallen asleep?

Harrison had written to Thurloe on September 11 suggesting that Henry should now be made Lord Lieutenant of Ireland as 'a most open manifestation of that affection in the one and a further engagement to a perpetual reciprocation in the other and of general influence and advantage both at home and abroad'. But Henry had recoiled upon himself. Thurloe was troubled by thoughts that Henry had fallen ill, there being 'no letters from Ireland these three posts'. Later in the month Henry sent a personal letter to Richard pouring out his troubles with a freedom he had never been able to use with his father. On September 18 he wrote:

Since his late highness was pleased to place me in this station, I have met with nothing but toil and disquiet of body and mind and have thereby so exceedingly impaired my health that it is not possible for me to undergo the like any longer.

Fauconberg wrote on September 28 to Henry in cipher that he was to be made Lord Lieutenant. On October 6 Henry wrote to Thurloe that 'the very thought of it puts me into confusion'.

It was not until November 27 that the body of Oliver Cromwell was given an official burial after an attempt at embalming and a laying-in-state in Westminster Abbey. The numbed reaction of his death had now given way to plots and rumours of plots. The army was well to the fore in these affairs and Thurloe reported to Henry that 'there are some secret murmurings in the army as if His Highness were not General of the Army as his father was'. There was a strong rumour that Fleetwood had been designated to succeed as Lord Protector and, although Fleetwood supported Richard, certain army officers were for Fleetwood being given power. In October army officers met and demanded that a general be appointed commander-in-chief of the army and that in future no officer would be cashiered without a council of war being convened. Fleetwood was suspected of instigating the demands of the army. Richard replied that Fleetwood was already a Lieutenant General of the army and commanded it under the Lord Protector. Dissatisfaction was also reflected in the army in Ireland and Cornet Richard Whalley, a cousin of Cromwell, was dismissed from Henry's own regiment for refusing to recognise Richard as Protector. Fauconberg warned Henry that 'matters are drawing towards ruin and speedily if not prevented'. On October 20 Henry wrote to his brother: 'I thought those whom my father had raised from nothing would not so soon have forgot him and endeavour to destroy his family before he is in the grave.'

Henry had plenty of problems of his own with which to deal. The soldiers and financiers were now more than anxious to settle on their estates for, if a restoration of the monarchy were to come about, a different land distribution might be made. The soldiers were out for payment and there was a great deal of discontent, especially among the regiments stationed in the province of Munster many of whose allotments fell in the inhospitable regions of Kerry, still a stronghold of numerous guerilla bands.

Richard now confirmed Henry's appointment as Lord

Lieutenant of Ireland. Henry wrote on November 3 thanking him for the honour but confessing he had been in doubt whether to accept it. He deemed a visit to England more necessary than ever. Those in England 'render me a persecutor of good men and handle my reputation so rudely with their cobblers' thumbs that they have already begot a doubt amongst some good men (even my friends) whether all be well'. He begged Richard to give him permission to return. At the same time he wrote to Lord Broghill wishing 'with all my heart' that Richard had the benefit of Broghill's presence in London. On November 2 he had received a note from Fleetwood congratulating him on his new office which angered him, and to which he wrote an impassioned reply about the conditions in which he found himself. Fleetwood replied on November 9.

I do wonder what I have done to deserve such a severe letter from you . . . as for your coming to England, I am not the hinderer of it . . . I know of no design to keep you in Ireland, and shall be as glad to see you here as those who pretend more.

Henry's attackers were still Anabaptists. The leader of the current wave of attacks was Sir Hierome Sankey, whom Henry once thought a 'moderate man'. Sankey had, on October 22, 1652, ordered a survey of Kilmainham Manor, Leinster, to be carried out in his favour. He had been awarded 3,000 acres by lot and was supposed to have these lands awarded in Co. Kerry but he demanded lands in the better placed province of Leinster. The demand was rejected and Sankey turned wrathfully on Petty and Henry. In November an anonymous pamphlet was published in Dublin while Petty, who was now secretary of the Council of Ireland, was away in London on business for Henry. The pamphlet compared Henry to Henry VIII and Petty to Cardinal Wolsey, making a series of charges of dishonesty and corruption in the allotment of land to soldiers and financiers. If Sankey did not actually write the pamphlet he, at least, inspired it. It was 'a simple and salacious paper which truly I set nothing by' wrote Henry to Thurloe. It was referred to a body of forty leading army officers who then appointed a committee of seven to consider the facts. This committee asked Petty and his Committee of Distribution to reply to the charges by providing an authentic book of records showing in detail what had been done with the army's allotments. An order to this effect was published by the Irish Council on December 20, 1658. Petty answered the charge, saying that if facts were gone into it would be found that he was still owed sums of money for his work. The four civilians on the committee supported him but the three officers thought there were charges of corruption to be answered.

News that there was to be a new Protectorate Parliament arrived on November 29. Thurloe wrote to Henry that such a Parliament was 'a thing always usual at the beginning of every prince's reign' but the real reason was the poor financial state of the Commonwealth. Ireland was to send thirty members. The financial problems were more acute in Ireland and Fleetwood found he could only send £14,000 to Henry 'which was more intended for a supply to keep up the English coin amongst you than in answer to what the necessity of your forces doth want'.

Henry's letters had become brief and irregular again because of an illness. 'My indisposition hath been so and is so great that I have not written of late to my friends, and I hope both you and they will excuse me if I am able to do not more than sit and look on,' he wrote to Thurloe. But when Richard Pepys, a member of the Irish Council, died on January 2 in Dublin, Henry found he had to do more than 'look on'. There was the election to organise for the first parliament of Richard's Protectorate, due to sit on January 27, 1659. In spite of the cloud of suspicion hanging over him, Petty was among those elected, being returned for Kinsale and also for West Looe, in Cornwall.

Lord Broghill had come out of his retirement to represent Cork and started a dispute with Vincent Gookin, now representing Youghal. Broghill left for London with his sister, Lady Ranelagh and her daughters. En route for Bristol, just passing Minehead, the ship struck a shallow. Broghill hastened on deck and narrowly avoided having his brains beaten out by the detached rudder. His authority calmed the crew and the sails were taken down and the rudder secured under his orders. The ship reached Bristol in safety.

No one had any illusions about the new Parliament. Richard had opened it asking that it especially consider the settlement of arrears of pay for the army. Richard only had the support of half the House while there was a strong opposition of moderates, fifty republicans and an infiltration of Royalists. The first business was the introduction of a Bill agreeing 'to recognise and declare His Highness Richard, Lord Protector, to be Lord Protector and Chief Magistrate of England, Scotland and Ireland'. This was finally passed on February 14, 1659, by 223 votes to 134 votes. The Royalist John Barwick wrote to Sir Edward Hyde two days later:

> The proceedings at Westminster are so full of distraction that it is probable they will end in confusion. For the one party thinks the Protectorists cannot stand, and the other that the Commonwealth cannot rise, and those that are indifferent men hope both may be true; and then the conclusion will be easy to forsee and foretell.

The conclusion being the restoration of the Stuart monarchy.

One debate held a special interest for the English colonists in Ireland. On March 23 the House debated whether the members from Ireland should, with those from Scotland, sit in the House or sit in their own legislatures. Major Ashton, representing Cos. Meath and Louth, preferred a separate legislature in Dublin on the grounds that Ireland should have no share in running England. Arthur Annesley, for the city of Dublin, had the same opinion basically because Ireland would be overtaxed by an assembly where she was always in a minority. At that moment Ireland very unfairly paid £900 a month tax while Scotland paid £500 and his prayer was 'that they might have some to hear their grievances in their own nation seeing they cannot have them heard here'. Sir Thomas Stanley, representing Cos. Tipperary and Waterford, said that they spoke not for Ireland but for the English in Ireland 'language, habit, laws, interests being in every respect the same in kind'. He was in favour of the Union for free born Englishmen beyond the Channel had a natural right to be heard in the sovereign Parliament. The vote was 156 to 106 for the retention of the members from Ireland.

The day after this debate, on March 24, Sir Hierome Sankey rose in his place and delivered a startling speech.

> I open the highest charge against a member of this House that ever was: such news has not been of a long time; a high breach of trust. It is against a great person—the charge consists of several articles—1, bribery; 2, imposing money and lands. He is both cook, caterer and is Commissioner and Surveyor, and had the disposing of two million acres of lands. He is a man of great parts, and has greatly wronged them. His name—Dr. Petty.

Petty was absent and, after a short debate, it was agreed that Petty be asked to attend the House on April 21 to answer such charges. Thomas Brampfield, the Speaker, wrote to Petty on March 26 informing him of Sankey's allegations.

'Here be foul things ...'

Henry completely supported Petty. He wrote to Thurloe on April 11: 'I believe Parliament will find him as I have represented him. He has curiously deluded me these four years if he be found a knave ...' He added that 'Petty is not the only mark aimed at ...' The Anabaptist officers, led by Sankey, were determined to pillory Petty for the delays in the colonisation scheme and Sir Charles Coote actually wrote to Henry on March 29 advising him to drop his support of Petty.

On April 21 Sankey rose in the House to level six charges against Petty.

1. That the said Dr. Petty hath received great bribes.

2. That contrary to the Act 1653 ch. 12 p. 249 in Scobell's Collections, he hath made it his trade to purchase a vast number of debentures, he himself being the then Chief Surveyor, and hath used all other means to necessitate others to sell their debentures to him, or else denied to set them out their lands.

3. That by fraudulent and indirect means he hath got into his hands vast sums of money from the state, possessing himself of many thousand acres of land that he hath no right unto, having no claim thereto by lot or consent.

4. That he used many foul and unwarrantable practices during his employment of being surveyor and commissioner to the great wrong of others and the dishonour of the Commonwealth.

5. That the said Dr. together with his fellow Commissioners have placed many debentures upon the security which of right belonged to them.

6. That he, the said doctor, together with his fellow Commissioners have totally disposed of retaining part of the army's security contrary to law, the debt still remaining and chargeable upon the said.

Petty replied to all six charges in order. On the first charge he declared: 'I have not made profit enough to defray the incident charges of office.' On the second charge 'the vast sum of debentures I have bought are under £7,000 ... I never meddled with lands or debentures till this surveyorship, such as it was, was at an end ...' As for charge three, 'I never received money ... until I had first sufficiently tortured by reference, reports, examinations of all kinds'. On charge four 'I know not what answer to make ... the practices which I have used, both as a surveyor and Commissioner, are such as I can glory in ...' 'As to the two last ...,' charges five and six, 'I shall say nothing to them more than to tell you that my fellow Commissioners are grave persons, men of tried knowledge and integrity, not apt to deceive or easy to be deceived.'

He ended his speech to Parliament:

I have, sir, been so weary of the calumnies I be under that I have often endeavoured to bring myself to a trial, and I was to have been tried and heard within three or four days after I received your summons, but my adversaries had done more for me than I was able to do for myself, they have brought me to the best trial, to the highest and noblest judicature: I say, they have brought me to this fountain of justice, and I willingly throw myself into it to be washed from all that is foul and superfluous about me.

Sankey was given the opportunity to reply. He was on his feet and angry at the good impression Petty had made. Sankey was an excitable and a boring speaker and while he delivered his tirade, words tripping over each other in his excitement and indignation, the House fell to talking amongst itself. One member stood up and moved that Sankey put his charges in writing and the House proceed to the next business. Another member said the matter was already in writing as Sankey had his papers. A third member urged Sankey to proceed with the charges.

Why, then, Mr. Speaker, continued Sankey, there is Captain Went-worth came with an order for the liberties of Limerick; but the doctor said, Captain will you sell? will you sell? No, said the Captain, 'tis the price of my blood. Then, said the doctor, 'tis bravely said: why, my noble Captain, the liberties of Limerick are meat for your masters, meaning the Lord Deputy. Now, Mr. Speaker, who dishonours the Lord Deputy, the doctor or I? In my judgement, now, the doctor does. Then, Mr. Speaker, comes Lt. Colonel Brayfied for land, but the doctor asked whether he would sell. He said, no. Then, said the doctor, littleman, littleman, there is land for you beyond the moon. I have more yet, Mr. Speaker, there be fouler things yet, this is but half . . .

But the House was restless and kept interrupting. One member stood up and cried: 'Mr. Speaker, I admire that you forget yourself as to hearken to these private quarrels and neglect the public.' But another cried that Sankey should proceed and doggedly Sankey continued:

Mr. Speaker, I must speak, for I have foul things. Why, there is Balleboy, the barony of Balleboy, Mr. Speaker, the doctor has 7,000 acres in the barony of Balleboy, that he has no right to. And then there is the odd pence that he has taken all to make this debt swell; he has 18,000 acres and his debentures but amount to 5,000 acres. For our debentures, Mr. Speaker. come many times to five shillings and two pence, he take the two pence to himself and pays only 5s Then there is another thing, Mr. Speaker, I have it here in my papers, and that is Strafford's survey, which never cost him £20 and received £1,600 for it. These be foul things.

Another exasperated member again moved that the charges be put in writing. It was promptly seconded and Sankey was ordered to present them within one week. Sankey interrupted:

Mr. Speaker, I have but one short motion to make which is that all the original maps and books of reference which the doctor keeps, contrary to the Act of Parliament, may be brought into the Exchequer: for those are the books upon which we hold our estates, those are the records, and if we have not those Mr. Speaker we may be all undone.

Dr. Petty was on his feet: 'Mr. Speaker, the surveys upon which the soldiers deed are and must be grounded are already delivered into the Exchequer, and are kept there as records.'

The next day was Saturday and the House dissolved. San-

key accosted Petty in the corridor and said he expected repa-
rations. Petty replied that he did so as well. Sankey then
said he had not done with Petty but would continue to press
his charges against him. The doctor said he would await his
summonses with pleasure and walked away. A week passed
and Sankey did not produce the charges, so Petty decided
to return to Ireland reaching Dublin on May 12. Lord
Aungier had written to Henry on the evening of April 21 to
say 'all that troubles me is to consider that a person so rarely
qualified as is our learned doctor should be necessitated to
trifle away his time (like Don Quixote) in giving battle to
windmills and barbers' basins'.

Petty had returned to Ireland bringing a letter from
Fleetwood urging Henry to return to England to discuss
the increasingly perilous situation. There had been a rebirth
of the Leveller Party led by John Wildman, who, it was
rumoured, had plotted to kill Cromwell as early as 1647, and
Maximilian Petty (no relation to Sir William). A number of
pamphlets on social and constitutional programmes were
being published by the party. In February senior army officers had contacted the republican party, led by Haselrig and
Ludlow, to press a petition about the freedom of the military.
The attacks of Parliament on the military, who had been
Cromwell's instrument of obtaining power, led to a fresh
meeting in April ending in the presentation of a 'humble
address' on April 6 insisting in strong terms on the danger
to 'the good old cause' from intrigues of Royalists. Fleetwood had placed himself at the head of the movement which
refused to obey Richard in order, not to overthrow the Protectorate, but to merely grasp power himself. Towards the
end of March those opposed to Richard, like Fleetwood and
Desborough, formed the Wallingford House Party (the name
of Fleetwood's residence) as opposed to Richard's Whitehall
Party. Lord Broghill was alarmed by the growing opposition
of the army officers to Richard. At a meeting of the Council
of Officers on April 14 he spoke against the proposal to purge
the army by forcing every officer to swear that the execution
of Charles I was 'lawful and just' and bringing those who
refused before courts martial. Broghill advised Richard to
dissolve the Council, which he did, but the army officers

realised that Broghill was behind the measures. Broghill did indeed make an effort to steer Richard on a strong course against the extremist republicans and hard line Protectorate men but with senior officers like Fleetwood pitted against him he only just escaped from London while plans for his arrest were being drawn up. Most of the Munster regiments were personally loyal to Broghill and he headed towards their protection.

Fleetwood and Desborough, playing a delicate political game, urged Richard to dissolve Parliament, throw in his lot with the army and establish strong rule, as his father had done. 'I will not have a drop of blood spilt for the preservation of my greatness which is a burden to me,' declared Richard. But on April 21 he signed the order dissolving Parliament which was carried out on the following day. But Fleetwood's plan misfired. The army now demanded the recall of the Long Parliament which Cromwell had dissolved in 1653 and the re-establishment of the Commonwealth or republic as opposed to the Protectorate. There was nothing Fleetwood or Desborough could do to stem the tide. On May 26, 1659, the army invited the Long Parliament to re-assemble and the following day some forty-two survivors collected in the Painted Chamber at Westminster.

'I have resisted great temptation . . .'

The Royalists had not lost the opportunity to capitalise from the unsettled situation. On March 16 Petty reported to the Admiralty that a picaroon out of St. Sebastian had been raiding the Irish coast and had managed to escape from two frigates sent after her. It had, by all accounts, switched to raiding the north-west coast of England but had now returned and was lying off Dublin. It had raided seven or eight ships out of Chester bearing goods for Ireland. In April Captain Richard Cowes of the *Paradox*, out of Kinsale, was able to report that he had captured a galleon which had been commanded by Captain Nicholas Johnson, who had a commission signed by James Stuart. The galleon had

been one which 'hath this spring greatly annoyed and infested these parts'. The booty consisted of two guns, and
thirty-five men taken prisoner.

Generally speaking, Dr. Jones felt the country was fairly
peaceful. It was true, he said, in a letter to Thurloe, that the
Catholic clergy were coming over from Flanders 'more than
ordinarily' but 'the Irish are generally so quiet and certainly
without great assurances of powerful assistance from abroad,
they will not readily and rashly attempt what they are stirred
up into'.

The authorities in Dublin managed to seize a large consignment of Catholic books on April 22 'for the further
seducing and confirming of the Irish in their obstinate and
superstitious principles'. Robert Aiken of Dublin offered
the revenue officials £5 to allow the consignment through.
He claimed they were his uncle's books but when questioned
more closely said they belonged to Christopher Cleere of
Drogheda. Both men were arrested. Among the books were
a few copies of a work in Latin, published the previous
month in Innsbruck, entitled *Threnodia Hiberno-Catholica
sive Planctus Universalis Totius Cleri et Populi Regni
Hiberniae* which gave a detailed account of the suffering of
the Irish Catholics and their clergy. The work was written
by Father Maurice Conry OFM, a native of Thomond, who
studied at St. Isidore's College, Rome. In 1650 he had been
a member of the Irish Franciscan College in Prague where
he was made a Professor of Theology. He was on the domestic
council of the College in 1652. Very soon afterwards he
went to England on a mission and was arrested. For a time
he was held in London and then taken to Bristol where for
two and a half years he was imprisoned with the Quaker
James Naylor. He was released early in 1658 on condition
of banishment and went to Rome where he was asked to
examine two Quakers who had arrived there with the purpose of converting the Pope. In 1659 he was in Innsbruck
where his *Threnodia* was published. He returned to Ireland in 1660. In trying to describe the desolation of Ireland,
Father Conry wrote despairingly:

What shall I yet say? time would fail me to narrate the martyr-
doms of chiefs, nobles, prelates, priests, friars, citizens and others of

the Irish whose purple gore has stained the scaffold almost without end . . .

The Franciscan Father Seamus Carthún, writing from the bleak prison of Inishbofin, was not at such a loss. He poured out his feelings in a poem

> *Ataid a teampla mar barr peine*
> As the ultimate pain, the churches
> without altar, without mass or adoration,
> the most pitiful situation, as horse stables,
> not a stone left upon a stone.

The Presbyterians were more active in looking at the possibilities thrown up by the unstable government. Patrick Adair recalled: 'The true Presbyterians in the meantime were heartily active and concurring in all these passages in order to the King's restoration, and with a view to a happy settling of religion according to the first undertaking in Scotland.' In the meantime, on April 8, they held a Presbytery at Ballymena which became known as the Synod of General Presbytery. At this meeting Lt. Colonel William Cunningham, on behalf of Henry, arrived with a letter asking that John Greg, minister of Newtownards, be sent to places where only Catholics, High Prelates (Anglicans) and Anabaptists lived, and preach there. Henry promised to give support and encouragement to this. The Presbytery agreed to send Greg, Gabriel Cornwall, George Wallace and a man called Shaw to visit such places for three months.

Henry was feeling more expansive about the idea of freedom of conscience and he had even given the Irish in Connaught permission to prepare an address to Richard setting forth their concern on the oath of abjuration and the penalties for not going to Protestant churches. The army in Ireland was demanding greater freedom from civil government. A soldier named Lyll had been condemned to death by court-martial for murder but Henry had submitted the case to London for advice. On March 22 Thurloe suggested that it was not safe to execute the man but that he should be handed over to the civil authorities for trial. Henry remarked that the case was 'influential upon government of our army; mutineers now craving to be tried at common law and intend to bring action bitterly against their officers that correct them'. The power of the officers, and thereby the army, was being decreased.

At the end of April Henry left Dublin for a week and according to Samuel Bathurst was 'about twenty miles off, taking his pleasure'. When Henry returned from his rest he found that his brother Richard had been deposed in a republican *coup d'état*.

A Committee of Public Safety had been established with Fleetwood, Haselrig, Sir Henry Vane, Ludlow, Sydenham, Salway, John Jones, John Lambert, Desborough, Berry and Scot. The Committee had recalled the Long Parliament which Cromwell had disbanded in 1653. Out of the 160 members only forty could be found but 'about 80 more are capable of sitting. It is expected they will speedily join them'. A formal letter announcing the new government was sent to Henry on May 10 signed by Fleetwood and Lambert. Henry, without waiting for orders from England, published his own proclamation and despatched William Bury, Colonel Lawrence and Dr. Henry Jones to London with despatches and requests for further instructions.

When the Long Parliament assembled the excluded Presbyterian members led by the English west country Royalist, Sir George Booth, with Prynne and Annesley, proceeded to Westminster to take their seats. But they found themselves still excluded. Speaker William Lenthall was in the chair and on May 13 a Council of State was formed. It was decided to reinstitute the Commonwealth form of government and on May 25 Richard formerly submitted to the new government and resigned office as Lord Protector.

The Protectorate had gone. A broadsheet declaimed:

> Hail sacred Commonwealth!
> Did interest or gain your souls inspire?
> If your great Hero were alive again,
> He'd little thank such mercenary men
> That clawed the Father and when he was gone,
> Eat up the words and then forsook the son.

Fleetwood kept his post as head of the military and was confirmed in his appointment as commander-in-chief of the armed forces of the Commonwealth.

In spite of the confusion Dr. Petty was worrying Henry

on May 5 that ' I hope I shall be permitted to proceed with
my vindication at Dublin if this be a time for any particular
business less than the preservation of the whole'. When the
new Parliament met Sankey had renewed his attack on
Petty in order to deprive him of the 'benefit of the Act of
Indemnity then passing'. Sankey now drafted eleven accusations of corruption against Petty and dated them Tuesday,
July 12, 1659. According to Petty himself, he had actually
invested £7,469 of the money paid him by the government in
land speculation; he had a further £3,181 due to him from
the army plus £2,025 in army land debentures, plus £1,263 in
mortgage redemptions and a further £2,025 in payment for
labour and distribution for which 18,482 acres had been
awarded him. He still had a considerable personal fortune
in cash assets.

On June 7 Parliament decided that the administration of
the government of Ireland 'shall be by Commissioners
nominated and authorised by the Parliament and not by
any one person and that Colonel Henry Cromwell be made
acquainted with the resolutions of this House concerning
the government of Ireland and that he do forthwith repair
to the Parliament to acquaint them with the state of affairs
there'. It was ominous that the order referred to *Colonel*
Henry Cromwell, thereby ignoring his Protectorate appointments as Major-General and Lord Lieutenant.

Five Commissioners were appointed by the Council of
State to run Irish affairs. They were Colonel John Jones,
William Steele, Robert Goodwin, Matthew Tomlinson and
Miles Corbet. Ludlow's name was put forward but rejected
by twenty-six votes to twenty-two. The republican general
was, however, appointed by Fleetwood as Lieutenant General
in command of a regiment of horse and a company of foot.
Steele and Corbet were the only two Commissioners in Ireland and on June 14 Speaker Lenthall wrote to them asking
them to administer the affairs of the country 'until the
arrival of one or more Commissioners named for that affair
from England'.

The Royalists hoped that Henry would resist Parliament
but on June 15 Henry wrote a formal letter of resignation.
This letter was sent via Petty and Colonel Edmund Temple.

To Fleetwood Henry openly admitted: 'I cannot but be troubled at what has so lately befallen my relations and do acknowledge that others may very honestly do what I cannot do so handsomely, I have resisted great temptations to their authority.'

The Royalists had hoped that Henry might declare for the restoration of the Stuarts. It was not such a far-fetched notion as might have been thought at first glance. Henry's brother-in-law, Lord Fauconberg, was already in touch with the Royalists and Charles Stuart had ordered Sir Edward Hyde to send Edmund Villiers to Lord Broghill to 'assure Lord Broghill of all that he can wish for from the King if he will perform this service and that he may likewise undertake to Henry Cromwell that he shall be gratified in all that he will propose and it will be in the King's power as soon as his declaration shall be known to send over men, money and arms, and for this the King hath the absolute promise of those who are very well able to perform it'. The Royalists did not believe 'the general discourse of Henry Cromwell's submission'. They did not think he would give in so easily to the new regime, and were partly right. Henry had, in fact, proposed that the army in Ireland declare for the Protectorate but finding hesitation among the officers until they knew of the attitude of the army in England, he had called to Dublin the only regiment he counted loyal to himself and despatched Cornet Henry Monck to his father, General George Monck in Scotland, to see what action he was taking. The new Parliament had their suspicions but Nathaniel Fiennes told Thurloe that Henry was incapable of maintaining control of the army in Ireland.

Henry certainly had many Royalist friends who must have made some attempt to make him join their cause. Lady Thurles, Lord Ormonde's mother, was friendly with Henry and regarded him as 'the person from whose hands I do expect a settlement after all my sufferings'. Her daughter-in-law, Lady Ormonde, was also a frequent visitor to Henry's house. Henry O'Brien, the seventh Earl of Thormond, was also no stranger to Henry in whose house he was to meet Lady Reynolds, the widowed sister of Henry's wife, whom he eventually married. Above all, Lord Broghill was a close friend and Broghill had just arrived back in Ireland convinced that the restoration of the Stuart monarchy was the only solution to the problems of the country.

Henry was no royalist and, when he realised that the Anabaptist officers, who had opposed his rule, were not willing to stand for the Protectorate he submitted to the new government. He announced that he would retire to his house in Phoenix Park, leaving Colonel Thomas Long in command of Dublin Castle garrison. The two Commissioners, Corbet and Steele, still suspected that Henry might make a last minute attempt to raise the army and Hardress Waller was sent with troops to make sure he vacated Dublin Castle. Long, known to be friendly with Henry, was also relieved of his command. However, Henry, as good as his word, retired to Phoenix Park and wrote a letter to Parliament which was published by *Mercurius Politicus*, June 23–30:

I intend (God willing) to take shipping hence for England as soon as convenience of shipping can be had (which I daily expect of that side) and so to attend the Parliament in observation to their pleasures signified by your letters to me ...

With Henry out of harm's way, the Commissioners issued orders for the arrest of Lord Broghill, who was known to have had a meeting with his royalist brother Lord Cork at Bennett's Bridge to discuss the new turn of events. Against the advice of his friends Broghill immediately went to Dublin and appeared before Steele and Corbet. By 'artful reasoning' he persuaded them to let him return to Munster on condition he create no disturbance there. On June 13 Thomas Howard wrote to Charles Stuart that Broghill desired him to come to Ireland. Broghill's brother Francis, Viscount Shannon, was now in The Hague carrying messages to the royalists. Hyde wrote: 'the King looks upon Lord Broghill as a person who may be instrumental to do him service there (Ireland) ...'

Henry Cromwell left Ireland on June 27, 1659, and arrived in London on the evening of Saturday, July 2. On the following Wednesday he was sent for by the Council of State. He spent some time

...acquainting them fully (says the *Mercurius Politicus* of June 30–July 7) in what conditions he left the affairs of that nation, giving them to understand that all officers, both civil and military, and generally the whole people were in perfect peace under obedience and authority of the Parliament.

Having made his report he was allowed to repeat the report directly to the House of Commons where he delivered a bitter speech.

I see here Sydenham, Lambert and many more that were once Flanders laced with the titles of Lords, who are now again content to be but plain Colonels, and may thank God for that too! Come my masters, a colonel's pay is better than nothing. I do not envy Pride for dying a Lord, for life is sweet, though it be enjoyed in mean condition, especially to men that are not much troubled with that thing called courage and a high spirit, such as my brother and I...

I was lately Lord Deputy of Ireland, but now poor, miserable, dejected, rejected, disrespected, unprotected Henry Cromwell. But 'tis no matter since you have done it, whom I ought to flatter lest a worse thing befall me...for I know you will never believe any son of my father to be real. Alas, the people would think us bastards, I mean my brother and I, were we not like our father in some things.

He ended his speech in what was to be a strangely accurate prophecy.

...take heed of your good friend Mr. Lambert, for it concerns you being the end of a Parliament to have a care of coming under the lash; give your friends life, hang your enemies, grow rich, and let your obedient servant go home to the country.

> Where I like to hermit poor in pensive place obscure
> Do mean to spend my days of endless doubt
> To wail such woes as time cannot rescue
> Where none but you shall ever find me out
> And at my gates despair shall linger still
> To let in death, when you shall please to kill.

The Parliament granted Henry's plea and announced that Colonel Cromwell 'hath liberty to retire himself into the country whither he shall think fit upon his own occasions'. On September 5 the Council of State granted a licence 'for Colonel Henry Cromwell to transport from Ireland to any part of England his horses, goods and household stuff custom free'. He was, however, allowed to retain his estates at Portumna.

Henry turned to his father-in-law, Sir Francis Russell, who had an estate at Chippenham. Here he wrapped himself in private grief which was accentuated by the death of his eldest child, Elizabeth, who had died on July 17, within a few days of his arrival, and who was buried at Chippenham. His brother Richard was in retirement at Hursley, weighed down by enormous personal debts. The house of Cromwell had truly fallen.

CHAPTER 5

EDMUND LUDLOW

'Ludlow is the man desired...'

On July 8, 1659, Lieutenant General Edmund Ludlow received a commission as commander-in-chief of the army in Ireland. At the same time his republican colleague John Jones was appointed to the Irish Commission. Jones, who had an Irish estate valued at £3,000 a year, had been appointed to the Committee for Public Safety on May 7 and then nominated to the Long Parliament's Council of State. On July 8 a letter was sent by Sir Edward Nicholas, Charles Stuart's secretary, to Monsieur Momperson in Flanders.

We hear Henry Cromwell had barely submitted to Parliament, as his brother has done, but the rebels hear nothing from Montague or Monck that satisfies them. Tell no one but your Lt. Colonel that I have advised you to put yourself in readiness.

To this he added, on July 10:

Sir Hardress Waller, a rigid Presbyterian, commands as Major-General in Ireland. His daughter is married to Ingoldsby, governor of Limerick, who vaunted that he would withstand this Government to the wearing out of his old shoes. All ports for Ireland waylaid him, so he sailed for Dieppe and thence for Ireland where, if disturbed, he will arm the Irish. Ludlow is the man desired as Lord General of the forces in Ireland.

In May Ingoldsby had supported Richard and the Protectorate and defiantly declared that he would hold Limerick 'to the wearing out of his old shoes'. In danger of arrest, however, he had fled to France and his command was given to Colonel Robert Barrow, the former Anabaptist governor of Co. Down.

Ludlow and Jones immediately set out for Ireland and it was while they were en route to Holyhead that they heard the Royalists, taking advantage of the situation, were organising a rising under the Presbyterian Royalist, Sir George

Booth. Ludlow and Jones were greeted at Ringsend by Colonel Theophilus Jones. It had been decided that each Commissioner would chair meetings of the Commission for one month and that Ludlow, as commander, should chair the first meeting. He was styled 'Excellency'. He had brought to Ireland a letter of credit for £30,000 which added weight to his promises to pay the army.

The Commissioners immediately turned their attention to the state of the country. Petty had just finished a thirty volume census in which the overall population of Ireland was stated as being 500,091. In spite of transportations, deaths by sword, pestilence and famine, the Irish still outnumbered the English in a ratio of seven to one. Petty's information was not really reliable, for Gaelic speaking Scots were classed as Irish while other nationalities, such as German Protestant, were classed as Scots. In the main cities the Irish still outnumbered the English, except in Dublin itself, where there were 2,321 Irish to 6,459 English. Clearly, from the English viewpoint, the colonisation was not successful.

What worried Ludlow was the danger of insurrection either by Royalists or by the pro-Cromwellian factions around such people as Ingoldsby. The army in Ireland now consisted of six regiments of horse, eleven regiments of foot and one dragoon regiment. Ludlow felt that the army should be immediately purged of any dissident elements. To undertake this task he set up a Committee for the Nomination of Officers. Colonel John Hewson, the former governor of Dublin, was appointed as commander-in-chief of foot regiments, Ludlow taking over command of Henry Cromwell's regiment of foot. Ludlow felt considerably easier in mind when this reorganisation of the army was completed.

It was now confirmed that Sir George Booth had led a Royalist uprising in Chester. On July 30 Ludlow decided to supply a brigade to assist in suppressing those 'who are endeavouring the engaging the Commonwealth in blood and confusion'. A force of 500 horse and 1,000 foot was agreed upon. Lieutenant Colonel Daniel Axtell was to command the foot and Hierome Sankey was to command the horse. When the brigade left it was under strength, consisting of 845 foot and 474 horse. The voyage was not without incident for

Major Thomas Rowles of Ludlow's foot regiment was drowned en route. The brigade was quartered near Chester until August 29 when they were sent north to reinforce John Lambert's army.

Ludlow set about suppressing any Royalist sympathisers in Ireland and arrested various suspects, including Hugh, Viscount Montgomery, Lord of Ards. Montgomery, whose estates were in Co. Down, had surrendered to Cromwell at Clonmel in April, 1650. He had gone to Holland as an exile but petitioned to be allowed to return. After payment of a £3,000 fine he was allowed to settle at Mellifont, at the house of his brother-in-law, Viscount Moore. After a while the Commissioners had made him move his lodgings nearer to Dublin Castle in case he was involved in any Royalist plots. His young wife died and in despair he threw himself into Royalist political plottings, was arrested and taken to Kilkenny where he fell ill. He was imprisoned in Naas, Leixlip and finally Dublin where Henry Cromwell, because of his illness and the extortion of a promise not to act in any way prejudicial to the Protectorate, released him on February 13, 1657. As a prominent Royalist he was high on the list of suspects.

John Vernon was appointed as a special emissary between Ireland and England on August 2 and a few days later Ludlow decided to call in the arms of the Dublin militia when it became known that the Royalist army was nearing Chester. He gave orders that 100 men be sent to Beaumaris Castle, Anglesea, to be put under John Jones, the governor of the garrison, to keep open communications should Chester be captured.

On the same day, August 6, Ludlow decided to mount an operation to arrest and detain all people who would probably be involved in any Royalist plottings in Ireland. A second list of people to be detained was made out a few days later.

The situation was worrying. On August 9 Bulstrode Whitelock, on behalf of Parliament, wrote to inform Ludlow that Chester had fallen to the Royalists and that Irish troops were leaving Spain for Ireland, Scotland and Flanders. He advised Ludlow to act with extreme caution. On August 22 Captain Richard Edmonds, High Sheriff of Cos. Longford and Westmeath, was discovered to be fighting with the Royalists in Chester. Ludlow sent Colonel Brayfield to confiscate his property. Other Royalist suspects were rounded up. In June, 1659, Dr. Jeremy Taylor, an Anglican minister, had arrived in Ireland and taken up residence between Lisburn and Portmore, preaching to congregations in the half ruined church of Kilalla. Taylor, a Royalist, was an outspoken critic of the regime in England. On August 11 Lieutenant Colonel Brian Smith, the governor of Carrickfergus, was ordered to bring Taylor 'under safe custody' to Dublin to appear before the Commissioners. Taylor had been favoured by Archbishop Laud and trusted by Charles I. He was imprisoned until the following year when he was appointed Anglican Lord Bishop of Down, Connor and Dromore.

Another Royalist minister named Heritage Badcock was arrested. Panic was setting in and many felt the Royalists would topple the government. Ludlow prepared to defend Dublin, causing searches to be made for priests on August 23 and ordering all beggars and vagabonds to be cleared from the city on August 26. But news arrived that the Royalists had been defeated by Lambert's army, and this was confirmed on September 3 in a letter from Sir Harry Vane, President of the Irish Council in London.

The news gave Ludlow only a partial relief because the activity from the Tory guerilla bands, stimulated by the news from England, had increased. On September 5 Ludlow ordered that no Irish inhabitant or 'Popish Recusant' in Co. Wicklow was to be permitted to have 'arms or habiliments of war'. The same day Sir Harry Vane wrote to Ludlow pointing out the dangers of an invasion of Ireland and gave him 'power to arm such well affected persons in Ireland in the nature of a militia, and to fill up the troops and companies of horse and of foot of the standing army there, in such numbers for the preservation of the peace and security of the nation as they shall think fit . . .' On September 15 Lieutenant Francis Rowlestone, who in April 1657 had received a reward for his activities against the Tories, was ordered to enter into negotiations with a well known Tory leader, Garrett Kinsellagh, and two others, in order to offer them an amnesty if they would hunt down other Tories on behalf of the Commonwealth. On October 14 Colonel Henry Pretty was ordered to employ twenty Irishmen, with guns and ammunition, to hunt Tories for three months in Cos. Carlow and Kilkenny. Lt. Colonel Nelson was given a similar order applying to King and Queen's counties (Offaly and Leix).

After a brief spurt of activity the Tory bands were quiet until after the Restoration but they lasted long after the Cromwellian age. The last law was passed against Tories in 1776. Toryism gave rise to the Anglo-Irish nursery rhyme:

> Ho! brother Tadhg, what is your story?
> I went to the wood and shot a Tory,
> I went to the wood and shot another,
> Was it the same or was it his brother?
>
> I hunted him in, I hunted him out,
> Three times through the bog and about and about,
> Till out of a bush I spied his head
> So I levelled my gun and shot him dead!

Activity on behalf of the Catholic clergy was also worrying the new regime, but even more disturbing was the inter-marriage between English soldiers and Irish Catholics which had continued in spite of decrees designed to prevent such practices. On September 9 the Commissioners learnt that many soldiers, especially those stationed in Connaught and Co. Clare, had married 'Irish Papists contrary to sundry declarations'. Ludlow asked that an inquiry be set up and that it should take 'such proceedings ... as shall be agree-able to the rules and discipline of the army'. On September 13 Justices of the Peace were asked to suppress the practice of 'the Irish Papists in divers parts of this land, yearly and in superstitious manner, by frequenting wells and otherwise to observe days in memorial of the patrons or pretended tutelary of saints'. On December 9, Colonel John Jones issued a further order for the suppression of Catholic Christmas holidays which, he said, were only calculated to 'uphold idolatry and superstition derived from the Church of Rome'.

In October, 1659, the new Primate of Ireland, O'Reilly,

had finally arrived at Passage, Waterford. He reported to
the Vatican:

> I came in the month of October to Passage, a maritime town of
> Ireland situated in the province of Cashel. Crossing the Sound which
> is there I came down into the Province of Dublin where I visited
> en route the Vicars General of Ferns, and Leighlin in turn and
> then the pastors of the diocese of Kildare (there was no superior
> there). From them I learned the state of their churches, as also that
> of the Metropolitan City of Dublin. In the diocese of Ferns there
> were at that time, i.e. at the end of last October, only 8 priests; in
> Leighlin 4; Kildare 6, in Dublin 7; and in Ossory more than 12. The
> Vicar Apostolic of Ossory did not meet me, though he was in his
> own diocese, whereby I would be able to know the whole position
> there more exactly. But it was not permissible to delay there.
> On the ninth day after my arrival in the kingdom, I betook my-
> self into the province of Armagh, in which Anthony, Bishop of
> Meath, met me in his own diocese (there are 60 pastors in it) work-
> ing like a busy bee in the hive of the lord. Finally, going down
> further towards the north, I reached my own diocese (where the
> pastors number only 26) and there I remained for the whole winter.

News of another revolution in England sent Ludlow hurrying back to London. The days of the Commonwealth were
numbered.

'Against ambitions and tyranny . . .'

The man who had led the latest military coup was 'the dar-
ling of the army', John Lambert, now in his fortieth year.
He had fought in the Civil War as one of Fairfax's commanders, and had been a strong supporter of the Protectorate from 1653 when Cromwell first dissolved Parliament.
He had taken no part in the military plottings against
Richard Cromwell of whom he declared 'we are all for this
honourable person that is now in power'. However, he did
urge that limitations be put on the Protector's powers. 'The
best man is but a man at best. I have great cause to know it.'
He had been appointed commander of the forces ordered to
suppress Booth's rising. He had defeated Booth at Winwick
Bridge near Northwick, Cheshire, on August 19, 1659, and
recaptured Chester on August 21 and Chirk Castle on

August 24. It was proposed that Lambert be appointed
Major-General in gratitude for the victory but Parliament
rejected the proposal. Lambert's officers were angered at the
refusal and held a meeting at Derby where they drew up
*The Humble Petition and Proposal of the Officers Under
Command of Lord Lambert in the late Northern Expedition.*
Hierome Sankey's brigade of the army from Ireland sent
copies of the petition to the Commissioners and army officers
in Dublin asking for their support. Ludlow was against
bringing the army into conflict with Parliament saying that
England would never submit to military rule. He announced
that he intended to go to England and wanted to place the
military and civil government in the hands of the Commissioners. They objected to this and asked Ludlow to appoint
a military leader before he left. Hardress Waller was regarded as a time server by Ludlow, although Waller, as
Major-General, was the highest ranking officer in Ireland.
Sankey was obviously too fanatical, so he appointed Commissioner Colonel John Jones.

Ludlow had been determined not to be kept as an exile
in Ireland, as had happened to Henry Cromwell, and he had
a clause written into his commission allowing him to return
to England at a time of his choosing. On reaching Beaumaris
Castle he learnt that John Lambert had marched on London,
dissolved Parliament and established a Committee of Safety.

On October 12 Parliament had decided to cashier Lambert and other officers as being trouble-makers. Lambert
collected the regiments who adhered to him and marched on
Westminster, surrounding it on October 13 and barring
members of Parliament from entering. He told Ludlow a
few days later 'he had no intention to interrupt the Parliament till the time he did it, and that he was necessitated to
that extremity for his own preservation, saying that Sir
Arthur Haselrig was so enraged against him that he would
be satisfied with nothing but blood'. The Council of Army
Officers now made Lambert Major-General and a Committee
of Safety was set up which included Fleetwood. The poet
Milton said Lambert's ambition 'abused the honest natures'
of the soldiers. The Royalists fully expected Lambert to

make himself Lord Protector and Lord Hatton even suggested that Charles Stuart marry Lambert's daughter.

General George Monck did not favour this latest turn of events and was in touch with Ludlow by October 20 demanding reinstatement of Parliament. His intention was to 'prosecute this business against ambitions and tyranny to the last drops of my blood, till they (the Parliament) be restored'. On November 3 Cornet Henry Monck reported to his father that the army in Ireland was neutral on Lambert's take-over. Henry Monck had misread the situation, however, for fourteen senior Anabaptist officers supported Lambert. John Jones had written a rebuke to Monck, declaring that any division in the army would be 'found in issue to be nothing else but the opening of the door for the common enemy to come in'. However, Henry Monck told his father that Sir Charles Coote and Theophilus Jones could be counted on for any support in restoring Parliament.

The government in London was now a semi-military junta and England was soon torn by riots. In London mounted troops clashed almost daily with the people, and the courts of law ceased to sit while traders simply shut up their shops. People began to call for a new free Parliament or for the reinstatement of the Long Parliament with the excluded Presbyterian members. Monck openly declared his support for such moves on November 3. Lambert went north to oppose Monck, stationed in Edinburgh, and tried to negotiate with him.

The troops in Portsmouth declared for Parliament on December 3 and the entire naval fleet followed their example on December 13. The authority of Parliament was established in London on December 24. Ludlow was depressed with the growing split. He saw that if the Long Parliament met with the excluded members there would be little to stop the restoration of the monarchy and so destroy all hopes of the republic he had worked for. Two days before Parliament was due to meet he slipped out of London and left for Ireland, in a bid to rally the army there to the Commonwealth cause.

In Ireland, however, a similar struggle had taken place.

There was strong dissatisfaction with John Jones' support of the new military junta. A broadsheet asked:

Whether or no any national man of England can or may expect any good from a parliament when the army is in power at the same time in the nation?

On December 13 Hardress Waller and Theophilus Jones led a *coup d'état* by taking over Dublin Castle and declaring for the restoration of Parliament. They wrote a letter to Speaker Lenthall announcing their reasons. It was subsequently published as *A Perfect Narrative of the Ground and Reasons Moving Some Officers of the Army in Ireland to the Security of the Castle of Dublin*. Commissioner John Jones was arrested and taken to Athlone while Miles Corbet and Colonel Tomlinson were placed under house arrest in Dublin.

Theophilus Jones emerged as the leading spirit in this coup, having acted in close liaison with General Monck. At first Theophilus Jones had petitioned John Jones and the Council of Officers to consider the situation but when he saw that they were inclined to favour Lambert he had enlisted the help of Sir Hardress Waller. Theophilus Jones' group had intercepted orders from the military junta in London for their arrest and Jones had immediately initiated his plan with the aid of Captain Bond and a company of foot. Having captured Dublin Castle he found himself in charge of the only sizeable magazine in Ireland whose 500 barrels of gunpowder had only just been replenished.

Sir Charles Coote secured Galway, Lord Broghill seized Youghal, Bandon and Kinsale, and one by one all the garrisons in Ireland declared for Parliament with the exception of Duncannon. Colonel Cooper, the governor of Carrickfergus, the only person who might have given trouble, had died in his chair a week previously. Brayfield, the governor of Athlone, found himself betrayed to Coote, and two companies of his regiment at Carrickfergus had mutinied in sympathy with Monck. Monck was informed of the support of the army in Ireland and Sir Hardress Waller became the acting commander-in-chief. The 'Irish' brigade which had supported Lambert in England now supported Parliament and Daniel Redmond, who was already in contact with the

Royalists, arrested Hierome Sankey on December 21. Hardress Waller and Theophilus Jones offered to send six troops
of horse to aid Monck in taking the field against Lambert.

Ludlow was in despair. He wrote: 'It was my judgement
that if either the Parliament or the Army should entirely pre-
vail against the other in this juncture, it would hazard the
run of both.'

With the restoration now a certainty in his mind, Ludlow
felt he could utilise the army in Ireland to prevent it, without realising that the army was now controlled by his avowed
enemies. Theophilus Jones had already written to Parliament:

> ... we cannot but take notice of the carriage of Lt. General Lud-
> low in this revolution, who having an opportunity to return hither
> or there appear for Parliament, yet hath not made use of it towards
> this restitution as he might have done. We find by the same letter,
> that his disaffection begins to be salved, and therefore how unsafe
> it is to confide in him, when what his civils allow, his conscientials
> destroys; we humbly refer to your consideration.

Ludlow arrived just off his home at Monkstown in the
frigate *Oxford*. He was told about the situation by a Captain
Lucas who brought him a letter from the Army Council
which told him he would not be allowed to land in Ireland
and would be arrested if he attempted to do so. Captain
Lucas suggested that he go personally to the Council and
exert his authority but Ludlow answered that he knew their
principles too well to trust himself in their hands—their
attachment to Parliament was merely feigned and their real
design was 'to bring in the son of the late King'.

The army were all in agreement that they wanted the
restoration of the Commonwealth and not a monarchy or a
Protectorate. On December 22, there was a General Council
of Officers of the Armies of England, Scotland and Ireland,
which issued ten resolutions. The first three stated: '1, that
the government of England, Scotland and Ireland and the
dominions and territories thereunto belonging be in the way
of a Free State and Commonwealth. 2, That they will not
have kingship to be erected in these nations nor any single
person to exercise the office of chief magistrate over the same.
3, That there be no House of Lords or Peers.'

Although the military junta had collapsed on December 26 General George Monck decided that Parliament must be given some stability and to this end he decided to intervene to prevent the suicidal folly of his fellow officers in London. Lambert was now facing him with an army of 12,000 men across the Tweed. Although Lambert was stronger he did not attack and there was a lack of resolution among his officers. Monck sent his brother-in-law, Thomas Clarges, to Fairfax, the old general who was still remembered from the days of the Civil War and who still bore, unstained, the responsibility for the New Model Army's victories. He had opposed the King's execution and, following it, had withdrawn from public life. Monck felt that if Fairfax were with him the country would be his. Fairfax agreed to support Monck but the problem now was how to organise a joint rising of Yorkshire forces loyal to Fairfax and Monck's forces when Lambert's army was between Yorkshire and Coldstream, where Monck had his headquarters. Fairfax's young cousin Brian, home for Christmas from Cambridge, undertook to ride a wild route over the snow-covered hills and frozen rivers of Cumberland to Monck's camp. On December 30 the uprising of Monck and Fairfax began.

'Ireland alone grieves and mourns'

During the last two days of December the Yorkshire gentry joined Fairfax and on January 1, 1660, they met the 'Irish' brigade who, with the removal of Sankey from command, reinforced their numbers. Fairfax turned and marched on the city of York, commanded by Colonel Robert Lillburn, the brother of the former Leveller leader. Monck's army was also on the move and its vanguard had crossed the Tweed with General Monck following on January 2. Lambert's army simply melted away and he was left with a handful of officers and fifty troopers. The reinstated Long Parliament in London issued orders to all forces opposing Monck and Fairfax to disperse to their former quarters. Lillburn surrendered York. On February 3 Monck was in London and issued a demand on Febuary 11 that a freely elected parliament must replace the Long Parliament by May 6. With his northern army to back him, Monck issued an ultimatum to Parliament to issue writs for elections to all vacant seats in the House within six days. Ten days later, having received no satisfaction, Monck made the excluded Presbyterian members, those who had opposed the execution of Charles 1 and who had been forcibly ejected in 1649, take their places. The Long Parliament, outnumbered by their old opponents, was powerless. The restoration of the monarchy was inevitable and in March the Long Parliament finally dissolved itself and provided for the summoning of its successor.

It had been to prevent this turn of events that the republican Ludlow had hastened back to Ireland, where he found that a *coup d'état* had taken place and the republicans he had left in charge removed or arrested.

While wondering what next to do, waiting in Dublin Bay in the frigate *Oxford* on December 31, Ludlow was joined by the republican Commissioner Miles Corbet. Corbet had been placed under arrest while on his way from church, but managed to elude his captors and get aboard Ludlow's frigate. Ludlow decided to head for Duncannon where the governor, the republican Captain Skinner, greeted him warmly. Waterford was as hostile as Dublin and Ludlow was not allowed to re-victual his ship. The story was allowed to spread that he had deserted from Parliament. Supplies were difficult to come by and cattle, which would have relieved the beleaguered republican garrison, were driven off by Colonel Edmund Temple. The siege of Duncannon was organised by Colonel Thomas Scot, the son of the regicide Thomas Scot. Ludlow appealed to the governor of Waterford, Colonel William Leigh, whom he had allowed to retain command during the 1659 purge. He thought Leigh was of republican sympathies but Leigh refused to mobilise his regiment stationed in the area.

Ludlow received an open letter from the leaders of the coup, which was dated January 10 and signed by Waller, Jones, Broghill and Coote.

You went to London to represent things to the Parliament and stayed there all the while that by force they were kept from sitting, and as soon as ever, through providence, they were restored to them you hastened away hither, without any application to them. This being the matter of fact we leave it to all sober men to make inference.

Ludlow replied, in a letter dated at Duncannon Fort on January 21, saying that their letter 'was rather intended for the informing of others than the satisfying of me in the grounds of what you resolved upon touching the blocking of this place'.

But time was running out. On January 19 articles of impeachment were read in the Commons against Ludlow, Corbet and Tomlinson. Ludlow was ordered to surrender Duncannon to either Sir Charles Coote or Theophilus Jones. It was Sir Charles Coote who was appointed commander of the army and he immediately purged it again, placing relatives in control of major regiments.

Ludlow's plight was now desperate. He had hoped for help from Colonel Pretty, whose regiment was based in Carlow, but Lieutenant Colonel Edmond Temple of Peter Wallis' regiment (formerly Henry Cromwell's own regiment) had taken Pretty prisoner and joined forces with Scot in besieging Duncannon. Captain Skinner observed that the men outside the fort were insulting his soldiers with expressions 'in use among the worst kind of cavaliers. "God damn them!" "Go to your prayers!"'

Ludlow and Corbet managed to slip out of Duncannon on board the *Oxford* and make their way to London where, in spite of their impeachment, they took their seats in the House on January 30.

Although those in Dublin, with the exception of Sir Hardress Waller, who genuinely seemed to believe his fellow conspirators' platitudes about upholding Parliament, were in close contact with Monck and his ultimate aim, they decided to force Monck's hand by establishing a Convention in Dublin to discuss the restoration of the old, pre-1641, Irish Parliament. The Convention met on February 7, 1660, with Sir James Barry (afterwards Lord Santry) as Speaker. The Presbyterians were much in prominence with Sir John Clotworthy in attendance, as well as Patrick Adair. As chaplain of the Convention a Mr. Cocks, a Presbyterian minister, was chosen. On February 27 Lord Broghill was received among its members 'with great joy'. In London the Council of State demanded the Convention be dissolved. The Convention refused but, at the same time, repudiated any idea of separation from the English Parliament.

Sir Hardress Waller, the republican and regicide, suddenly realised, too late, that his fellow conspirators had not been concerned with the preservation of the Commonwealth but with the restoration of the monarchy. He seized Dublin Castle with some loyal soldiers and made an effort to arrest Coote, Jones and Broghill, but the Dublin garrison were tired of barrack-room revolutions, and overcame Waller and his men and handed him to Coote. He was held at Athlone before being taken to England.

On February 16 Sir Charles Coote and his officers declared themselves in favour of a freely elected Parliament. Two days later Broghill and his men made a similar declaration.

> If the said excluded Members be readmitted they must either be the greater or the lesser number in the House: If the lesser, wherein the danger of their admission? If the greater, where is the justice of their exclusion?

Broghill began to make the final moves. He sent his brother Francis, Viscount Shannon, to Brussels with an invitation to Charles Stuart to come to Ireland and be crowned. Charles Stuart received Broghill's invitation 'with a great deal of joy'. Sir Charles Coote had, at the same time, sent Sir Arthur Forbes to Charles Stuart with a similar declaration. Charles Stuart was preparing to accept the invitation to go to Ireland when Sir John Grenville arrived from Monck offering the restoration of the monarchy in England.

On March 8 Lord Broghill, Sir Charles Coote, Sir John Clotworthy and Sir William Bury were appointed Commissioners to manage the civil government in Ireland. On March 30 the Dublin Convention sent Clotworthy and William Aston to London to seek confirmation of the Cromwellian Settlement in view of the new developments. On April 25 the Convention Parliament was established in London and the restoration became a certainty. There was a great deal of opposition to these moves and on February 2 part of the army mutinied. Eleven days later Lambert was arrested in connection with the mutiny and on March 5 he appeared before the Council of State which sent him to the Tower of London. In the face of the restoration the republicans now sought an alliance with the Protectorists, led by Lambert. On April 10 Lambert escaped from the Tower and issued a declaration asking all those opposed to the restoration to assemble at Edgehill. Only six troops of horse and a few officers came. Many republicans distrusted Lambert and refused to turn out in support. Others like Ludlow, who had been elected to the Convention Parliament on April 4 for Hindon, could not break through the tight security in the country. On April 22 Colonel Richard Ingoldsby, the brother of the former governor of Limerick, Henry Ingoldsby, and Colonel Streeter, met Lambert at Daventry and accepted his surrender. Lambert gazed sadly at the people cheering his defeat and reminded Ingoldsby of the words Oliver Cromwell had said as the people had cheered them as they marched northward on the Scottish campaign: 'Do not trust to that, these very persons would shout as much if you and I were going to hang.'

The republicans still in Parliament, like Ludlow and Jones, refused to have any part in the proceedings to restore Charles Stuart. Their elections were declared invalid.

On May 14, 1660, Charles Stuart was formerly proclaimed as King Charles II in Dublin, a few days after a similar proclamation in England, and three days later the Dublin Convention adjourned until November. On May 25 Lord Broghill and Sir Charles Coote went to London to greet the new King. General Monck was appointed Lord Lieutenant of Ireland and Lord Roberts became his deputy, although neither visited Ireland.

The restoration of the monarchy was greeted with great enthusiasm by the majority of Irish Catholics who thought that Charles II would reverse the Cromwellian colonisation policy. Peter Talbot, now titular Archbishop of Dublin, wrote to Lord Ormonde hoping that the mediation of the French and Spanish Kings would not be needed to persuade Charles II to restore the Irish estates to their former owners. Talbot's fellow-Royalist, the Franciscan Father Peter Walsh, published *A Continuation of the Brief Narrative and the Suffering of Ireland under Cromwell*, in London in 1660, in an effort to gain sympathy. In October, 1660, he wrote to Ormonde exhorting him to maintain the 'natural supporters of royalty' against Presbyterians, Anabaptists, Quakers, Independents and Fifth Monarchy men. He also urged that the Irish clergy should make a royal address to Charles II to try to efface the bad impression left by their share in the insurrection of 1641.

But many Irish, who had supported the Confederacy against both English King and English Parliament, men like the Primate O'Reilly, had little hope for a just settlement from the new monarchy. After the winter of 1659/60 O'Reilly had set off on a tour of Ireland listing the number of priests in each area. His activities were becoming known to the administration, who made concerted efforts to capture him.

> When this storm arose I left the work unfinished and from that time on I am keeping myself in hiding places and caves. Nevertheless, I have meanwhile ordained 13 priests, two from my own diocese, six from Clogher, two from Kilmore, two from Dromore and one from Killaloe in the province of Cashel.

A Provincial Council of the Church, the first to be held in Ireland in over ten years, was held at Cloone, in the parish of Killow, Co. Longford. O'Reilly was president, assisted by Abbott Thomas Quinn of Assaroe. It was found that the church was split into two political camps, those who supported O'Reilly, still believing in the principles of the Confederacy, and those who followed Walsh and the union with England.

Ormonde had encouraged Walsh in the drawing up of a remonstrance to be presented to Charles II on behalf of the Irish Catholic clergy. It denied Papal power in temporal affairs, judged the insurrection of 1641 as unlawful and rejected any Papal or foreign interference with the crown of Charles II. Walsh presented this remonstrance to Charles II early in 1662 but as no Irish clergyman had signed it, it was returned. Walsh managed to get twenty-four Irish priests, who were living in London, to sign it including Bishop Oliver D'Arcy. The remonstrance succeeded only in widening the split in the Irish Catholic Church. Walsh's own Franciscan Order at Louvain censured his stand as being

offensive to the dignity of the Pope. Walsh replied in a
pamphlet in 1662 entitled *The More Ample Account*. Pope
Alexander was embarrassed by Walsh's persistence in drawing attention to indirect Papal power. Walsh, however, succeeded in getting 120 priests released from Irish prisons by
his subservience to the new King. He returned to Ireland
in August, 1662, and lived in Kennedy's Court, Dublin, near
Christchurch. His rival Peter Talbot accused him of dressing
more gaily than became a friar and of singing and dancing.

Walsh's battle with Primate O'Reilly continued with Walsh
demanding a general meeting of the Irish clergy to see
whether the majority supported the King and the union.
This meeting finally took place in June, 1666, in Dublin.
Lord Ormonde's efforts to influence the proceedings and make
the Irish clergy declare their loyalty to Charles II had an
opposite effect. At the end of the meeting Ormonde had
O'Reilly arrested for his opposition and banished. Archbishop
Eamonn O'Reilly died in Louvain in 1669.

In spite of the fact that by 1662 there were 275 diocesan
clergy and many regular clergy, with O'Reilly begging the
exiled bishops to return to the country to recruit and train
priests, the authorities continued to enforce the penal laws
against the Irish Catholics. In exile the Bishop of Ferns,
Nicholas French, wrote in his book *The Unkind Deserter*:
'The Catholics of Ireland are excluded from all commerce
which the very Turks do grant to their Christians.'

John Lynch, Archdeacon of Tuam and Vicar-Apostolic of
Killala, also in exile in southern France, published *Cambrensis Eversus* two years after the restoration with a dedica-
tion to Charles II pointing out: '... while your other kingdoms are delirious with joy, Ireland alone grieves and
mourns.'

On August 26, 1660, Dr. Anthony Geoghegan, Bishop of
Meath, reporting to the Vatican wrote: *'Vibo in cavernis
adhuc et caeteri mael vocationis et status* ... I live still in
the caverns of the earth as do all other members of the
clergy.'

The Catholic Church was not the only ·sect to suffer in
Ireland after the restoration. The Restoration Parliament
was overwhelmingly Church of England and it was to the

Anglican Established Church that most favours went in Ireland. Among the first acts of Charles II was the reestablishment of a hierarchy. James Bramhall was appointed Anglican Primate in 1661. All the estates held by the Church in 1641, which had been confiscated under the Commonwealth or Protectorate, were restored, as were tithes, and a glebe, the land attached to a parish church, was provided in every parish. From 1661 the new parliament in Dublin did everything possible to hinder meetings of all other denominations, Presbyterians, Independents, Anabaptists, Quakers, and others who, with Catholics, were classed as enemies of the (Anglican) Church and State.

'Others notoriously guilty ...'

For those who had helped to engineer the restoration of the monarchy there were rewards to be gained from a grateful Charles II. Lord Broghill was appointed Lord President of Munster and governor of Co. Clare, and on September 5, 1660, was created first Earl of Orrery. Broghill was to die on October 16, 1680, honoured as a poet, playwright, a brilliant soldier, an experienced politician, a vigorous pamphleteer, a graceful romancer and the initiator of the Restoration heroic drama. His greatest work, the romance *Parthensia*, had been published in five parts during the Protectorate.

Sir Charles Coote had been confirmed by Charles II as Lord President of Connaught and made governor of Queen's County (Leix) and Receiver-General of Composition Money in Connaught and Thomond. On September 6, 1660, Charles II created Coote first Earl of Mountrath but the new title did not benefit him long for he died of smallpox on December 18, 1661 and was buried in Christ Church. Of his father, who had come to Ireland as an adventurer in search of his fortune, Archdeacon Lynch had commented that he was 'the Raven' but Sir Charles Coote was 'a bad crow from a bad egg'. Coote's brother Richard was created first Baron Cloony; Sir John Clotworthy became first Earl of Massereene. Henry Ingoldsby was made a Baronet by Charles on August

30, 1660. Theophilus Jones was made a Privy Councillor and Scoutmaster-General for life. He was also given command of a troop of horse. His brother, Dr. Henry Jones, was appointed Anglican Bishop of Meath in May, 1661. He was to die in 1682. James Butler, the now fifty-year-old twelfth Earl of Ormonde, who had spent ten years with his King in exile, was created first Duke of Ormonde on March 30, 1661, and made Lord High Steward of England, carrying the crown at the coronation of Charles II. He then returned to Ireland as Lord Lieutenant with increased influence and power.

Those who had been prominent in the Cromwellian administration and who had, unlike Coote and Broghill, refused to accept the restoration or work for it, were rewarded in other ways.

Richard Cromwell, the deposed Lord Protector, fled abroad in the early summer of 1660, pursued by debtors, to die on July 12, 1712, under an assumed name. Henry Cromwell, thanks to the intervention of Broghill, lived in quiet retirement in Spinney Abbey, Cambridge, drawing an income from his Irish estates which he had been allowed to keep. He died in 1674. Fleetwood was excluded from all offices of public trust and died some time after the restoration in obscurity. His wife, Bridget Cromwell, died before him and he was to marry for a third time. John Lambert was exiled to Guernsey but on June 2, 1662, he was arraigned for High Treason and sentenced to be executed. Charles commuted the sentence to life imprisonment. Lambert died in 1683. On May 15, 1660, Thurloe was arrested and charged with High Treason but was acquitted. On June 29 he retired to Great Milton, Oxford, where he died on February 21, 1667.

In spite of the promise Charles had made, that his restoration would be followed without any persecution of people prominent in Cromwell's administration, the Royalist party forced the new government to try several people for 'the wellbeing of the kingdom'. The first to be tried and executed was the Fifth Monarchy leader, Major-General Thomas Harrison who had done much to bring about the execution of Charles I. 'Where is your good old cause now?' jeered a spectator as he ascended the gallows. Harrison clapped a hand to his breast: 'Here it is and I am going to seal it with my blood.' The republican, Sir Henry Vane, although not a regicide, was executed on the personal intervention of Charles II.

Of those who commanded in Ireland Sir Hardress Waller was sentenced to be hanged, drawn and quartered. He had escaped to France early in 1660 but, being a man of principle, he had returned to defend the cause he had fought for. Tried on October 10, 1660, he refused to plead to a Royalist court. His sentence was suspended on October 16 and he was imprisoned in the Tower of London before being transported to Mount Orgueil Castle, Jersey, where he died in the autumn of 1666.

John Jones had been elected to the Convention Parliament but his election had been declared void on May 18. He made no attempt to escape the restoration and was arrested while walking in Finsbury. He was tried on October 12 and made no attempt to justify or defend himself. He was executed on October 17 and died with courage and dignity. Miles Corbet, whose election to the Convention Parliament had also been declared void, went into hiding and left England. He was arrested in Holland and was tried and executed on April 19, 1662. John Cooke, the Chief Justice of Ireland during the Commonwealth and Protectorate, who had been Parliament's solicitor at the trial of Charles I, was arrested by Coote, tried and executed on October 16, 1660.

Former Adjutant-General William Allen was tried, but given a sentence of banishment. Hercules Huncks, whose regiment was disbanded in Ireland in 1653, was one of three officers to whom the King's death warrant was addressed. He turned informer against his fellow officers, in particular Daniel Axtell, and was allowed to go free. Axtell was found guilty of commanding the halberdiers at Charles I's trial and executed on October 15. Colonel Peter Stubber was also accused of being a halberdier but he vanished from Ireland. His estates were given back to John Fitzpatrick. Colonel Robert Phayre, the former governor of Cork, was classed as a regicide but was allowed to turn State's witness with Colonel Hughes, against Colonel Francis Hacker who was found guilty of actually carrying out the instructions of the execution warrant on Charles I. Phayre was discharged from prison on March 28, 1661. Colonel John Hewson, the former governor of Dublin, who had served on the Committee of Safety during Lambert's coup and had suppressed a demonstration in London calling for a free parliament, killing three and wounding 20, fled abroad in May, 1660. He died in Amsterdam in 1662.

Ludlow, as a regicide and arch-republican, was high on the list of those who were to be tried and executed. He hid himself in London on Charles's return and, day after day, he heard of the arrests of his friends. A reward of £300 was offered for his capture. He managed to leave the country, travelling to Geneva via Paris. He became a bogey-man to the Royalists. In October, 1661, he was said to be lurking in Cripplegate, London, ready to lead an attack on Whitehall. In July, 1662, he was about to head an insurrection in the West Country. In November, 1663, he was reported to be at Canterbury disguised as a sailor plotting some new rising. However, he had removed to Lucerne in April, 1662, and then, in September, had taken up residence at Vevey where the government of the canton of Berne granted an Act of Protection to him and his two fellow regicides, William Cauley and John Lisle. A series of attempts by English government agents to assassinate him led to the fatal shooting of Lisle at Lucerne on August 11, 1664. Similar attempts to kill or kidnap Ludlow continued until 1669. After the revolution of 1688 Ludlow returned to London and, in August, 1689, he found he was about to be arrested and so returned to Vevey to write his memoirs. He died there in about 1692.

As the momentous events of the restoration continued the charges of corruption against William Petty were forgotten. But Petty still smarted. Early in 1660 he had a 185-page book published at St. Paul's, London, plus a lengthy contents table, which he entitled *Reflections upon some Persons and Things in Ireland by letter to and from Dr. Petty*. This was to be the complete answer to the charges of Sir Hierome Sankey, 'an Anabaptist who hath so often endeavoured to supplant me in my employment'.

Petty maintained that he had acquired his estates in

Ireland 'by and for debentures bought at the dearest rates in the openest markets'. He attacked Sankey and the Surveyor-General, Benjamin Worsley, whom he called Sankey's 'jackal', but was full of praise for Henry Cromwell.

> I, finding the Lord Henry Cromwell, to be a person of much knowledge and integrity to his truth, as also of a firm faith and zeal to God and his church and withall to have translated me from a stranger to his bosom, thinking me worthy of the nearest relations to himself, and one whom when all tricks and devices were used to surprise me by foul play, would still be careful I might have fair play, I did (as in justice and gratitude I was bound) serve him faithfully and industriously: I was his secretary without one penny of reward, I neglected my own private affairs to promote his and consequently I preferred his interest before any man's and I served his friends *ceteris paribus* before his enemies.

The work was full of mistakes and the printer apologised for all the errors in the book because he was not acquainted with Ireland or Petty's references and 'was forced to guess at many interlined and imperfectly obliterated words and sentences, as also the true places of many of them'.

Petty was plagued until the end of his life by accusations of trickery and corruption. His extraordinary ability was matched by a reputation for an equally extraordinary greed, therefore some of the charges were probably well justified. Sankey was clearly not relying on his imagination alone in many of his charges. Petty was an immensely resourceful man, whose teeming brain produced new schemes one after the other. After the restoration he went back to his scientific life, remaining a resident in Dublin but making frequent trips to his estates in Kerry. He founded the Royal Society of Ireland, reorganised Dublin's College of Physicians and lived to herald Newton's *Principia*. He died at his house in Piccadilly, London, almost opposite St. James' Church, on December 16, 1687, of gangrene in his foot occasioned by the swelling of gout. His widow became Baroness Shelbourne and his son the first Baron. Petty was buried with his mother and father in the churchyard at Rumsey, in Hampshire.

'This caps all their tricks'

Ireland now waited in tense expectation to hear whether the Cromwellian colonisation was to be revoked. Many of the banished were returning from Connaught and Co. Clare to reclaim their estates. Many thought that Charles II would naturally take their side against those who had supported the Commonwealth and Protectorate.

The transplantation scheme had certainly not been successful. The native Irish had not been removed and many native chiefs were still in possession of their lands, such as Séafra Ó Donnchadha an Ghleanna, known as Geoffrey O'Donoghue of the Glen to the colonists, and a chief of the O'Donoghue clan of Gleann Fleasg (Glen Flesk). Séafra had managed to retain his estate and castle at Killaha, in spite of the confiscations going on around him.

But while Séafra had managed to survive the confiscations and others were confident of a reversal of the colonisation, the poet Dáibhí Ó Brudair of Cnoc Rátha did not like the turn events seemed to be taking. When Ormonde arrived back as Lord Lieutenant he expressed his feelings in a poem entitled *Nach ait an Nós*—How queer this mode:

> *Mairt atá gan béarla binn*
>
> Woe to him who cannot simper English
> since the Earl has come across to Ireland:
> so long my life upon Conn's plain continues
> I'd barter all my poetry for English.

Dáibhí went to Limerick for the first time in 1660 and, although he returned to his native Cork from time to time, he settled there. But because of the destruction of the bardic system, and the attendant loss of patronage, he sank increasingly into poverty. In Limerick he composed his best poems on the hardships suffered by his countrymen. He was to be hounded in the last four years of his life by the authorities, and after a long struggle against poverty and tyranny died in January, 1698. In 1692 he had written a sad lament for a still conquered Ireland entitled *Do chealg mo chom*—Pierced has been my breast.

> Pierced has been my breast severely with full many a disease
> at the journey of those gallant chiefs who laboured for our weal
> for in the land they loved to dwell is now, as far as I can see,
> no one that has been left unrobbed or free from want but serfs
> and churls.

Charles II had given much hope to Ireland when he concluded a speech to Parliament on July 27, 1660, with the words:

> I hope I need say nothing of Ireland, and that they alone shall not be without the benefit of my mercy. They have showed much affection to me abroad, and you will have a case of my honour of what I promised them.

It was not until December 30, that year, that Charles made a firmer declaration regarding the land settlement. A number of specially named Royalists were to have their estates returned to them and the Cromwellian colonists would be compensated with other estates of equal value. But such estates could not be found in Ireland and the exact working out of the settlement was left to the new Irish Parliament. In May, 1661, a Parliament of the Anglo-Irish and the new English colonists was ceremoniously opened in Chichester House, Dublin, with Sir Audley Mervyn as Speaker. In all, 339 members were returned from the thirty-two counties and 108 boroughs, plus representatives from Trinity College. They were all Protestants, mainly Anglicans, but all were animated by the Cromwellian interest. Jeremy Taylor, the Bishop of Down and Connor, opened the Parliament with a significant sermon entitled 'Rebellion—the son of witchcraft'. It was plain that those Irish who had taken part in the insurrection against the English colonists would certainly not receive any return of property while only the 'Old English' colonists who had remained loyal to King or Parliament would benefit. The proposals for the settlement were embodied in the Acts 14 and 15 of Charles II, 1662. All lands in the possession of Cromwellian financiers before May 7, 1659, were secured to them; those whose claims had not been fully satisfied were to have the deficiency made good out of territory assigned to them as a body but not yet distributed. Catholics found innocent of taking part in the 1641 insurrection and those who had followed the King to exile abroad, and eighteen special nominees of the King, were to be restored to their estates. Among these nominees were influential individuals such as Westmeath, Clanricarde, Clancarty, Mountgarret, Taafe and others. Many claimants were left unsatisfied because there was simply not enough land to be distributed. Cromwellian colonists resented having to give up even a part of their estates and recovery was slow and troublesome, even for those who were entitled under the Act to recover something. Jonathan Swift, born in Dublin seven years after the Restoration, was to write of the 'Old English' some years later:

> The Catholics of Ireland ... lost their estates for fighting in defence of their King. Those who cut off the father's head, forced the son to fly for his life, and overturned the whole ancient frame of government ... obtained grants of those very estates the Catholics lost in defence of the ancient constitution, and those they gained by their rebellion what the Catholics lost by their loyalty.

The Catholic Bishop of Ferns, Nicholas French, wrote bitterly in a work entitled *Sale and Settlement of Ireland*: 'Is not this a blessed Declaration, which provides in so large a manner for so many different interests; a declaration that satisfies the natives and yet dispossesses none of the Cromwellists?' He was being more than prophetic when, speaking of the dispossessed 'Old English' colonists, he added:

> If this cannibal English interest gives no quarter to the children of the English, may not the posterity of those very adventurers and soldiers, after an age or two, be likewise devoured?

The conquest, confiscations and colonisation of William of Orange proved French's prophetic comment.

As for the native Irish, it was Séafra Ó Donnchadha an Ghleanna who summed up his people's impotent rage at the Stuart confirmation of the Cromwellian confiscation in a poem

> *'s barra ar an gcleas ...*

> This caps all their tricks, this statute from overseas
> That lays the switch on the people of Heber the Fair;

A crooked deal has robbed us of our claim
And all our rights in Ireland are swept away.

The Gaels are stripped in Ireland now at last
And now let the grave be dug of every man,
Or let them get their pass and cross the waves
And promise to stay gone to their dying day.

Although the English are stronger now than the Gaels,
And though their fortunes are better for some time here:
Relying on their titles, they will not yield a field,
On their backs God's anger will pour down in streams.

He died in 1678 before he saw what further tricks and burdens Ireland was to suffer.

But, in spite of the brutal and methodical way in which the confiscations and colonisation was carried out from 1652 to 1660, its success was only partial. The Irish nation survived. True, the ownership of the soil had now changed hands and the colonists had taken the chief places in towns and were dominant in industry, commerce and the professions: true, there was a deep cleavage on religious grounds and Ireland was beginning to assume her more modern features and appearance, but it was equally true that given time the colonists would have been absorbed into the Irish Nation as they had been in the past.

Father Francis Molloy, writing in a book entitled *Lochrann na gCreidmheach* (Light of the Faithful), published in 1675, observes 'no language is well understood by the common people of the island except Irish alone'. Primate O'Reilly, at the first Catholic Convention in 1660, had made sure that all candidates for the priesthood were to learn to read and write Irish well. Most colonists found that they had to learn the language and their children naturally became bilingual or monolingual in the majority tongue. This was even more pronounced among the ordinary soldiers of whom a great number married Irish women and were in a short space of time completely absorbed into the Irish nation. Ludlow had seen this process as early as 1659. He had noted that many of the soldiers, especially those stationed in Connaught, had married Irish Catholics and although some professed Protestantism Ludlow said they might 'justly be suspected to continue Papists'. That the absorbing power of

Irish culture had survived the Cromwellian colonisation was witnessed by an Englishman, Robert Molesworth, who observed, in his book entitled *A True Way to Render Ireland Happy and Secure* published in Dublin in 1697:

We cannot so much wonder at this when we consider how many there are of the children of Oliver's soldiers in Ireland who cannot speak one word of English.

Time for assimilation was something that Ireland did not have. A generation later came the Williamite wars, confiscations and colonisation which were to reshape the face of Ireland. In his book *The Political Anatomy of Ireland*, published in London in 1691, William Petty commented that 'The Irish will not easily rebel again, I believe, from the memory of their former successes, especially of the last...' But it was that very memory, indeed the memory of all their conquests and the subsequent confiscations and colonisations, that kept alive in the Irish the spirit to keep striking for their freedom. The Irish scholar Ruairí Ó Flaithearta, severed from his ancestral territory in Connaught, articulated the feelings which were to cause generation after generation of Irish to rise up in an attempt to strike off the imperial yoke:

I live a banished man within the bounds of my native soil; a spectator of others enriched by my birthright; an object of condoling to my relations and friends, and a condoler of their miseries.

SOURCES AND ACKNOWLEDGEMENTS

After considerable deliberation, I have decided not to use copious footnotes for source references because I do not wish to claim an academic status for this work to which I feel that it is not entitled. The sources for the quoted material in the text, all of which is contemporary, are self evident and all sources are listed in the bibliography. The only liberty I have taken with quoted material has been to standardise erratic seventeenth-century spelling into modern spelling for easy readability.

Regarding source material: difficulty awaits anyone researching material on the Commonwealth and Protectorate period in Ireland. That which would have provided a rich source of information no longer exists. The fifty-six manuscript volumes of records kept by the administration during the period 1650–60, called *The Books of the Commonwealth*, were totally destroyed in 1922 when, in the opening minutes of the Irish Civil War, Free State artillery opened fire on Republican positions in Dublin's Four Courts, which houses the Public Records Office of Ireland. No complete copies were known to have been made of these invaluable records. However, extracts from the manuscripts were published in the Maynooth Journal *Archivium Hibernicum* in 1917 and 1918 as 'Commonwealth Records' and in R. Dunlop's two volume collection of *Ireland Under the Commonwealth* in 1913. These have proved most invaluable.

The historians of this period have tended to ignore the wealth of material in Irish, in particular the poetry of the time whose political comments show more vividly than anything else the hopes and feelings of the ordinary Irish people of the period. Many of the poems of this period are still unpublished. In spite of the destruction of manuscripts since the seventeenth century there is known to have been a considerable number of poets writing in this decade but unfortunately no one appears to have published a study in depth of this period. I am much indebted to Professor Brían Ó Cuív of the Dublin Institute for Advanced Studies who gave me valuable help with these sources.

Another overlooked source of material has been the reports, mainly in Latin, from Catholic priests writing 'underground' in Ireland during this period to the superiors of their various orders in Rome and elsewhere. References to where these records are housed can be found in such works as Moran's *Spicilegium Ossoriense*. There are also works, such as *Threnodia Hiberniae-Catholica* etc., published in such places as Innsbruck, Antwerp, Lisbon, Louvain by exiled Irishmen of the day. I would like to thank Mrs. Mary Buck, Librarian of the Catholic Central Library, London, for her help in referring me to such sources.

An important source of information about the trials, held under Commonwealth auspices in 1652–4, of those accused of massacres in 1641–2 is Mary Agnes Hickson's two volumes *Life in Seventeenth Century Ireland*. Ignoring the flagrantly biased introduction and editing, the volumes contain depositions and trial reports which are not only invaluable for the student of 1641/2 but explain much of the Cromwellian attitude to the Irish. Also, it dispels the commonly held belief that only Irish Catholics were tried for alleged massacres of Protestant colonists. The documents relating to the trial of Scottish colonists for the murder of Irish Catholics at the Isle of Magee disprove this belief. The conscientious Commissioners for the Administration of Justice took down many depositions from the Irish, some of which had to be translated from Irish into English, for the purposes of prosecution. References as to where the original depositions and trial documents may be found, mainly in the archives of Trinity College, Dublin, are given in Miss Hickson's study.

Regarding works containing references to the Irish in Barbados and West Indies generally, I would like to thank J. C. Tudor, CMG, High Commissioner for Barbados in the United Kingdom.

There is still much research on this period that could be done. During the period many Irish families settled in Spain where some became prominent, the O'Neills and O'Donnells in particular. In Spanish archives there could well be a considerable wealth of contemporary documentary work on the seventeenth century defeats of the Irish. But probably only years of painstaking specialised study will bring such work to light.

I would like to express my thanks to my good friend Pádraig Ó Conchúir who kept a paternal eye on the production of this work, who read the manuscript and made several helpful suggestions. Lastly I would also like to thank another good friend, John D. Cully, who helped me by his criticism.

BIBLIOGRAPHY

State Papers

Acts and Ordinances of the Interregnum, edited by C. H. Firth and R. S. Rait, 3 vols, HMSO, London, 1911.

Calendar of State Papers, Domestic Series, edited by Mary Anne Everett Green, Vols for 1650–1660, London, 1875–1886.

Calendar of State Papers, Colonial Series (America and West Indies) edited by W. Noël Sainsbury, Vol. for 1547–1660, Longmans Green, London, 1860.

Calendar of State Papers, Ireland, edited by J. P. Mahaffy, Vol. for 1647–1660, HMSO, London, 1903.

Calendar of State Papers, Ireland (Adventurers for Land 1642–1659) edited by J. P. Mahaffy, HMSO, 1903.

Calendar of the Clarendon State Papers, edited by W. Dunn MacRay, 5 vols, Clarendon Press, Oxford, 1876.

Thurloe's State Papers, edited by Thomas Birch, 7 vols, London, 1742.

Published Collections

ABBOTT, W. C., Writings and Speeches of Oliver Cromwell, 4 vols, Cambridge, Massachusetts, 1937–1947.

DUNLOP, Robert, Ireland under the Commonwealth, 2 vols, Manchester University, 1913.

HALLER, William, and DAVIES, Godfrey. The Leveller Tracts 1647–1653, Columbia University Press, 1944.

HICKSON, Mary Agnes, Ireland in the Seventeenth Century or the Irish Massacres of 1641–42 (Depositions with introduction), 2 vols, Longmans Green, London, 1884.

JENNINGS, Brendan, and GIBLIN, Cathaldus, Louvain Papers 1606–1827, Irish Manuscript Commission, Dublin, 1918.

MORAN, Patrick Francis, Spicilegium Ossoriense: History of the Irish Church from the Reformation to the year 1800, M.H. Gill, Dublin, 1878.

PENDER, Séamus, A Census of Ireland circa 1659, Stationery Office, Dublin, 1939.

WOLF, Don M., Leveller Manifestoes of the Puritan Revolution, Thomas Nelson, London, 1944.

SIMINGTON, Robert C., The Civil Survey 1654–1656, Stationery Office, Dublin, 1931.

Periodicals

ANALECTA HIBERNICA (Journal of the Irish Manuscript Commission) No. 4, October, 1932: *Documents Relating to the Irish in the West Indies* edited by Rev. Aubrey Gwynn, SJ.

ARCHIVIUM HIBERNICUM (Maynooth) Vols VI (1917) and VII (1918)—*Commonwealth Records;* Vol XIII (1948) *Threnodia Hiberno-Catholica* introduced by Brendan Jennings, OFM; Vol XIV (1949) *Irish Priests Transported Under the Commonwealth* by Kevin MacGrath; Vol XV (1950) *Sanguinea Eremus Mortyrum Hiberniae Ord. Eremit SP Augustini* presented with introduction and notes by F. X. Martin, OSA.

CELTICA (Dublin) Vol IV (1958)—*Brian Mac Giolla Phádraig* le Cuthbert Mhág Graith, OGM.

ENGLISH HISTORICAL REVIEW (London), Vol XIV—*The Transplantation into Connaught* by S. R. Gardiner.

FREEMAN'S JOURNAL (Dublin) January 24, 1871—*Erasmus Smith.*

JOURNAL OF THE KERRY ARCHAEOLOGICAL AND HISTORICAL SOCIETY No 3 (1970)—*A Poem on Seafraidh Ó Donnchadha an Ghleanna* le Pádraig Ó Rian.

JOURNAL OF CORK HISTORICAL AND ARCHAEOLOGICAL SOCIETY, Vol V No 44 (second series)—*Ancient History of Kerry* by Jarlath Prendergast, OFM.

PUBLICATION OF THE AMERICAN ECONOMIC ASSOCIATION, Vol IX No 4 (August, 1894) *Sir William Petty; a study in English economic literature* by Wilson Lloyd Bevan.

STUDIA HIBERNICA, No 2 (1962) *Scribhenoiri Gaeilge na Seachtú hAois Déag* le Cainneach Ó Maonigh.

Essays

BUTLER, Sir William, *Oliver Cromwell in Ireland* in Studies in Irish History, Irish Literature Society, Dublin, 1903.

MILLET, Benignus, *Survival and Reorganisation 1650–1695* in A History of Irish Catholicism, Vol III Fasc. 7, M. H. Gill, 1968.

Contemporary Journal

MERCURIUS POLITICUS, editor M. Needham, June 6, 1650–June 7, 1660.

Contemporary Writings

The Declaration of Sir Hardress Waller, Major General of the Parliament Forces in Ireland and the Council of Officers there, Dublin Castle, 1659.

The Declaration of Sir Charles Coote, Lord President of Connaught, and the officers and soldiers under his command, January 19, 1660.

A Letter from Sir Hardress Waller and Several Gentlemen at Dublin to Lt. General Ludlow with his answer to the same, London, 1660.

A Copy of a letter from an Officer of the Army in Ireland to His Highness, the Lord Protector, concerning his changing of Government, Waterford, June 24, 1654.

The Lord Henry Cromwell's Speech in the House, 1659.

ADAIR, Rev. Patrick, A True Narrative of the Rise and Progress of the Presbyterian Church in Ireland 1623-1670, C. Aitchinson, Belfast, 1866.

BIRCH, Thomas, The Life of the Hon. Robert Boyle, London, 1744.

BOATE, Gerard, Ireland's Natural History ... published by Samuel Hartlib, London, 1652.

GILBERT, John T. (editor), A Contemporary History of the Affairs in Ireland 1641-1652 (An Aphorismical Discovery of Treasonable Fraction), 3 vols, Irish Archaeological and Celtic Society, Dublin, 1879-80.

GOOKIN, Vincent, The Great Case of Transplantation in Ireland Discussed ... by a well wisher to the good of the Commonwealth of England, London, 1655.

GOOKIN, Vincent, The Author and Case of Transplanting the Irish into Connaught Vindicated from the Unjust Aspersions of Col. Richard Lawrence by Vincent Gookin Esq., London, 1655.

HOGAN, Edmund (editor), The History of the Warr of Ireland from 1641 to 1653 by a British officer of the regiment of Sir John Clotworthy. McGlashen and Gill, Dublin, 1873.

HUTCHINSON, Lucy, Memoirs of the Life of Col. Hutchinson by his widow Lucy, George Routledge & Sons, London, 1906.

KELLY, Matthew (editor), Cambrensis Eversus: or the refutation of the authority of Giraldus Cambrensis on the History of Ireland by John Lynch. 3 vols. Celtic Society, Dublin, 1848.

LAWRENCE, Richard, The Interest of England in the Irish Transplantation Stated ... by a faithful servant of the Commonwealth, London, 1655.

LUDLOW, Edmund, The Memoirs of Edmund Ludlow, Lt. General of Horse in the Army of the Commonwealth of England, edited by C. H. Firth, 2 vols, Oxford, 1894.

MAC FIRBISIGH, Duald, The Chronologies, edited by J. O'Donovan, Irish Archaeological Society, Dublin, 1844.

MEEHAN, C. P. (editor), The Portrait of a Pious Bishop, of The Life and Death of the Most Rev. Francis Kirwan, Bishop of Killala, trs. from the Latin of John Lynch. James Duffy, Dublin, 1884.

MEEHAN, C. P. (editor), The Geraldines, trs. from the Latin of Brother Dominicus de Rosario O'Daly. James Duffy, Dublin, 1847.

O'FLAHERTY, Roderic, A Chorographical Description of West or H-Iarr Connaught, London, 1684.

PETTY, Sir William, Reflections upon some Persons and Things in Ireland, London, 1660.

PETTY, Sir William, The Political Anatomy of Ireland, London, 1691.

PETTY, Sir William, The History of the Survey of Ireland Commonly called the Down Survey, Dublin, 1851.

TALBOT, Peter, The Politicians Cathechisme for his instruction in divine faith and moral honesty written by N. N. Antwerp, 1658.

VENABLES, Robert, The Narrative of General Venables, edited by C. H. Firth, Longmans Green, London, 1900.

WALSH, Peter, Continuation of the Brief Narrative and the Sufferings of Ireland under Cromwell, London, 1660.

General

ASHLEY, Maurice, Cromwell's Generals, Jonathan Cape, London, 1954.

BAGWELL, Richard, Ireland Under the Stuarts and during the Interregnum, 3 vols, Longmans Green, London, 1909.

BROWN, Louise Fargo, The Political Activities of the Baptists and Fifth Monarchy Men in England during the Interregnum, Oxford University Press, 1912.

BUCHAN, John, Cromwell, Hodder & Stoughton, London, 1934.

DE BLACÁM, Aodh, Gaelic Literature Surveyed, Talbot Press, Dublin, 1919.

ESSON, D. M. R., The Curse of Cromwell, A History of the Ironside Conquest of Ireland 1649–1653, Leo Cooper, London, 1971.

FIRTH, Charles H., DAVIES, Godfrey, The Regimental History of Cromwell's Army, 2 vols. Clarendon Press, Oxford, 1940.

FITZMAURICE, Edmond, The Life of Sir William Petty 1623–1687, John Murray, London, 1895.

FRANCISCAN FATHERS OF DHUN MHUIRE, Killiney, editors, Father Luke Wadding: Commemoration Volume, Clonmore & Reynolds, Dublin, 1957.

FRASER, Antonia, Cromwell: Our Chief of Men, Weidenfeld & Nicolson, London, 1973.

GARDINER, Samuel Rowson, History of the Commonwealth and Protectorate 1649–1659, 4 vols, Longmans Green, 1903.

GARDNER, Phyllis, The Irish Wolfhound, Dundalgan Press, Dundalk, 1931.

HARLOW, Vincent T., A History of Barbados 1625–1685, Clarendon Press, Oxford, 1926.

LYNCH, Kathleen M., Roger Boyle, First Earl of Orrery, University of Knoxville, Tennessee, Press, 1965.

MACLYSAGHT, Edward, Irish Life in the 17th Century, 3rd edition, Cork, 1969.

MAHAFFY, John P., An Epoch in Irish History—Trinity College, Dublin, 1591–1660, T. Fisher Unwin, 1903.

M'GEE, Thomas d'Arcy, The Irish Writers of the 17th Century, James Duffy, Dublin, 1846.

MORAN, Patrick Francis, Historical Sketch of the Persecutions Suffered by the Catholics of Ireland Under the Rule of Cromwell and the Puritans, James Duffy, Dublin, 1862.

MURPHY, Denis, Cromwell in Ireland: A History of Cromwell's Irish Campaign, M. H. Gill, Dublin, 1883.

O'BRENNAL, Martin A., Ancient Ireland, Dublin, 1885.

O'BRIEN, George. The Economic History of Ireland in the Seventeenth Century, Maunsel & Co, Dublin, 1919.

O'DONNELL, Terence, Father John Colgan, OFM, 1592–1658, Assisi Press, Dublin, 1959.

O'HART, John, The Irish and Anglo-Irish Landed Gentry When Cromwell Came to Ireland, M. H. Gill, Dublin, 1884.

PEASE, Theodore Calvin, The Leveller Movement, Oxford University Press, 1916.

PRENDERGAST, John P., The Cromwellian Settlement of Ireland, 3rd edition, Mellifont Press, Dublin, 1922.

RAMSEY, R. W., Henry Cromwell, Longmans Green, London, 1933.

ROGERS, Edward, Some Account of the Life . . . of a Fifth Monarchy Man, London, 1867.

RONAN, Myles V., Erasmus Smith Endowment, Talbot Press, Dublin, 1937.

RUSHIN, J. P., Carmel in Ireland: a narrative of the Irish province of Teresian, or discalced Carmelities AD 1625–1876, Burns & Oates, London, 1897.

SALAMAN, Redcliffe N., The Influence of the Potato on the Course of Irish History, Browne & Nolan, Dublin, 1943.

SALAMAN, Redcliffe N., The History and Social Influences of the Potato, Cambridge University Press, 1949.

SEYMOUR, Rev. St. John D., The Puritans in Ireland 1647–1661, Clarendon Press, Oxford, 1921.

STEVENSON, John, Two Centuries of Life in Down 1600–1800, M'Caw Stevenson & Orr, Belfast.

STRAUSS, E., Sir William Petty: Portrait of a Genius, Bodley Head, London, 1954.

TOWNSHEND, Dorothea, The Life and Letters of the Great Earl of Cork, Duckworth, London, 1904.

WEDGEWOOD, C. V. Oliver Cromwell, Duckworth, London (2nd revised edition) 1973.

Irish sources

DE BRÚN, Pádraig, Ó BUACHALLA, Breandán agus Ó CONCHEANAINN, Tomás, Nua-Dhuanaire, Cuid 1, Dublin Institute for Advanced Studies, 1971.

MAC ERLEAN, John C. Dháibhidh Uí Bhruadair (Poems of David Ó Bruadair) Irish Texts Society, London, Vols 11, 12 and 13.

Ó DHONNCHADHA, Thadhg, Saothar Filidheachta an Athar Padraigín Haicéad, M. H. Gill, Dublin, 1916.

UA DUINNÍN, Pádraig (P. S. Dinneen), Filidhe Mora Chiarraighe, M. H. Gill, Dublin, 1929.

UA DUINNÍN, Pádraig, Danta Phiarais Feritéir, Ofig Díolta Foillseacháin Rialtais, Dublin, 1934 .

UA DUINNIN, Pádraig, Danta Shéafraidh Uí Dhonnchadha an Ghleanna, Chonnradh na Gaedhilge, Dublin, 1902.

Ó MUIRGHEASA, Énrí, Dhá Chéad De Cheotaibh Uladh, Ofig Díolta Foillseacháin Rialtais, Dublin, 1934.

O'RAHILLY, Cecile, Five Seventeenth Century Poems (title & notes in English only) Dublin Institute of Advanced Studies, 1952.

Ó'RAITHBHEARTAIGH, Toirdhealbhach, Maighistrí san Fhilidheacht, Ofig Díolta Foillseacháin Rialtais, Dublin, 1932.

French sources

GOBLET, Yann Morvan, Les Noms de lieux irlandais dans l'oeuvre géographique de Sir William Petty, Paris, 1930.

GOBLET, Yann Morvan, Transformation de la géographie politique de l'irlande au xviie siècle dans les cartes et essais anthropogéographiques de Sir William Petty, Paris, 1930.

PASQUIER, M., Sir William Petty: Ses idées économiques, Paris, 1903.

INDEX